Warren Koontz M.D.

DICKENS AND THE RHETORIC OF LAUGHTER

DICKENS
AND THE RHETORIC
OF LAUGHTER

James R. Kincaid

Oxford

At the Clarendon Press

1971

Oxford University Press, Ely House, London W. 1

GLASGOW NEW YORK TORONTO MELBOURNE WELLINGTON
CAPE TOWN IBADAN NAIROBI DAR ES SALAAM LUSAKA ADDIS ABABA
DELHI BOMBAY CALCUTTA MADRAS KARACHI LAHORE DACCA
KUALA LUMPUR SINGAPORE HONG KONG TOKYO

PRINTED IN GREAT BRITAIN
AT THE UNIVERSITY PRESS, OXFORD
BY VIVIAN RIDLER
PRINTER TO THE UNIVERSITY

For Sue

'Dead!' replied the other, with a contemptuous emphasis. 'Not he. You won't catch Ned a-dying easy. No, no. He knows better than that.'

Martin Chuzzlewit

Preface

'Rhetoric of laughter' simply means the use of laughter to persuade. In Dickens, our laughter affects very strongly our notion of what the novel is, and the vision of that novel is partly defined by the nature, quantity, and control of our response. All this is obvious enough, and I regret that a phrase as pretentious as 'rhetoric of laughter' needs to be used at all. I could, however, think of nothing else that was any clearer— 'humour' and 'comedy' can mean almost anything—and 'rhetoric of laughter' at least distinguishes the approach from one that consists of extracts from funny scenes. All the same, it is exactly the sort of phrase Dickens would have attributed to the Circumlocution Office.

I am grateful to many critics who are not specifically cited here, partly because their influence is so pervasive that it goes beyond phrases and isolated notions and partly because my British editors and publisher allowed themselves some good natured derision over my American and mindless pedantry in footnoting. I do not mean, by all this, to slip plagiarized material by and blame it on the publisher. I am, of course, fully responsible for the material, its errors, misrepresentations, and omissions.

However, the faults would have been even greater and more obvious without the help of many friends. I am especially grateful to Arthur A. Adrian, who introduced me to Dickens and patiently showed me how to read him, and who has been, ever since, a model of precise and intelligent scholarship and a warm and generous friend. To my colleague Richard D. Altick I owe a great deal indeed: he read the entire manuscript with care and tolerance (in a few places, agreement), allowing me the benefit of his enormous knowledge of Dickens and of the nineteenth century, of his tact, and of his good nature. My wife, Suzanne M. Kincaid, has worked closely with me throughout. I might add that she did *not* help much with the typing, flipping cards, and the like—I did that—but by reading Dickens and thinking about him. I have also been helped by the conversation, prodding, and cynical barbs of my friends at Ohio State University, especially Arnold Shapiro, who read a version of the chapter on *Oliver Twist* and made excellent criticisms of it.

This work was supported in part by a grant from the Ohio State University Development Fund, and I would like to express my thanks to that agency. I am also grateful to the College of Humanities and especially to my chairman, Albert J. Kuhn, for arranging time off.

Earlier and shorter forms of Chapters 3 and 4 appeared in *PMLA* and *Dickens the Craftsman: Strategies of Presentation*, ed. Robert B. Partlow, Jr. (Carbondale, Ill: Southern Illinois Univ. Press, 1970). The reading of *Pickwick Papers* used in Chapter 2 was in part presented in an article in *Nineteenth-Century Fiction*. I am grateful to the respective publishers for permission to use some of this material.

Contents

1 Introduction

IN the midst of the dark-Dickens revolution, Fred W. Boege wrote, 'Dickens is still read for his fun, but he is being read more and more for the profound, brooding sense of evil in life that informs his work and causes his name to be coupled constantly with Dostoevsky's'.[1] Surely one need not make this choice or this distinction. Edmund Wilson and G. K. Chesterton, so remote from each other in many ways, still saw the same writer, and both saw further that his fun was very serious and his seriousness often funny. Wilson noted 'a trace of the hysterical'[2] in Dickens's humour, and Chesterton more pointedly complained that 'the frivolous characters of Dickens are taken much too frivolously'.[3]

I want to examine the part laughter plays in our response to both early and late novels and to demonstrate not so much how serious *Pickwick* is and how funny *Little Dorrit* is as how our laughter is used in both cases to cement our involvement in the novel's themes and concerns. Instead of approaching the novels through imagery, structure, or theme, this is an attempt to approach them through humour, one of Dickens's most certain rhetorical tools, and through the resulting laughter, one of the most complex and intimate responses a reader can make. Laughter implies, among other things, a very solid agreement with a certain value system, and Dickens is masterful in using that agreement for subtle thematic and aesthetic purposes. He can use it to reinforce the feeling of freedom and the opposition to order and bureaucratic sterility in *The Pickwick Papers*, to undercut the apparent bourgeois comfort of *Oliver Twist* and force us into at least temporary

[1] 'Recent Criticism of Dickens', *NCF*, viii (1953), 187.
[2] 'Dickens: The Two Scrooges', *The Wound and the Bow* (New York, 1947), p. 14.
[3] *Appreciations and Criticisms of the Works of Charles Dickens* (London, 1911), p. 57.

sympathetic alignment with the world of Fagin and Sikes, to make effective the pathos of *The Old Curiosity Shop*, to define more emphatically the structural principle of contrasts in *Barnaby Rudge*, to urge us into agreement with an extremely sophisticated and worldly value system in *Martin Chuzzlewit*, to create an ambiguous response to the narrator in *David Copperfield*, to attack the very bases of comedy in *Little Dorrit*, and to reassert a final and limited comic view in *Our Mutual Friend*. Every time we laugh at Sam Weller's witty attacks on the law, we are moving a step further from our usual position of commercial safety; laughter at Sim Tappertit implicates us in his final crippling; laughter at Mr. Micawber forces us to take a position on the crucial thematic issues of imagination-irresponsibility-freedom as opposed to fact-prudence-imprisonment. I should say at the outset that Dickens's variety in this regard is all but overwhelming, but his success seems to me so complete as to necessitate some examination of the details.

I shall, then, examine the several novels I have mentioned—*The Pickwick Papers, Oliver Twist, The Old Curiosity Shop, Barnaby Rudge, Martin Chuzzlewit, David Copperfield, Little Dorrit*, and *Our Mutual Friend*—in terms of their appeals to laughter, not primarily to judge the success or failure of those appeals or to examine Dickens's techniques as a humorist,[4] but to understand the individual novels better by more sharply defining our reaction to them. More specifically, I wish to show how Dickens controls our response to his humour and integrates that response into the entire novel. The primary emphasis, however, will be literary, not psychological. Our sensitivity to humour will be used, much as our sensitivity to patterns of imagery has often been used, in order to articulate more clearly and thereby understand more completely our experience with the novels. With Dickens, the reader's laughter is important evidence for the critic and becomes a valuable tool for literary criticism.

[4] It is not possible to avoid technique entirely; to some extent and in some cases Dickens's technique is vital in determining our laughter and is integral to his vision (see pp. 5–8). The emphasis, however, is important. Instead of studying Dickens's techniques (or style or historical influences) using the novels primarily as evidence, I mean to study the novels, using laughter as a critical tool.

1. DICKENS AND LAUGHTER

'The greatest humourist whom England ever produced,—Shakespeare himself certainly not excepted':[5] these lines began the obituary notice in the *Spectator*, and John Forster picked them up in the first sentence of his biography a few years later: 'Charles Dickens, the most popular novelist of the century, and one of the greatest humorists that England has produced, was born . . .'[6] No one has ever really questioned these judgements; in fact, Edmund Wilson's decision is undoubtedly not only tactful but also accurate: 'In praise of Dickens' humor, there is hardly anything new to say.'[7] We have, no doubt, had enough praise.

What we have not had, as countless symposia, introductions, and bibliographies solemnly announce, is anything very much beyond praise.[8] It is commonplace now to suggest that the once orthodox view of the dark Dickens was one-sided, that the early novels have been neglected, and that studies of his humour are needed. But there is, at the same time, a widespread and understandable uneasiness at seeming to promote either a return to appreciative collections of funny scenes or a rash of dull explanations of jokes. As Henri Bergson says, the analysis of laughter is likely to leave a very bitter after-taste,[9] and Freud makes it very clear just why we do not want to know why we laughed: we laughed in the first place only by 'keeping our conscious attention at a distance',[10] but more fundamental is our natural disinclination to examine our own

---

[5] 'Charles Dickens', xliii (1870), 716.

[6] *The Life of Charles Dickens*, notes by A. J. Hoppé, i (London, 1966), 3.

[7] *The Wound and the Bow*, p. 13.

[8] There have been a few excellent discussions of Dickens's humour, and these have aided me greatly in this study, though none has used the same approach. Of the earlier critics, Chesterton is clearly the best on this subject, though his remarks are often evocative in the woolliest way. Of the more recent studies, four are exceptionally perceptive: V. S. Pritchett, 'The Humour of Charles Dickens', *The Listener*, li (1954), 970–3 ; Mark Spilka, *Dickens and Kafka* (Bloomington, Ind., 1963) ; Barbara M. Cross, 'Comedy and Drama in Dickens', *WHR*, xvii (1963), 143–9 ; and Northrop Frye, 'Dickens and the Comedy of Humors', *Experience in the Novel*, ed. Roy Harvey Pearce (New York, 1968), pp. 49–81.

[9] 'Laughter', *Comedy*, ed. Wylie Sypher (Garden City, N.Y., 1956), p. 190. Further references will be cited in the text.

[10] *Wit and Its Relation to the Unconscious*, trans. A. A. Brill (New York, 1916), p. 238. Further references will be cited in the text.

aggressive, exhibitionistic, or egoistic impulses. There is also
a suspicion that any such study will ignore the later novels.

However, I think we have made an over-facile and generally
false distinction between the dark and the funny Dickens,
and between the early and the late novels. I agree on the
whole with the dominant movement of Dickens criticism in
the last twenty years and have, like many others, been taught
by it how to read his novels. I agree too that the overriding
impression of the novels after *David Copperfield* is very dark
indeed. But I think J. Hillis Miller has demonstrated persuasively how much organic unity there is in Dickens's career; at
any rate, there is certainly a consistency in his use of laughter,
terror, pathos, indeed all the tools at his disposal to support
his dominant themes and effects. It is true that the humour is
sometimes more closely integrated into the whole design in the
later novels, but it was 'serious' and organic to begin with. Even
Sairey Gamp is not autonomous and she is deadly serious.
The notion that humour declines or disappears in the later
novels likewise seems to me gratuitous and false. Laughter is
used in different ways in the later novels, but it is always
important. As Dickens said when writing *David Copperfield*,
'The world would not take another Pickwick from me now,
but we can be cheerful and merry. [*sic*] I hope, notwithstand-
ing, and with a little more purpose in us.'[11] Generally speaking,
as Dickens progressed he used humour for perhaps more
serious purposes, attacking and persuading the reader more
and more subtly. But generalizations on his progress in this
regard are dangerous; the laughter in *Oliver Twist* is as subversive in its blunt way as that in *Little Dorrit*. The contention
here, at any rate, is that the evocation of laughter is important throughout his career and that the early novels are
generally just as rewarding in this regard as the later ones.
Therefore, though the debt of this study to previous criticism
is very great, the pervasive distinction implied in almost all
of it between the serious and the funny is rejected. As a
natural corollary, the notion that the humour is somehow
detached from major concerns or that it functions mainly

[11] To Dudley Costello, *The Letters of Charles Dickens*, ed. Walter Dexter, 3
vols. (London, The Nonesuch Press, 1938), ii. 150, 25 Apr. 1849. This edition
will hereafter be cited as *Nonesuch Letters*.

as a holiday or relief and the notion that it is genial, soft, or humanitarian seem to me demonstrably false, but the demonstration is naturally more important than the assertion.

Some points of Dickens's technique

Though generalization is indeed risky and though this study is mainly concerned with the examination of the contribution laughter makes to individual novels, it is possible to indicate briefly some of the general outlines and characteristics of Dickens's humour:

i. *Perspective.* 'Nothing', said G. K. Chesterton, 'can be funnier, properly considered, than the fact that one's own father is a pigmy if he stands far enough off',[12] and Dickens is a master at controlling our distance from the matter at hand in order to evoke laughter. In its simplest form, the contrast of language and action can itself be funny; Taine noted how often Dickens's humour depended on 'saying light jests in a solemn manner',[13] and it is clear that the laughter at Mrs. Gamp and Mr. Pickwick, for instance, is made more boisterous by the 'disparity between the narrative voice describing the characters and the images they project of themselves'.[14] Of course the personality implied by the narrative voice can itself be very important in establishing laughter and creating a sense of security: 'Even a rabbit, were it suddenly to materialize before us without complicity, could be a terrifying event. What makes us laugh is our secure consciousness of the magician and his hat.'[15] But with Dickens we are not always conscious that the magician is there; he has a tendency to behave like his rabbit. The variety and continual fluctuation of Dickens's point of view makes possible the wildest contradictions in general discussions of this subject: Taylor Stoehr repeatedly cites the effects Dickens gains by the 'absence of the narrator from the scene' and says the dominant effect is one of 'detached immediacy';[16] Robert Garis says that the

[12] *William Blake* (London, 1910), p. 16.
[13] *History of English Literature*, trans. H. Van Laun, ii (New York, 1879), 352.
[14] Cross, p. 144.
[15] Maynard Mack, 'Introduction' to *Joseph Andrews* (New York, Rinehart, 1948), p. xvi.
[16] *Dickens: The Dreamer's Stance* (Ithaca, N.Y., 1965), pp. 58, 61.

first and continuing impression 'in Dickens's prose is of a voice manipulating language with pleasure and pride in its own skill' and says our constant impulse is to applaud.[17] Both are right, depending on which passage from Dickens one examines. The fact is that Dickens's use of the narrative voice is highly variable and that the use he makes of it to promote laughter simply cannot be reduced to precept, though it is an important factor that must be accounted for in individual cases.

ii. *The use of the concrete.* One aspect of Dickens's humour often noted is that it is rooted in the specific and continually manifests itself in the vivid and exact details which George Orwell called the 'florid little squiggle[s] on the edge of the page'.[18] Though again difficult to generalize about, the revivi- fication of the concrete almost always serves an organic rather than a marginal purpose and is part of Dickens's constant campaign against deadly forms and machinery. Those flower- ing annuals, for instance, which are stuffed in Pumblechook's mouth (Orwell's illustration of the squiggle) clearly suggest (among other things) everything which Pumblechook is not. The very vividness of the image serves as an indictment of the grey, hypocritical world of Pumblechook and its earlier reflec- tion in Pip.

iii. *The force of the idiom.* Related to the use of the concrete is the fact that much of the force of Dickens's humorous characters rests in their absolutely distinctive language. His ability to catch with precision and subtlety the idiom of his comic characters has often been praised and perhaps has meaning only in specific characters. It is true, though, that with characters like Mr. Micawber and Sam Weller their diction suggests a separate and complete world, and Dickens demands that we pay close attention to the nature of that world. It very often serves as an implicit commentary on another world. Mr. Micawber's verbosity provides not only insight into his own habit of mind but also a criticism of David's values; Silas Wegg's artificial and pathetic (if also predatory) imaginative life protests against the world of Podsnap.

[17] *The Dickens Theatre: A Reassessment of the Novels* (Oxford, 1965), p. 16.
[18] *Dickens, Dali and Others* (New York, 1946), p. 61.

iv. *Savagery*. John Middleton Murry has argued that Dickens's 'comic vision was the fiercest that has ever been in English literature, so savage as to be sometimes all but unbearable'.[19] Though it flies in the face of received notions concerning Dickens's genial gaiety, I think Murry's statement is accurate. Not all of Dickens's humour is as potentially vicious as that evoked in the quarrel between Mrs. Gamp and Betsey Prig, the scene Murry refers to, but anyone who examines the basis of laughter in the line of sex-starved women that runs through Rachael Wardle, Sally Brass, Miggs, Charity Pecksniff, Mrs. Skewton, to Lady Tippins, or in the alternate line of henpecked husbands from Mr. Pott, Mr. Bumble, Sampson Brass, Gabriel Varden, Mr. Chillip, to Rumty Wilfer will not think this humour, at least, very genial—certainly not in its appeals.

v. *Darkness*. Related to the savagery of much of Dickens's humour is the fact that it is often dark to the point of grotesquerie. This issue has often been discussed and in any case is best treated in relation to individual novels, so it will only be touched on here. The important point is that Dickens often asks us to laugh at the very subjects he is, in other parts of the novel, asking us to sympathize or be angry with: death, loneliness, improvidence, rigidity, spontaneity, cruelty . . . the list could be extended indefinitely. Dickens confronts us, time and again, with these contradictory lures and, time and again, uses our alternate responses to intensify our relationship to his principal appeals. Ruskin's famous statement, 'I believe Dickens to be as little understood as Cervantes, and almost as mischievous',[20] is suggestive here of the subtlety and darkness of Dickens's humour. The ambiguity with which he mixes the funny, terrifying, and pathetic in his villains is a case in point, but again detailed discussion must wait for specific cases.

The preceding generalizations are meant to suggest only a framework for analysis, but they are perhaps misleading in that they point mainly to Dickens's humorous techniques. But it is the tendency of his humour which seems to me most important, along with his use of that tendency as a rhetorical

---

[19] *The Times*, 14 July 1922, p. 11b.
[20] Letter to Charles Eliot Norton, 8 July 1870, in *The Works of John Ruskin*, ed. E. T. Cook and Alexander Wedderburn (London, 1903–12), xxxvii. 10.

tool. I am not primarily concerned with just how Dickens gets us to laugh at Sairey Gamp, but I am concerned both with what meaning our laughter expresses and with the use Dickens makes of that meaning in terms of the entire novel.

2. THE NATURE OF LAUGHTER

Laughter is such an intricate and explosive subject that in discussing it some degree of oversimplification is inevitable. The muddle of various approaches, the innumerable categories, and the rancorous critical in-fighting connected with this topic make it necessary to be as discriminating and, at the same time, as eclectic as is sensibly possible. The analyses that follow, therefore, though depending primarily on the work of Sigmund Freud and Henri Bergson, will also employ the arguments of related theorists: Rapp, Piddington, Kimmins, Gregory, Grotjahn, and others.[21] In the absence of any generally accepted (or acceptable) single theory of laughter, I cannot hope to provide a synthesis which will cover all kinds of laughter; the test should be the applicability of the theory to Dickens's novels.

The first step toward a workable theory of laughter seems to me to be a necessary distinction between laughter and comedy.[22] Though the two are often closely related, there is apparently no necessary or absolute tie between the genre and the effect. As Wylie Sypher says, 'Comedy may, in fact, not bring laughter at all; and certain tragedies may make us laugh hysterically.'[23] Of course, the problem in Dickens is both simpler and more complex than this statement implies. While there are few of his novels to which the term comedy would apply at all as an adequate and total description, he was pre-

[21] For useful summaries and critical surveys of various theories of laughter, see the following: Max Eastman, *The Sense of Humor* (New York, 1921); C. W. Kimmins, *The Springs of Laughter* (London, 1928); D. H. Munro, *Argument of Laughter* (Melbourne, 1951).

[22] In order to avoid a profusion of terminology, I shall use 'comedy' as a reference to the genre and its values only and not as a synonym for anything funny. The general term used here for anything evoking amusement will be 'humour'. It is true that Freud used this term with very special meaning; when the restricted meaning is intended, Freud's name will be introduced.

[23] 'The Meanings of Comedy', *Comedy*, p. 205. This same distinction is convincingly developed by L. J. Potts, *Comedy* (London, 1948), p. 19 and by Herbert McArthur, 'Tragic and Comic Modes', *Criticism*, iii (1961), 36.

occupied with traditional comic values and symbols: freedom, justice, rebirth, flexibility. Despite the fact, then, that few novels have the simple vision or clear direction of comedy, the terms of the genre are often relevant, even when they are treated with such bitter irony as in *Little Dorrit*. A discussion of the details of comedy can be postponed until the next chapter, however, since Dickens's first novel is one of the great English comedies and helps to define the genre.

One unavoidable issue, however, appears in most theoretical analyses of laughter and must be dealt with before a more general discussion can be attempted: the degree to which laughter expresses (if it does at all) hostility, aggression, the vestiges of the jungle whoop of triumph after murder, and other unpleasant impulses. The corollary to this issue is the debate over whether laughter is incompatible with sympathy, geniality, or indeed with any emotion. Roughly speaking, the dark-laughter theorists spring from Thomas Hobbes;[24] the genial-laughter theories from Jean Paul Richter.[25] Without retracing the steps of this very tortuous, often confused, and usually truculent argument, one can, I think, accept the reasoning of Arthur Koestler, which is based on the simple fact that nearly all the important writers on the subject have,

[24] There are, of course, earlier theorists who suggest the darkness of laughter or its incompatibility with strong feeling—there is a hint of this in Aristotle's cryptic remarks—but Hobbes's formulation seems to have had the most influence on later discussions. He argues that 'laughter is nothing else but *sudden glory* arising from some sudden *conception* of some *eminency* in ourselves, by *comparison* with the *infirmity* of others, or with our own formerly' (*Human Nature*, in *The English Works*, ed. Sir William Molesworth, iv [London, 1840], 46). Among those later Hobbesian positions, the following are most notable: Charles Baudelaire, 'On the Essence of Laughter', *The Mirror of Art*, trans. and ed. Jonathan Mayne (London, 1955); Edmund Bergler, *Laughter and the Sense of Humor* (New York, 1956); Henri Bergson's 'Laughter'; Freud's *Wit*; Anthony M. Ludovici, *The Secret of Laughter* (London, 1932); and Albert Rapp, *The Origins of Wit and Humor* (New York, 1951). The Hobbesian argument is best suggested and perhaps most concisely illustrated by Prince Hal's comment in *1 Henry IV*: 'Falstaff sweats to death and lards the lean earth as he walks along. Were't not for laughing, I should pity him' (II. ii).

[25] This view enjoyed a vogue in the late eighteenth century and throughout the nineteenth century; the most famous statement of it is in George Meredith's *An Essay on Comedy*. Stuart M. Tave's *The Amiable Humorist* (Chicago, Ill., 1960) is an intelligent analysis of the development and manifestations of the anti-Hobbesian theory. Of its few twentieth-century exponents, the most strenuous is Max Eastman (*The Sense of Humor* and *Enjoyment of Laughter* (New York, 1921 and 1937)).

for hundreds of years, noted 'a component of malice, of debasement of the other fellow, and of aggressive-defensive self-assertion . . . in laughter—a tendency diametrically opposed to sympathy, helpfulness, and identification of the self with others'.[26] I find this argument and the evidence given by the theorists cited above (see note 24) conclusive. The important point, though, is the relevance of Koestler's conclusions to our subject. Even if there *is* genial or harmless laughter, I think it is very rare in Dickens.

There are, of course, genial characters in Dickens and even sympathetic characters at whom we laugh. But there is no necessary contradiction. One of Henri Bergson's most important distinctions, which, if noticed, would silence almost all of his critics, applies here. After arguing that 'laughter has no greater foe than emotion', he adds, 'I do not mean that we could not laugh at a person who inspires us with pity, for instance, or even with affection, but in such a case we must, for the moment, put our affection out of court and impose silence upon our pity' (p. 63). The key phrase is 'for the moment'; our ordinarily active sympathy is temporarily withdrawn in the process of laughing. And it is this moment of required 'anesthesia of the heart' (p. 64) that Dickens manipulates so tellingly. It does no good, then, to cite Mr. Pickwick as a refutation of Bergson; Bergson has allowed for Mr. Pickwick. He admits the possibility of our affection and explains our derisive laughter in a brilliant essay that, though often attacked for its narrowness, has particular relevance to Dickens.

Bergson sees the basis of all laughter in the conflict of the rigid and mechanical with the flexible and organic; the key is *something mechanical encrusted on the living*' (p. 84). He sees laughter as, above all, a *'social gesture'* (p. 73), the corrective by which society humiliates in order to preserve itself from the deadening effects of what Matthew Arnold called 'machinery' —political, ideological, social, and psychological rigidity. Therefore, *'we laugh every time a person gives us the impression of being a thing'* (p. 97) and, of course, at the converse.

This transposition of the functions of persons and things is, as Dorothy Van Ghent and others have shown,[27] the basis of

[26] *Insight and Outlook* (New York, 1949), p. 56.
[27] Dorothy Van Ghent's arguments are stated in 'The Dickens World: A

Dickens's animism, which is, in turn, one of the keys to his vision and his technique. It is also at the core of much of his most significant humour, and Bergson provides us with an extremely important means of approaching that humour. The long procession of mechanical humans and living things in Dickens suggests not only his typically Victorian position as revivifying artist, not only his vision of human beings fundamentally isolated from one another and from their environment, but also a use of laughter as a rhetorical tool to enlist his readers in a protest against isolation and mechanistic dominance and in support of imaginative sympathy and identification with others. The fact that the reader is largely unconscious that his responses are being directed makes the rhetoric no less vivid or successful. Through his animism, Dickens continually uses laughter as a rhetorical support to thematic issues, and Bergson is assuredly the chief theorist of animism.

But there are other appeals to laughter in Dickens and other uses made of the reader's response to humour. Bergson's clarity and lucidity become simplistic if stretched too far, and one is forced to turn to more subtle and complex theorists, principally Freud.[28] Freud's work on laughter, though by no means universally accepted, comes about as close to that position as any single statement reasonably could. More important, his concept of laughter is far more flexible and inclusive than most, and takes into account two factors in laughter that are often separated and treated as exclusive: the offensive release of aggression, hostility, or inhibition and the defensive protection of pure pleasure, joy, or play. Though the complexity of Freud's argument makes it extremely difficult to summarize,[29] a brief discussion is essential.

The major part of Freud's work on laughter was published

View from Todgers's', *SR*, lviii (1950), 419–38 and in the chapter on *Great Expectations* in *The English Novel: Form and Function* (New York, 1953), pp. 125–38. Dickens's animism had previously been noted, most prominently by H. A. Taine, *History of English Literature*, ii. 340–41; however, it has been investigated intensively only since Miss Van Ghent's studies.

[28] As a matter of fact, Freud agreed with Bergson's theories and saw them as coincident with a part of his own formulation (*Wit*, p. 338).

[29] There is, however, a successful and extremely useful summary and clarification by Martin Grotjahn, 'Sigmund Freud and the Psychoanalysis of Jokes', *Beyond Laughter* (New York, 1957), pp. 1–21.

in 1905 under the title, *Wit and Its Relation to the Unconscious.*
Here he first distinguishes between the technique and the
tendency of jokes, and devotes the first section to an analysis
of technique, mainly the details of grammar, syntax, and
vocabulary which form the surface matter of jokes. In this
long analysis, Freud finds the techniques of jokes similar to
those used in dreams: condensation, displacement, substitution, and like disguises. This similarity between wit-work and
dream-work establishes the connection to the unconscious
which he explores in the second section of the book. This part
involves an analysis of the matter or tendencies which lie at
the core of jokes and which the techniques have partially and
necessarily disguised. He begins with wit, that form of produc-
ing laughter which functions most like dreams, and shows
that it originates in aggressive or obscene tendencies.[30] The
aggressive or obscene idea is activated in the unconscious but
disguised by the wit-work (or technique) so that the psychic
energy initially aroused can be safely relieved. If the joke is
successful, the source of laughter in the teller and the listener
is the same: 'the economy of psychic expenditure' (p. 180),
or in other words, the efficient use of energy previously needed
for repressing the dangerous idea by removing the apparent
danger and releasing the energy in laughter. In addition to the
pleasure aroused from release, there is also play pleasure: the
infantile and pure joy in nonsense, playing with words, and
combating order. To summarize to this point, then, jokes can
be analysed as to technique and tendency, though it is likely
that the technique in most cases is mainly the disguise and
the tendency the *cause* of the laughter. We laugh because we
are permitted to express the energy from hostility or aggression
openly; the release plus the infantile joy of word play account
for the pleasure in laughter.

By far the least important and persuasive part of Freud's
analysis follows, an account of our pleasure in the comic. Here
Freud discusses the laughter at stupidity, the naïve, caricature,
repetition, and the like, explaining it as differing from wit in
its psychic location (foreconscious rather than subconscious),

---

[30] Freud also postulates 'harmless wit', wit without tendency; but though
he devotes considerable space to this subject, his demonstrations are usually
considered quite unpersuasive; see Grotjahn (pp. 10–11), who argues that there
simply is no such thing as harmless wit.

in its moving beyond words into action and behaviour, and in the fact that it is based on an explicit comparison of ourselves with another's limitations. The pleasure in this case is provided by the feeling of superiority, as Hobbes had said, plus a release of inhibition energies temporarily unnecessary in the face of such childish action. Freud remarks on his indebtedness to Bergson at this point, and Bergson is clearer and more satisfactory in this area.

Both wit and the comic, Freud argued, are incompatible with strong emotion (p. 371), which is one reason why they must be presented in a disguised form. In the final section of the book, supplemented by a paper published in 1928,[31] Freud discusses humour, which he describes as a way of dealing with pain. His best example of humour concerns the prisoner on the way to the gallows who remarks, 'Well, this is a good beginning to the week' (*IJP*, 1). For the prisoner, this comment represents a way of combating pain by denying its province; it is the rebellious assertion by the ego that it is invulnerable (*IJP*, 2–3). More important, the pleasure for the listener is derived from an 'economy of sympathy' (*Wit*, p. 374). We are prepared to respond with pity, but pity is found to be superfluous and the energy first called up for sympathy can be released in laughter. More generally, he speaks of the 'economized expenditure of affect' (*Wit*, p. 371), in which the energies associated with any strong emotion are aroused, then shown to be unnecessary, and are thereby available for laughter.

Actually, Freud recognized quite clearly that his categories were analytical conveniences and that, in practice, wit, the comic, and humour were intermixed. For our purposes, the most important uses of Freud will be: the distinction between technique and tendency, and the general dominance of the latter as a cause of laughter; the dual pleasure source of laughter; and the concept of economy and its explanation of the way in which aggression, inhibition, and strong feelings of sympathy or fear can be turned into laughter.

This is the general outline, then, of the approach to laughter to be used here. It does not, of course, constitute a complete theory of laughter, and it is perhaps incomplete because it

---

[31] 'Humour', *International Journal of Psychoanalysis*, ix. 1–6. Further references will be cited in the text as *IJP*.

concentrates almost entirely on the laugher to the exclusion of the means of evoking laughter. An appropriate (at least forceful) apology for both limitations is offered by Samuel Johnson, who chides 'definers' of comedy for having fiddled with useless definitions of techniques of arousing laughter 'without considering that the various methods of exhilerating [the dramatist's] audience, not being limited by nature, cannot be comprised in precept'.[32]

To supplement, in a minor way, the arguments of Bergson and Freud, a few subsidiary points should finally be considered:

i. *Laughter and order.* One of the reasons laughter has always been identified in some way with the form of comedy is that their main impulses are similar: the restoration of order or equilibrium. Behind comedy lie the ritual pattern of resurrection[33] and the movement to a new society; though the origin of laughter is not so clear, certainly one of its functions is the restoration of 'social equilibrium'.[34] Paradoxically, the movement towards order is paralleled by an impulse towards freedom. Like comedy, which progresses 'from law to liberty' (Frye, p. 181), laughter moves from restraint to release and from a world of mechanistic restriction to a world of childhood and play. Though we laugh always in chorus, either real or imagined, the society we create by our laughter is generally opposed to what we ordinarily think of as society; in the desire to cleanse the existing order of absurdity and rigidity, laughter is always dangerously close to anarchy. This is only a way of saying that laughter is a means of having it both ways: it reassures us of our social being (we are part of a chorus), but also, and perhaps more basically, of our own invincible and isolated ego. Even if we could always laugh at Falstaff[35] (and Shakespeare makes it by no means this easy), we are not only rejecting him but also providing ourselves with a way of glorying in his display of the primacy of the libido. We are

[32] *The Rambler*, no. 125 (28 May 1751), ed. A. Millar (London, 1763), iii. 106.
[33] See F. M. Cornford, *The Origin of Attic Comedy* (London, 1914) and Northrop Frye, *Anatomy of Criticism* (Princeton, N.J., 1957), pp. 212–15.
[34] This is the central thesis of Ralph Piddington's *The Psychology of Laughter: A Study in Social Adaptation* (London, 1933).
[35] Falstaff is Freud's best example of the 'comic', a means of providing for laughter by utilizing the energies of inhibition, now superfluous in the face of a completely uninhibited man.

preparing for the triumph of Hal, in one sense, but perhaps in another and deeper sense we have already experienced the triumph of Falstaff.

Thus laughter both confirms and denies society and is, from a social viewpoint, implicitly subversive. It moves towards a coalition, but it is a coalition of joyful people dedicated to freedom and play; order is, at best, secondary. Who could imagine the wonderful social group assembled at the end of *Pickwick*—Mr. Pickwick, the Wellers, Tracy Tupman, Snodgrass, Winkle, the Wardles, and the rest—really constituting a society that would function at all? Every reader of the novel has imagined just that, and our conviction is a testament to the ambiguity of laughter: its paradoxical movement towards both order and freedom. The freedom is potentially absolute, but the order is deceptive: the world of Stiggins and Serjeant Buzfuz, which is to say the world of law and organized religion, is rejected in favour of the world of Tony Weller and Bob Sawyer. Laughter confirms society, but strictly on its own rather deceptive terms.

ii. *Laughter and the grotesque.* Though this very complex subject can only be touched on here, the grotesque is present in one form or another in most of Dickens's novels. It generally concerns itself with the demonic aspects of existence or, more generally, with a perception of 'the terrors and absurdities of internal and external traps'.[36] In one sense, whether or not we laugh depends on the relative strength of 'the terrors and [the] absurdities', but more important is the nature of the power given to the ego to resist the terror or dismiss it. The funny grotesque is a form of what Freud called 'humour', and its most consistent manifestation in Dickens comes from the sense of estrangement evoked by his animism (discussed above). The most important, though rather obvious, point to make is that there *is* a balance involved: that our laughter moves close to the desperate or the hysterical as the balance shifts to terror and that we may dismiss the threat with our laughter now, only to have it reappear a few pages later, all the stronger for coming on us in our presumed safety.

[36] Spilka, *Dickens and Kafka*, p. 243. Spilka's treatment of the grotesque in Dickens is extensive and rewarding.

iii. *Vulnerability and immunity provided by laughter.* As the last sentence suggests, laughter provides a kind of immunity which may become a special kind of vulnerability. Laughter implies the sort of commitment which is so complete that it is unable to avoid rebuffs; it assumes complicity and sanctity and is therefore especially vulnerable to attack, as anyone knows who has had his own laughter met with icy stares. Having released the energies ordinarily used to guard our hostilities, inhibitions, or fears, we are especially unprotected if the promised safety which allowed us to laugh proves to be illusory. Imagine the fat old man who slipped on the banana peel being suddenly identified as our brother, now seriously hurt; the custard pie containing sulphuric acid; the train really hitting the funny car and killing the Keystone Cops. These are extreme examples, of course, and Dickens's technique is much more subtle, but one of his more successful tactics involves just this sort of combined immunity-vulnerability which laughter creates and which makes us so open, even if just for an instant, to the deepest attacks.

iv. *Laughter and the narrative.* The preceding arguments all imply a more orderly and complete kind of analysis than is possible outside the restricted world of the joke: the ordinary Dickens novel contains perhaps five thousand jokes. But even if one were to analyse each one of these (God help us), there would still remain the other appeals to humour: images of funny faces and absurd postures, conventional funny situations, and the like. Discussing all of these would still leave one of the most important causes of laughter unaccounted for: the cumulative effect. This can take many forms, from the snowball technique, in which one laugh makes us more ready for another, to the chuckle of anticipation which comes when we sense that Mr. Micawber is in the wings, about to make another entrance. Our memory builds up associations which can act reflexively and set us laughing without apparent local cause. Dickens appeals to this reflexive laughter most obviously in his use of tags to accompany so many characters.[37]

[37] It is also possible to view the tag as a form of caricature and thus a kind of insult which appeals to our unconscious sense of superiority; see Grotjahn, p. 49.

But the problem is still more complicated: our laughter is conditioned not only by memory but by anticipation of the future course of the narrative. The expectation of a happy ending can induce a mood of comfort or euphoria particularly suited to laughter; conversely, the anticipation of a sad or frightening ending makes us seize all the more readily on nearly any excuse to laugh.[38] There is also the whole area of tone to account for, since it helps to create and sustain a certain mood. Finally, one must obviously just assume (there is no way to prove it) that the text examined does, in fact, provoke amusement, internal or external, and that a smile or chuckle, internal or external, is at least related to a fully fledged laugh and involves the same tendencies.[39] At any rate, the term laughter will be used generally to describe the many manifestations of amusement.

3. DICKENS AND RHETORIC

Dickens said so little about his own practices as a humorist, and that little is so contradictory, that it is almost without value for criticism. He spoke at one time about being required 'to restrain myself from launching into extravagances' in the enjoyment of his 'preposterous sense of the ridiculous'; on the other hand, he said later that he had 'such an inexpressible enjoyment of what I see in a droll light, that I dare say I pet it as if it were a spoilt child'; and he sometimes implied in letters to potential contributors to his journals that they should 'administer' humour as a relief. Dickens's direct comments mix the obscure and the superficial and tell us little or

[38] This point is made by Kimmins (*The Springs of Laughter*, p. 64), who says that in this case the amount of laughter far exceeds the apparent provocation. This kind of laughter is often called 'relief', though it seldom functions so simply. It partially explains, however, the approval expressed at Dick Swiveller and the disappointment at the performance of Mr. Venus and Silas Wegg. The former does, for some, help to alleviate the gloom; the latter, apparently, do not, and we are angry at their presumed failure. The interesting parts of these reactions are our dogged anticipation of relief and our unexamined assumption that it should be there. In Dickens, the assumption is most often invalid and the anticipation purposefully thwarted.

[39] See Charles Darwin's *The Expression of the Emotions in Man and Animals* (Chicago, Ill., 1965 (originally published 1872)), pp. 206–9, for the most authoritative arguments on this subject.

nothing about his practice. Perhaps one of his more indirect statements is more revealing: 'You write to be read, of course.'[40] Naturally, a good many writers do write to be read, but the rhetorical emphasis is important. Dickens held as an unquestionable assumption the notion that one wrote *to* someone. And though I do not want to present him as a calculating journalist, easily and cheaply manipulating the feelings of his readers, the evidence for Dickens as a rhetorician, a man constantly aware of and in touch with his audience, is, as has often been recognized, very strong. He spoke of his relationship to his public as 'personally affectionate and like no other man's', and he loved to tell the story of the lady who stopped him to ask if he would let her *'touch the hand that has filled my house with many friends'*.[41] Certainly Dickens did think of his novels, at least partially, as periodic communications with his affectionate readers; he wrote with the reader very much in mind; and he was very much concerned with that reader's feelings: 'You cannot interest your readers in any character unless you have first made them hate, or like him.'[42] The emphasis on emotional response is significant. Further, as John Butt and Kathleen Tillotson suggest, he used John Forster 'as a judge of what the average reader would stand',[43] as a rhetorical sounding-board, in other words. Such famous queries to Forster, then, as the one concerning the projected evil course of Walter Gay—'Do you think it may be done, without making people angry?'[44]—can be seen not so much as a request for a critical opinion as an idea thrown out against a representative audience for testing. 'Does it make *you* angry?' is the real question. Forster was, among other things, insurance against a disruption of the affectionate communication.

Dickens's extreme sense of intimacy with his audience was partly responsible for his decision to publish his explanation of the separation from his wife and to embark on his series of

---

[40] To John Forster, *Life*, i. 419; to Edward Bulwer-Lytton, *Life*, ii. 273; to Percy Fitzgerald, *Nonesuch Letters*, iii, 393, 27 July 1864; to Miss Emily Jolly, *Nonesuch Letters*, ii. 679, 17 July 1855.

[41] Forster's *Life*, ii. 205 and ii. 221.

[42] To John Overs, *Nonesuch Letters*, i. 255, 12 Apr. 1840.

[43] *Dickens at Work* (London, 1957), p. 23.

[44] Forster's *Life*, ii. 21.

readings. If one can judge from his letters, what excited him most about these readings was the particularly warm and personal response of his audience: 'The affectionate regard of the people exceeds all bounds and is shown in every way. The audiences do everything but embrace me, and take as much pains with the readings as I do.'[45] The last phrase strikes exactly the right note in regard to Dickens's rhetoric: the reader must participate equally with the writer in the experience and in the theme. Dickens's use of laughter is a major element in allowing—indeed forcing—us to do so.

Again, this is not to say that Dickens planned his novels simply in terms of controlling our responses. Nor does this approach necessarily rule out the time-honoured view of Dickens as a deeply unconscious or hallucinatory writer. Both aspects are undoubtedly part of his art. Whether we see Dickens as consciously manipulating his work or unconsciously projecting his view of society does not really matter. It remains true in either case that the use of our laughter is an extremely powerful instrument of rhetoric, persuasive and incisive in its accuracy, and applicable to us in its contribution to the total vision contained in Dickens's novels.

[45] To John Forster, *Life*, ii. 359.

2 *The Pickwick Papers*

THE VISION FROM THE WHEELBARROW

'Vidth and visdom, Sammy, alvays grows together' (LV).

AT the very heart of *The Pickwick Papers* is the symbol of Christmas: 'Happy, happy Christmas, that can win us back to the delusions of our childish days' (XXVIII).[1] Christmas symbolizes the recapture of freedom and joy celebrated by this great novel, Dickens's one unequivocal comedy, in which all the energies are directed toward providing for the final and beautiful society radiating from Dulwich. *Pickwick* demonstrates how we can realistically maintain those 'delusions of our childish days' in the midst of brutal anonymity; it teaches us how to recall the sense of play in the midst of a world concentrating on superficial seriousness. It does more than teach, of course; it attempts to persuade, not only by appealing to our nostalgia for a lost childhood and a lost Eden, but by extending our awareness of what these worlds mean: *Pickwick* argues that, compared with sliding on the ice, elections and lawsuits are trivial things indeed. More than any other Dickens novel, this one is devoted to what Freud called the pleasure principle. It reopens channels of joy we had considered closed, and it does so primarily by laughter. For the first and only time in Dickens's writings, the aggressive element in laughter is truly secondary. Here our laughter is used constantly to preserve what might be called the vision from the wheelbarrow:

This constant succession of glasses produced considerable effect

[1] All quotations from the novels are taken from The New Oxford Illustrated Dickens (1948–58).

upon Mr. Pickwick; his countenance beamed with the most sunny smiles, laughter played around his lips, and good-humoured merriment twinkled in his eye. Yielding by degrees to the influence of the exciting liquid, rendered more so by the heat, Mr. Pickwick expressed a strong desire to recollect a song which he had heard in his infancy, and the attempt proving abortive, sought to stimulate his memory with more glasses of punch, which appeared to have quite a contrary effect; for, from forgetting the words of the song, he began to forget how to articulate any words at all; and finally, after rising to his legs to address the company in an eloquent speech, he fell into the barrow, and fast asleep, simultaneously. (xix)

The beaming countenance we all associate with Mr. Pickwick is provided for, time and again, by alcohol, used almost as a magic potion in this novel to settle quarrels, restore order, and, most important, to provide just this sort of warm and comfortable sanctity. It is true, however, that, particularly after his experience in the Fleet, Mr. Pickwick uses this magic less and less often; for though it is certainly never repudiated and always retains some potency, it is not always truly effective. It provides, in fact, something of a delusory victory, an escape from the real world. In a novel where the real world is defined largely as a 'legal fiction', there is nothing really wrong with escape, except that it seldom works. Even Mr. Pickwick is not allowed to sleep peacefully in the wheelbarrow. Captain Boldwig, following the rigid and impersonal ordering of people sanctioned by Serjeant Buzfuz, decides Mr. Pickwick is 'a drunken plebeian' and has him shipped to the pound. When Mr. Pickwick awakens, senses his position, and asks for his friends, the nameless, hostile mob throws eggs and turnips, screaming, 'You an't got no friends. Hurrah!' (xix). The brilliantly quick succession of events here suggests the final inadequacy of escape: the world of rigidity and anonymous hostility is always there. Escape is ultimately impossible; the only possibility is transcendence.

But to achieve that transcendence Mr. Pickwick must lose a great deal: his innocence and his vision of an idyllic world. The novel proposes a farewell to unqualified innocence rather than a celebration of it; Mr. Pickwick must for a time turn his back on the wheelbarrow and enter the Fleet. In the process, he moves from Eden into a fallen world. The novel is so comically satisfying, I suggest, precisely because it refuses the idyllic vision and insists on a world which is brutally real; it is so artistically persuasive because of the strength and imposed relevance of the central motif of initiation.[2]

The central fact of the novel is that Mr. Pickwick does change:[3] he must be educated. He must first learn the nature of the real world and, without becoming cynical or despairing, discover the limits of benevolence and innocence as effective agents in that world. He must suffer and emerge from that suffering less bland and more fully human. In the process he must undergo a reductive questioning of identity: Mr. Pickwick as a leader of men, a detached scientist, a gentleman, a benevolent man, and simply a human being. And, as in other literary educations, Mr. Pickwick is attended by his Fool, Sam Weller, likewise a tutor who subverts his position to educate the master whose defects he sees and fears, and who is nonetheless attached to him by love.

And despite his defects, his losses, and his necessary accommodations, Mr. Pickwick fully justifies the faith of his wise servant. His engagement with the world is finally triumphant, illustrating that the vision from the wheelbarrow can be preserved after all and that all the internal and external enemies that had seemed so threatening can be expelled or reconciled. The most important instrument of persuasion for the threefold function of preservation, expulsion, and reconciliation is our laughter.

Though the functions served by the humour in this novel are more straightforward and unified than in any other Dickens novel, they are still manifold. Most important, how-

---

[2] This theme is also discussed, though very differently, by J. Hillis Miller, *Charles Dickens: The World of His Novels* (Cambridge, Mass., 1958), pp. 1–35. The most suggestive treatment of Mr. Pickwick's development is by W. H. Auden, 'Dingley Dell and the Fleet', in *The Dyer's Hand and Other Essays* (New York, 1962), pp. 407–28. Auden sees Pickwick as moving from Eden into the fallen world and thereby losing his innocence. My debt to this brilliant essay is very great, though I disagree with Auden's view of the novel's ending. Other readings of the novel which are exceptionally worthwhile include: William Axton, 'Unity and Coherence in *The Pickwick Papers*', *SEL*, v (1965), 663–76 and Steven Marcus, *Dickens: From Pickwick to Dombey* (New York, 1965), pp. 13–53.

[3] Not that anyone except Dickens has really denied it. The real issue is the nature of the change and whether it is organic or arbitrary. Virtually every discussion of the novel has something to say on these points.

ever, are the controls exercised over the general areas of value and position. In terms of value, our laughter consistently works to expel the conservative and orderly and to reaffirm the free and generally uninhibited. Involved in this set of values is the rejection of law and the entire world of rigid and isolated principle for a world of flexible accommodation and humanity. Our laughter is, further, a defence against the terrifying suggestion of death and the even more terrifying suggestion of aloneness. In a society tending to ossify all human relationships and to make anonymity the common position, geniality, conviviality, even insults are welcomed and approved by laughter. Finally, laughter in *The Pickwick Papers* rejects all that is predatory and possessive, which is one reason why it is so uneasy about love, indeed about women in general, and creates such a thoroughly masculine atmosphere. The rejection of the predatory—in particular predatory females—makes for the almost complete elimination of sex from the centre of the new society and helps account for the particularly genial tone everyone notices in the novel. Though central to most comedies, sex is here not important as either a motivation or a blocking agent (the miniature comedy at the end involving Mr. Winkle acts, in terms of the whole, rather like a parody of the role of sex in traditional comedy). This is not to say that sex jokes are not present; there are hundreds of them, but they are nearly all negative and hostile, turning our aggressive laughter against sex itself. The ritual phallic celebration behind all comedy is very much muted here and the joyousness transferred to the spiritual. Free and uninhibited as the new society is, it is specifically a society of play, a wonderful childhood association in which sex is seen very largely as a threat.[4]

Laughter not only helps to eliminate sexual possessiveness and to define the standards of value on which the final society exists; it also seeks to enrol the reader in that society by

---

[4] The only real exception is Sam Weller, who compartmentalizes the aggressive sexuality of the entire final society. But it could be argued that just as Sam's cynicism is no longer necessary, so his sexuality makes him fit rather uneasily into the final society. At any rate, the separation of sex from the centre of that society is complete. Sam, by containing all of it, manages to suggest the traditional generative aspect of comic endings (all those little Wellers running around) without disrupting the gentle tone of the society.

defining his position in relation to its members. Starting from
a position very far removed from Mr. Pickwick, the reader is
asked to move gradually closer to him as the novel progresses
and to be at Dulwich waiting for him at the close of the novel.
The person who is first introduced, almost sneeringly, as 'the
immortal Pickwick', author of the Tittlebat paper, becomes
by the last chapter 'our old friend'. One could argue, as
Chesterton continually did, that the tone of the original
adjective, immortal, simply changes; that as the sarcasm
dissipates, Pickwick the pedant and fool becomes Pickwick
the god. But how do we allow this to happen? J. Hillis Miller
suggests that we take a position with the narrator and, along
with him, move gradually closer to the hero.[5] This is generally
true, I think, but perhaps oversimplified. The proper perspective towards experience is an important theme in the
novel, and Dickens uses one possible position of the reader as
a rhetorical demonstration of that theme. Mr. Pickwick must
drop his detachment and move to a full engagement with
experience; he must, in general, not treat people, their experiences, and feelings as things. But if we join the narrator
in laughing at Mr. Pickwick, the pretentious scientist who
sits 'as calm and unmoved' as a pickled Tittlebat (I) or who
reacts to alcohol 'like a gas lamp in the street' (II), we may
be showing our susceptibility to Mr. Pickwick's own limitation.
Dickens asks that we play Justice Stareleigh to the hero and
become equally detached and potentially just as callous. But
as the real pain and the equally real joy beneath the surface
are shown, detachment is likely to seem uncomfortable or at
least insufficient. As Dickens says of an uncontrollable horse,
'highly interesting to a bystander, but by no means equally
amusing to any one seated behind him' (v).

The narrative position, facetious and removed, can be
something of a trap, perhaps, to expose the egocentric illusion
of our own unique supremacy. We may find with a start that
we are laughing at least partly at ourselves: we had laughed
at the detachment of the naïve man, only to find that we are
equally detached. Even worse, it is suggested that our own
detachment is not at all naïve but worldly, professional,
cynical, and callous, and that the basis of our presumed

[5] *Charles Dickens*, pp. 26–7.

superiority to Mr. Pickwick is exactly that taken by Dodson and Fogg. When these two begin smirking at Pickwick, the rhetorical point is clear: we can justly laugh at Pickwick now only if we are willing to echo Perker's admiration of Dodson and Fogg and to accept their values. We have been able to avoid being fooled by Bill Stumps's scribbling only because we have long ago exchanged Pickwick's innocence for the paltry knowledge of Perker. So, I think the reader is likely to move towards the hero much more quickly than does the narrator, who waits behind a little, continuing his attack on detachment and smugness. In any case, as we move closer to Pickwick, we duplicate his own movement towards involvement. In this way, the novel's most important psychic progression is enacted in the reader. Like Mr. Pickwick, we too are initiated, primarily through the rhetoric of laughter.

The opening chapter of the novel establishes immediately both the central point of attack on the old society and the most prevalent source of humour: the divorce of language from any solid contact with reality or manageable meaning. Perhaps the most suggestive and thematically appropriate term in the novel, then, is the one Mr. Blotton uses in the first chapter to escape the unhappy position he is in: he had intended the word 'humbug' to apply to Mr. Pickwick only 'in its Pickwickian sense'. The novel exists largely to reverse our reactions to that term. We find that the use of the Pickwickian construction is not limited to this ridiculous club but is essential to the law (Dodson and Fogg are scoundrels only in a Pickwickian sense), religion (Stiggins imbibes only from a Pickwickian point of view), politics (Pott can be said to exist only in a Pickwickian sense)—in fact, all of organized society. In the end, we see that this usage is not really funny: even those exasperating women, Mrs. Bardell and Mrs. Weller, are victims of gammon and may become even slightly pitiable. The Pickwickian tyrants are not funny but vicious. The important and deeply ironic point is that only Mr. Pickwick and his group escape being Pickwickian. They alone successfully avoid the isolation created by a shifting, rootless language, and are able to escape from those in control who exploit this very fact. But it is not immediately apparent that there is any problem or that it was in any way related to this first farcical chapter. The laughter at the Club's circumlocutions is likely to establish all the wrong premises and to lead the reader into a position of detachment which, in the end, is itself Pickwickian.

However, the first section of the novel—up to the introduction of Sam Weller—does give some support to a false superiority and an accompanying derisive laughter by establishing very firmly the extreme limitations of Mr. Pickwick's initial position. It is made quite clear that Mr. Pickwick is limited by his *naïveté* (the basis for much of our laughter in the early stages), but more striking is the suggestion that his very innocence implies a kind of callousness. A man who insists that the world is rational and kindly not only looks foolish but may actually cause pain if the world is, in fact, irrational and cruel. His contact with others is bound to be incomplete. Dickens suggests this in an early (and admittedly untypical) entry Mr. Pickwick makes in his diary concerning the people of Kent. The very exaggeration of the callousness, of course, tempts us to dismiss it through laughter, but it is still the first of several important clues: 'Nothing . . . can exceed their good humour. It was but the day before my arrival that one of them had been most grossly insulted in the house of a publican. The barmaid had positively refused to draw him any more liquor; in return for which he had (merely in playfulness) drawn his bayonet, and wounded the girl in the shoulder. And yet this fine fellow was the very first to go down to the house next morning, and express his readiness to overlook the matter, and forget what had occurred' (ii). Mr. Pickwick is certainly not capable of irony; the narrator has a superabundance, of course, and some of it has clearly spilled over here, but still, through the facetiousness, creeps the slight hint of insensitivity and egocentricity.

More clarifying and persuasive, however, in this early section, is the light thrown on Mr. Pickwick and his values by his first important contact, Alfred Jingle. Jingle, significantly attracted by the notion of 'fun', rescues Mr. Pickwick and his friends from an attack by a mob, symbolic throughout the novel of a primitive hostility and a threat of anonymity. Jingle's rejection of the mob suggests what he soon makes explicit: that he finds a way of preserving his individual identity. As he insists, his life is 'not extraordinary, but singular' (ii). Though cynical by nature and unscrupulous by choice, Jingle maintains always an air of 'perfect self-posses- sion' (ii), which he supports by using two important weapons: Freudian humour and parody. He deals with his own poverty, for instance, by turning it into a joke about the enormous quantity of luggage he has; and clearly he struggles on from cricket match to soirée mainly in order to survive. As he says of the cricket team: 'flannel jackets—white trousers—anchovy sandwiches—devilled kidneys—splendid fellows—glorious' (vii). He preserves his 'self-possession' by denying the real identity of the others—flannel jackets and trousers only— and by covertly suggesting his own motivation—anchovy sandwiches. Jingle sees immediately through the artificialities of social behaviour and attacks the impersonal and the self- important wherever he finds them. In addition, he combats pain and personal attacks by laughing at them, thereby transforming them into a source of pleasure.

But there is an edge of the desperate in Jingle; he is very quick to refer to himself as from 'No Hall, Nowhere' in anti- cipation of attack. This same defensiveness accounts for his almost fatal lack of discrimination: he sees Mr. Pickwick and his friends as indistinguishable from Dr. Slammer or Mrs. Leo Hunter. They are all seen as threats or opportunities, and he reacts accordingly—generally with parody or hostility. Though his retort to Dr. Slammer is brilliant, it is no more aggressive than his response to Mr. Pickwick's announcement that he is 'an observer of human nature': 'Ah, so am I. Most people are when they've little to do and less to get' (ii). He proceeds to demolish in turn each of the other club members by treating them as 'poet, sportsman, lover', as distinct, clearly, from human beings. In one sense, he is right in attacking, and our responsive laughter is important in establishing Mr. Pickwick's limitations, but Jingle, though certainly wise, is also cynical and fails to respond to the possibilities in Mr. Pickwick. We are, therefore, given a slight justification for regarding him as a villain; his urge to survive makes him use the simply gullible, and the pretentious and vicious, alike. The justification is very slight, however, and

really constitutes a false lead. Jingle is clearly not the real
villain; in fact, his impulses are generally proper, and he is
often an index of values, directing our laughter towards all
that denies the flexibility and reality of the human spirit.
If Mr. Pickwick and his followers are included in this attack,
it is partly because they deserve it.

For instance, Mr. Pickwick uses the Pickwick Club itself
as a refuge from the harshness of the world and as a source
of easy and comforting identity. When asked if Jingle is a
member, he responds with indignation, 'Certainly not' (III).
The gentlemanly repulsion belies 'the beaming countenance
of the unconscious Pickwick' he lapses into a few lines later.
Jingle, he feels, is simply not part of the world he wants to
accept.

But Jingle's real world insists on thrusting itself on him.
Even the lugubrious Dismal Jemmy latches on to Pickwick's
aversion to the concrete and the awful:

'Ah! people need to rise early, to see the sun in all his splendour,
for the brightness seldom lasts the day through. The morning of
day and the morning of life are but too much alike.'

'You speak truly, sir,' said Mr. Pickwick.

.   .   .

'Did it ever strike you, on such a morning as this, that drowning
would be happiness and peace?'

'God bless me, no!' replied Mr. Pickwick, edging a little from the
balustrade. (v)

Pickwick readily assents to the abstraction—he can easily
live in the world of triteness, where death exists only in a
Pickwickian sense—but he violently resists its application to
himself. This may seem an involuted way of making the point
that he is comically unconscious, but his unconsciousness,
perhaps, is not so much a natural unworldliness as a defence
against reality. It is not Mr. Pickwick's impulse to defend
himself that is wrong, but the fact that he has not yet really
acknowledged the reality he is avoiding. He instinctively runs,
but there is no escape. Even the rescue from the second mob,
the faceless army, proposed by Mr. Wardle simply introduces
new problems and re-focuses old ones.

It is true that in some ways the Wardles' home represents
the desirable goal: the essence of the Christmas symbol. Even

in May there is a wood fire which Dickens says strongly
suggests Christmas (v), and 'Mr. Pickwick thought he had
never felt so happy in his life' (vi) as during the evening
games. But this lovely world has not yet been earned and is
symbolically wrecked at this early point by its own ineptness
and vulnerability; it must be purified and more clearly
defined. The purification is accomplished mainly by the
laughter at Joe and at Rachael Wardle. The fact that Joe is
here at all is important: in the midst of health and hearty
conviviality is this slightly sadistic eating-machine. What he
suggests, I think, is the divorce and separate embodiment of
some of the darker aspects of the central impulse toward
childhood. Joe embodies all the grasping and blatant physical
egocentricity particularly associated with childhood. By
laughing at Joe, we are asked not only to dismiss another
predatory instinct, but to make more comfortable the wheelbarrow vision, now partially cleansed.

The situations involving Rachael Wardle are slightly more
complicated. Though the general view of women in *Pickwick*
is by no means flattering, the humour derived from Rachael
Wardle is the harshest and most aggressive in the novel. This
weak old maid represents, ironically, a great threat to the
establishment of the final society and must be relentlessly
attacked by humour and finally dismissed. Marriage is, in a
very lukewarm way, sanctified by the Dulwich society, but
sex in general is not. Rachael Wardle in search of a man is
parallel to Dodson and Fogg in search of gullible clients, and
the laughter at her amounts to a dismissal of the selfish and
acquisitive in sexual love. What is surprising is the consistency
and harshness of the attack: Dickens obviously expects even
the very word 'spinster' to evoke laughter, and Rachael is
never around for long without the jokes on her age and condition beginning. Behind our laughter, of course, is the hostility
aroused by the notion of the sex impulse existing at all in the
old. But, though in most comedies our laughter insists that
sex belongs exclusively to the young, here it suggests that sex
(or more accurately the interest in sex) really is a part of age
and partakes of its absurdity. We are, of course, on the side
of the young in *Pickwick*, but youth is here defined more as a
spiritual than a physical condition (Mr. Pickwick is much

younger than Tommy Bardell in this sense), and the spiritual
condition is more than a little uneasy with the sex urge.

Along with sex, Dickens attacks through Rachael the more
thematically central opposition of conventional falsification
and concrete reality. Mr. Tupman's proposal scene, for
instance, takes place in a bower covered 'with honeysuckle,
jessamine, and creeping plants—one of those sweet retreats
which humane men erect for the accommodation of spiders'
(VIII). The proposal itself is likewise subverted and its language
ridiculed by the continual transference of emotion and movement to Miss Wardle's watering-pot: 'Here Mr. Tupman
paused, and pressed the hand which clasped the handle of the
happy watering-pot.' The emotion slithers along here from
point to point until it finally reaches the *happy* pot, the only
real object in this scene. Spiders and pots are measured
against the false attitudes and poses. 'Men are such deceivers',
Miss Wardle whispers softly, but the real deception and the
real danger lie in the divorce of language and personality from
any concrete basis. Our laughter is meant to reject just such a
separation.

Dickens reinforces this same thematic issue by allowing
Jingle to parody explicitly these conventional attitudes and
roles in winning Rachael. By the time we reach the climax
of this episode in the final scene at the 'White Hart', we are
eager to see all Rachael's notions of romance absolutely and
harshly crushed by reality:

'More than one-and-twenty!' ejaculated Wardle, contemptuously. 'More than one-and-forty!'
'I an't,' said the spinster aunt, her indignation getting the better
of her determination to faint.
'You are,' replied Wardle, 'you're fifty if you're an hour.' (x)

When a glass of water is proposed to revive the fainting Miss
Wardle, her brother counters with the demand that they
throw a *bucket* of water 'all over her; it'll do her good, and she
richly deserves it'. Only from a standpoint of complete exasperation is Wardle's notion that she somehow 'deserves it'
justified, but it is precisely that exasperation that the reader
is asked to share. The potential cruelty of the humour is thus
masked, and the laughter is used to demolish Rachael and the

sexually predatory and to form part of the strong artillery directed against false roles and meaningless conventional language.

The fact that Jingle wins here and must be paid off foreshadows, in one sense, the crucial acknowledgement of worldly defeat symbolized later in the paying off of Dodson and Fogg. But the differences are really more important than the similarities. Jingle is not a true enemy, as Dodson and Fogg certainly are. In fact, by attacking rigidity and blindness, he even provides Mr. Pickwick with an important object lesson. But at this point, Mr. Pickwick misplaces his anger and evades his education completely.

This evasion would not seem so serious, except that it indicates a lack of awareness, which in turn creates a certain insensitivity in his dealings with others. Even during the hilarious 'proposal' scene, this unpleasant aspect intrudes. Mrs. Bardell's primitive but very real reaction is entirely incomprehensible to him and becomes a 'very extraordinary thing' (xii). His confusion is, of course, partly caused by his innocence, but the key point is that his innocence results in a detachment which ironically shares the anti-human tendencies of the truly vicious. Though the law has none of Pickwick's innocence, it uses his tactics, disengaging itself and treating people and experiences as things. Mr. Pickwick's early *naïveté* unintentionally reflects in a small but significant way the self-conscious and deliberate inhumanity of the commercial society. His character during the first part of the novel is involved completely in his purpose, a 'scientific' trip to note 'curiosities'. He must be educated to see the cruelty of indifference and to see that it is not Jingle or Mrs. Bardell who is at fault. It is significant that it is at this point that Sam is signed on as Mr. Pickwick's valet, or, in terms of the central theme, his tutor. Mr. Pickwick has started the machinery of the main action of novel—Bardell *v.* Pickwick and the ensuing imprisonment. It is Sam's function to show him the details of the inner cogs of that social machinery and to persuade him that complete evasion is heartless and ultimately impossible. But his pupil is now all too well emblemized by his antiquarian discovery, the Bill Stumps rock, 'an illegible monument of Mr. Pickwick's greatness' (xi). Sam has no easy job.

But he is equal to the most demanding work. He is indeed 'the center of intelligence in the novel'[6] and the most important moral reference point we have. Like Jingle in his ability to see immediately through the artificialities of social behaviour, to construct witty attacks on the rigid institutions of language, and to combat pain through Freudian humour, he differs from him in being free from the necessity of continual hostility. Both Jingle and Sam are members of a guerrilla band, but Sam is much more selective about his targets, for he sees that some threats are more serious than others. He can be responsive to a good heart, as Jingle cannot, for he is much more secure in his own identity. He can accept with equanimity Mr. Pickwick's dehumanizing characterization of him as an 'original' and the probability that his own father doesn't know his name, whereas Jingle accepts a loss of identity only with his teeth gritted and strikes out indiscriminately in order to preserve himself. Sam certainly has the capacity for aggression, but also for gentleness. It should be made clear, however, that much of the humorous appeal of his language is very dark indeed; for instance, 'There's nothin' so refreshin' as sleep, sir, as the servant-girl said afore she drank the egg-cupful o' laudanum' (XVI). Notice that Sam manages here to include in the general attack on the stupid cliché a covert attack also on the price of aloof comfort and perhaps even on class snobbery. But despite this barrage of attacks, there is an enveloping genial purpose: the education of Mr. Pickwick into a world of pain and poverty, limitation and morality. One of his most important pedagogical tools is the comparison of the falsely genteel (in this case the cliché about sleep), associated implicitly with Mr. Pickwick's initial vision, to the concrete actuality (drunkenness, pain, and resiliency in this case) he must learn about. Throughout, he makes war on Mr. Pickwick in order to save him; the aggression is contained within a benevolent scheme. But it is aggression nonetheless. For Sam's first job is a negative one: to make Mr. Pickwick (and perhaps the reader) see the limitations of the 'scientific' position. He embarks on the education of his

[6] Marcus, p. 34. An extensive and often penetrating discussion of Sam's role is given by James A. Wright in an unpublished dissertation (Univ. of Washington, 1959), 'The Comic Imagination of the Young Dickens', pp. 51–89.

hero immediately; his first words in his job interview begin
the process:

'Queer start that 'ere, but he [Jingle] was one too many for you,
warn't he? Up to snuff and a pinch or two over—eh?'
'Never mind that matter now,' said Mr. Pickwick hastily. (xii)

Mr. Pickwick *hastily* dismisses the whole approach, perhaps
instinctively realizing the nature of the process which is just
beginning. For the education will be both difficult and painful.
He must find a balance between innocent benevolence and
knowing cynicism, between pride and humility; he must drop
the aloof defence of scientific observation and engage in a
true involvement. But he is understandably slow to do so,
and Sam thus begins, relentlessly forcing reality on to Mr.
Pickwick.

He receives a fine opportunity almost immediately from
the election at Eatanswill, an elaborate object lesson in the
dangers of egoism and ignorance. It is worth noting that
underlying all the wonderful absurdities of the election—Pott
and Slurk, Mrs. Leo Hunter, and the rest—is the central
proposition that elections themselves are vicious, precisely
because they work to magnify each isolated ego: 'the Eatanswill people, like the people of many other small towns, considered themselves of the utmost and most mighty importance'
(xiii). Our laughter tends to reject this egotism as well as to
diminish the importance of government and its suggestions of
order and restriction. It also protects us from the eradication
of personality which paradoxically results from such egotism.
Dickens suggests that a selfhood fed on formulated phrases
and conventional flattery may become enormous, but also
completely unreal: the individually important Eatanswill
electors, each with egos near bursting, merge quickly into an
indistinguishable mob. Our laughter, then, not only serves to
promote important comic values but to protect us from the
really great evil in the novel: anonymity. Both Mr. Pickwick
and the reader are shown that selfishness based on ignorance
provides no self at all. Eatanswill provokes laughter to teach
just that fact.

Mr. Pott, for instance. Master of the clichés of violence and
authority, he turns out to be nothing at all:

'It is a high treat to me, I assure you, to see any new faces; living as I do, from day to day, and week to week, in this dull place, and seeing nobody.'

'Nobody, my dear!' exclaimed Mr. Pott, archly.

'Nobody but *you*,' retorted Mrs. Pott, with asperity. (xiii)

One can almost hear the air escaping from the pricked balloon. Pott's distance from reality is exactly his distance from any true self, and the connection Dickens often makes between public tyranny and private impotence is based on this insight into the relation of reality and personality. Tyrants in Dickens live in a world of unreal language and rootless power and are invariably caught up by those wardens of the brutally concrete, their wives. We are asked to laugh at their hollowness and at every blow to their gaseous egos, and thereby affirm exactly what Sam is pushing Mr. Pickwick toward: a true selfhood based on firm knowledge.

Sam has a field day at Eatanswill:

'I never see men eat and drink so much afore. I wonder they an't afeer'd o' bustin'.'

'That's the mistaken kindness of the gentry here,' said Mr. Pickwick.

'Wery likely,' replied Sam, briefly. (xiii)

Pickwick's response forces Sam to drop the irony and explain more directly the bribery and corruption around them, but Pickwick's ignorance and corresponding distance from humanity astound his servant:

'Can such things be!' exclaimed the astonished Mr. Pickwick.

'Lord bless your heart, sir,' said Sam, 'why where was you half baptized?' (xiii)

Sam sees the real problem here in its full dimensions: for all his good intentions, Pickwick is only 'half baptized'; he is not yet fully human nor fully Christian. His education, then, must include not only knowledge but humanization. He must not only be introduced to the world but baptized into its concerns. Sam begins immediately with an anecdote (his favourite and most effective teaching aid) of his father's services in an election. Bribed to dump some electors in the canal, Tony complies, and Sam ends:

'You wouldn't believe, sir, . . . that on the wery day as he came down with them woters, his coach *was* upset on that 'ere wery spot, and ev'ry man on 'em was turned into the canal.'

'And got out again?' inquired Mr. Pickwick, hastily.

'Why,' replied Sam, very slowly, 'I rather think one old gen'l'm'n was missin'; I know his hat was found, but I a'n't quite certain whether his head was in it or not. But what I look at, is the hextraordinary, and wonderful coincidence, that arter what that gen'l'm'n said, my father's coach should be upset in that wery place, and on that wery day!'

'It is, no doubt, a very extraordinary circumstance indeed,' said Mr. Pickwick. 'But brush my hat, Sam.' (XIII)

Sam refuses to let Mr. Pickwick off with an easy evasion. He *very slowly* forces grim reality on to his master's hasty demand for comic reassurance. Sam's instinct is decidedly anti-comic, both here and in his dark similes. He hates the happy endings which deny reality, for he sees the cruelty of such self-satisfying evasiveness. He is not, of course, either gloomy or perverse; he is a corrective to those social forces which tend to dehumanize Mr. Pickwick. He insists on showing his master the brutality of elections, not to hurt him but to save him from greater harm. His cardinal point is that while ignorance may be bliss, if self-imposed it is inhuman. He believes that a full dose of reality is all that can save Mr. Pickwick, and in this belief he is completely optimistic in the same way that the novel itself is. Neither denies the darkness of this world, but both see that Eden can be transformed and preserved. It is Sam's job to accomplish this transformation, directly in Pickwick and indirectly in the reader.

Our laughter at the last story, for instance, is meant to accomplish the same thing for us as the lesson does for Mr. Pickwick. The story is partly an attack on *naïveté* as well as on elections, on Mr. Pickwick as well as Eatanswill. Sam parodies Mr. Pickwick's search for the 'hex-traordinary' and trivial and thereby directs our aggressive laughter toward the detached and the ignorant. In this way he is moving us toward a specific vision of Mr. Pickwick that anticipates already the final transcendence.

But Mr. Pickwick has a long way to travel; his characteristic response to any difficulty is either a dismissal of it as 'a very extraordinary circumstance indeed' or an impotent 'withering look', and he must first be made to see how inadequate these responses are. Even though he recognizes that he was the 'innocent cause' (xv) of Wardle's unhappiness (the conjunction of innocence and harm is significant) and leaves immediately in search of Jingle, he soon loses himself in the 'objects around him; and at last he derived as much enjoyment from the ride, as if it had been undertaken for the pleasantest reason in the world' (xvi). Again he shows himself incapable of a full response to human beings and turns to 'objects' instead.

He does almost find Jingle, of course, but is, along with Sam, taken in by him and Job, and made a fool of at the boarding-school. This first great humiliation does have an effect on him; he responds with a new coolness and a new deference to Sam:

'I don't think he'll escape us quite so easily the next time, Sam?' said Mr. Pickwick.
'I don't think he will, sir.' (xvi)

Even though he follows this with an absurd threat of physical reprisal, accompanied by some pillow-pounding, he has, at least partially, developed as a result of the education. Significantly, he never does defeat Jingle. He meets him at the Fleet and gives him money. But by then he has learned two important things: that Jingle is not an enemy but a victim and, more important, that one must accept the position of occasionally being cheated; paradoxically, he must accept an imperfect world in order to be perfect in it.

But now he has taken only the first step, and he tends soon after to evade even this position. Hearing the rumour of Winkle's indecent attachment to Mrs. Pott, he responds:

'Is it not a wonderful circumstance . . . that we seem destined to enter no man's house without involving him in some degree of trouble? Does it not, I ask, bespeak the indiscretion, or, worse than that, the blackness of heart—that I should say so!—of my followers?' (xviii)

Notice how close he comes to seeing the central point, that their innocence can, in fact, be harmful to others, and how quickly he evades its application: it is only his followers who are guilty of a 'blackness of heart'. He is, however, interrupted by Sam with a letter from Dodson and Fogg, informing him of the breach of promise suit. The circumstances are identical to the blackness of heart he had just denounced, but he ignores the connection: 'We are all the victims of circumstances, and I the greatest.' Even Sam, who never gives up hope, is depressed by this bit of egoistic self-justification. And our laughter is made to reject equally the ego and the evasion.

Sam rebounds, though, with even more grotesque stories (e.g., the pieman who used kittens for meat) to touch Mr. Pickwick, but Pickwick still resists and blindly demands to see Dodson and Fogg alone. Dodson and Fogg, each one certainly 'a capital man of business' (xx), symbolize the heart of power in the organized world and the chief enemies of all the values the book holds dear. Dickens describes Mr. Fogg as 'a kind of being who seemed to be an essential part of the desk at which he was writing, and to have as much thought or sentiment' (xx). This puts it precisely. Though humour cannot really dismiss the threat of Mr. Fogg, it does repudiate everything he stands for: the law, rigidity, order, dehumanization. Dodson and Fogg have the amoral and frigid success of awful machines, and Mr. Pickwick nearly mangles himself in their works. Sam, however, unceremoniously hauls him off and lectures him in a firm, unmistakably tutorial tone:

'Sam, I will go immediately to Mr. Perker's.'
'That's just exactly the wery place vere you ought to have gone last night, sir,' replied Mr. Weller.
'I think it is, Sam,' said Mr. Pickwick.
'I *know* it is,' said Mr. Weller. (xx)

Sam even omits the 'sir' in his earnestness.

It is at this point that the pedagogical corps is reinforced by the addition of Mr. Weller senior. Tony supplies rhetorical force not only to Mr. Pickwick but to the reader: he joins Sam in the attack on pretentiousness, callousness, and, not unimportantly, on women. He does a good deal to support the essentially masculine atmosphere of the novel, and his advice to those thinking of marriage—'pison yourself, and you'll be glad on it arterwards' (xxiii)—is never really repudiated. Most important, though, is his campaign against pretence; even women, he sees, are merely 'wictims of gammon' (xxvii).

Tony's war is symbolized most pointedly by his attack on the
hypocrisy of Methodism and its elaborate system of evading
realities, but it asserts itself in the form of brilliant parody
wherever it is needed. He instinctively forms an alliance with
Sam in his work with Mr. Pickwick and takes them away on a
field trip to Ipswich. On this trip they are given unconscious
but considerable aid by Peter Magnus, uneasiness personified,
worried even about the value of his own name. By laughing at
him, we are deriding his feeble attempts not only to bolster
his ego but also to establish his personality through things—
he pins his hopes for winning a wife on a hat and a suit. The
parallel to Mr. Pickwick is instructive.

But even more so are the lectures delivered by the Wellers:

'Not a wery nice neighbourhood this, sir,' said Sam. . . .
'It is not indeed, Sam,' replied Mr. Pickwick, surveying the
crowded and filthy street through which they were passing.
'It's a wery remarkable circumstance, sir,' said Sam, 'that
poverty and oysters always seems to go together.'
'I don't understand you, Sam,' said Mr. Pickwick.
'What I mean, sir,' said Sam, 'is, that the poorer a place is, the
greater call there seems to be for oysters. Look here, sir; here's
a oyster stall to every half-dozen houses. The street's lined vith
'em. Blessed if I don't think that ven a man's wery poor, he rushes
out of his lodgings, and eats oysters in reg'lar desperation.'
'To be sure he does,' said Mr. Weller senior; 'and it's just the
same vith pickled salmon!'
'Those are two very remarkable facts, which never occurred to
me before,' said Mr. Pickwick. 'The very first place we stop at,
I'll make a note of them.' (xxii)

Mr. Pickwick has, of course, missed the point. The Wellers
have discussed the neighbourhood in this way in order to make
the connection between the disagreeable streets and the human
poverty they announce; notice that Sam directs Pickwick to
'look here'. Without this pseudo-reflection, Pickwick (and the
reader) would undoubtedly have passed on in happy ignorance.
As it is, our laughter is directed by Sam's parody to reject
entirely the frame of mind which regards poverty as 'a wery
remarkable circumstance'. Pickwick, of course, falls back on
the pose of a scientific observer. But Sam is beginning to reach
his master-pupil. When he again bluntly insists on his tutorial

function, Pickwick is roused to protest but thinks better of it:

'You rayther want somebody to look arter you, sir, wen your judgment goes out a wisitin'.'

'What do you mean by that, Sam?' said Mr. Pickwick. He raised himself in bed, and extended his hand, as if he were about to say something more; but suddenly checking himself, turned round, and bade his valet 'Good night.' (xxii)

The bedroom escapade, from which Sam has just rescued Pickwick, brings them in contact with Mr. Nupkins, Magistrate, and the legal farce which follows acts, in part, as an educational foreshadowing of the major clash with Dodson and Fogg. In this freer and more bumbling courtroom, Sam can act as a chorus throughout, instructing Mr. Pickwick on the basis of the law as an instrument of the brutality of society: 'This is a wery impartial country for justice. . . . There ain't a magistrate goin' as don't commit himself, twice as often as he commits other people' (xxv). The major point of his attack, though, is directed at Mr. Pickwick's pose in the face of the law, on the abstraction of 'principle' that Pickwick uses as a prop to combat that institution:

'I shall take the liberty, sir, of claiming my right to be heard, until I am removed by force.'

'Pickvick and principle!' exclaimed Mr. Weller, in a very audible voice. (xxv)

Sam recognizes the dark facts which hide behind principle: self-delusion and self-gratification. One of the major points he must make with Pickwick is that the power of resiliency in the life force is greater than the depressing powers of cruel institutions. Principle, he sees, is the inflexible foundation of all these institutions, and he therefore attacks it. Immediately after the Bardell v. Pickwick trial, Sam again parodies this abstraction: 'Hooroar for the principle, as the money-lender said ven he vouldn't renew the bill' (xxxv). By juxtaposing the reality of the money-lender and the pun on principle against Pickwick's stance, Sam is, of course, attacking his master on the grounds of his ignorance and unrealistic behaviour. But beneath this he sees that Pickwick's principle is a means of escape, an unconscious but selfish attempt to preserve his own illusory image of his greatness, an image which can be finally broken only by the actual demonstration, in the Fleet, that this principle is harmful to others.

But even at this early trial the attack is both brilliant and intense. A large number of themes coalesce at Nupkins's court. Dickens appears to be using the chapter not only to foreshadow the great trial to come but also to make certain that his reader is primed with the proper attitudes and responses. Sam is not alone in asking us to react with aggression towards the law and Mr. Pickwick's principle; his rhetoric is reinforced in many ways. The simple fact that Jingle is present here, for instance, invokes the logical association, firmly established earlier in the novel, of Jingle's object—in this case, the law—with hollowness and pretence. By this same association, Nupkins becomes another Mr. Leo Hunter. Nupkins is, as a matter of fact, forced to be just as deferential as the husband of the poetess; in short, he is henpecked, and all the humour surrounding the castrating women is brought into play, Nupkins reduced to a cipher, and his professional tyranny shown to be a mask for a lack of power, even of being. Beyond Nupkins, there are dozens of supporting jokes and episodes here. One will have to suffice as an example: the case of the grandiose bit of hollowness, Mr. Grummer:

'My name's Tupman,' said that gentleman.
'My name's Law,' said Mr. Grummer. (xxiv)

Law and Grummer are indeed one: unreal, ridiculous, pretentious. When Grummer tries his high-handedness on Sam Weller, that instrument of reality simply knocks him down. Again our laughter is used thematically.

Before the great trial foreshadowed here, and the subsequent imprisonment, Dickens pauses to solidify the more positive position with three successive visions of childhood joy and freedom, contrasts to the unimaginative rigidity of the trial and prison and anticipations of the victory Mr. Pickwick will eventually gain. The first episode is the Christmas scene at Wardles', celebrating a symbolic defeat of death and the particular warmth and security of childhood: ' "This," said Mr. Pickwick, looking round him, "this is, indeed, comfort" ' (xxviii). Next there is the party at Bob Sawyer's, which amounts to a different form of the childhood vision: a celebration of lawlessness and a great reduction of all law and control into that symbol of pure rage, Mrs. Raddle. Because she suggests all morally restrictive value and because her application of it is so absurd—Mr. Pickwick is a 'willin', 'worse than any of 'em' (xxxii)—the whole issue of morality can be dismissed by laughter, and we are urged to accept a world which values good cheer far more than fiscal responsibility, smoking far more than working. Finally, there is the miniature comedy in Chapter xxxiii of the Wellers' overthrow of temperance, preceded by some 'Critical Sentiments respecting Literary Composition' by 'Mr. Weller the elder'. Tony's aesthetic position is both hilarious and very sensible. He associates poetry with gammon, with the unreal language used by officialdom to trick others: 'Poetry's unnat'ral; no man ever talked poetry 'cept a beadle on boxin' day, or Warren's blackin', or Rowland's oil, or some o' them low fellows; never let yourself down to talk poetry, my boy.' 'Poetry's unnat'ral', and Tony takes his Wordsworthian stand for the concrete reality closest to eternal values and against all commercial, bureaucratic, and immoral perversions of that reality. His chief objection to Sam's valentine is that the allusion to the profile-framing-finishing machine 'werges on the poetical'; it is certainly 'unnat'ral' at least. Tony's ethical fight against the poetical (as he defines it) is constant and is approved absolutely by our laughter and the values of the novel. He views the law, naturally, as a major poetic voice and thus sees that the only way to defeat it is to confound it by constructing something equally false: 'Never mind the character, and stick to the alleybi. Nothing like a alleybi, Sammy, nothing.' Though we may sometimes deride his notions of 'alleybis', they have a primitive aptness, but more important an ethical purity entirely missing from our more sophisticated but more corrupt knowingness. One of the points being made by our laughter is not that the law has its absurd aspects but *is* absurd and vicious and must be rejected, not just amended. This rhetoric of anarchic freedom is reinforced by the second half of the chapter, the beating of the Brick Lane Branch Temperance advocate, the deputy shepherd Stiggins. Typical of the Wellers' methods of subversion, this episode shows the joy available to a life of guerrilla warfare against the occupying armies of gammon. The laughter here supports the rejection not only of the ludicrous organization and Stiggins, its hypocritical leader, but of the whole notion of temperance as well. The position we are asked to take here is one familiar to us by now and likely to become more and more comfortable; the established order is fading and a free and somewhat chaotic joy taking over.

The victory of resilience and enlightened commitment celebrated in these three episodes is played off against the victory of legal rigidity in the great trial to follow. But we should notice that the rigidity is not only the law's, but Mr. Pickwick's as well. Principle, it is suggested, is just as rigid as the professional terminology it is supposedly attacking. It is true, of course, that Mr. Pickwick's principle is rooted in a moral reality that the law has long ago lost touch with: Dodson and Fogg *are* 'great scoundrels'. Perker's response to Mr. Pickwick's charge is very interesting: 'That's a matter of opinion, you know, and we won't dispute about terms; because of course you can't be expected to view these subjects with a professional eye' (xxxi). It is, of course, precisely the terms which do matter here, and Perker simply shows exactly how much he is like the Dodson and Fogg he cannot help admiring. In the law it is 'smartness' which is real; morality and ethics become a trivial 'dispute about terms'. Again, the vast legal fiction is a vocabulary which hides reality. Pickwick is, therefore, right in attacking it on these grounds; he is wrong, however, in using its methods. In forming the 'deliberate and irrevocable determination' not to pay Dodson and Fogg, he is forced to fight the law on its own terms, to take it seriously in other words, and the trial suggests that the law and the official society it represents are both too absurd and too dangerous to be met head-on.

Both the danger and the absurdity are united, as the trial shows, in the ability of the law and its society to dehumanize by manipulating people into things or forcing them into artificial, meaningless roles that deny their identity. Mr. Phunky becomes Mr. Monkey; Mrs. Bardell becomes a sympathetic victim of the scoundrel Pickwick, 'the ruthless destroyer of this domestic oasis in the desert of Goswell Street' (xxxiv);

Winkle becomes Daniel rather than Nathaniel; and Mrs.
Cluppins becomes Tuppins, Jupkins, and finally Muffins. All
this confusion about names and roles is more than a joke on
the court's stupidity, for the court, though stupid, is still all-
powerful. What is important is that it thrusts people into the
anonymity of things: 'A counsel, in the discharge of his duty
to his client, is neither to be intimidated, nor bullied, nor put
down; and . . . any attempt to do either the one or the other,
or the first, or the last, will recoil on the head of the attempter,
be he plaintiff or be he defendant, be his name Pickwick, or
Noakes, or Stoakes, or Stiles, or Brown, or Thompson' (xxxiv).

Mr. Pickwick's real person here is a matter of indifference;
for the law or for this society it doesn't exist. This fact suggests
that, underneath all, the law recognizes no people at all
because it is at war with natural life. Even the jokes about its
viewing anyone under eighty contemptuously as 'a very young
man' support this view. Our laughter is ultimately a defence
not only of the integrity of the human personality but of
existence itself, and the nature so firmly supported by the
Wellers is not in opposition only to artificiality but also to the
rigidity of the corpse. Sam's own part in the trial suggests this
defence of life:

'Have you a pair of eyes, Mr. Weller?'
'Yes, I have a pair of eyes,' replied Sam, 'and that's just it. If
they wos a pair o' patent double million magnifyin' gas micro-
scopes of hextra power, p'raps I might be able to see through a
flight o' stairs and a deal door; but bein' only eyes, you see, my
wision's limited.' (xxxiv)

Sam takes the cliché quite literally in order to attack not only
the rudeness of Buzfuz but his mechanical nature. Sam is
defending here an order which does make sense, one in which
eyes are only, but are really, eyes. The point of the attack on
clichés and the laughter at the rootless manipulation of
language ('Chops and Tomata sauce! . . . Gracious heavens!')
is that, for all its rigidity, the law, by destroying the basis of
language and personality, is ultimately chaotic; paradoxically,
the free society we are rooting and laughing for is, for all its
joyous liberty, maintained by an order based on the relation
of people and words to the concrete.

But Mr. Pickwick, though beaten by the law and temporarily humiliated, still doesn't fully realize how completely he has entered the clutches of organized life. Tony Weller is right: 'I know'd what 'ud come o' this here mode o' doin' bisness. Oh Sammy, Sammy, vy worn't there a alleybi!' (xxxiv). Mr. Pickwick has implicated himself in the very assumptions of the system and must be symbolically purified by imprisonment.

But before the Fleet, we have another pause in which Dickens re-forms his rhetorical troops—and our position. The episode at Bath provides an opportunity for an elaborate and systematic rejection of the falsity at all levels of society— Angelo Cyrus Bantam, M.C., for instance, has teeth which are 'in such perfect order that it [is] difficult at a small distance to tell the real from the false' (xxxv)—and a reinforcement of our support of naturalness, freedom, and flexibility (the 'routine' at Bath has 'a slight tinge of sameness'). There is a particular assault on the distortion of language to avoid reality: 'Hush, my dear sir—nobody's fat or old in Ba—ath.' The parallel footman's 'swarry' functions to spread the attack and make it clear it is not just restricted social satire.

At the opposite end, we are again introduced to the Jingle syndrome—the wonderful failures, Bob Sawyer and Ben Allen. We are urged to laugh here at the monstrous parody of prudence and restraint, and to celebrate the triumph of childhood which turns dull business into a joyous game. Dickens solidifies these dual aspects into one brilliant symbolic episode: Sawyer and Allen drink with Winkle a midday punch stirred with a pestle out of measuring vessels and 'a funnel with a cork in the narrow end' (xxxviii). They illustrate the creative powers of the flexible childish imagination to transform tedium and death into joy and vivid life.

The stage is thus set for the imprisonment. Mr. Pickwick has meanwhile been working in support of Winkle's romance, one of the first creatively outgoing things he has done and therefore a sign both of his developing humanization and his developing youth. As he becomes more involved, Mr. Pickwick becomes in certain key ways younger and therefore closer to the comic centre. Sam recognizes this and jubilantly takes part in the Winkle escapades. But he also recognizes that Mr. Pickwick's transformation and education are not yet complete, and he does nothing to resist his master's decision to go to prison. Just before Pickwick enters the Fleet, Perker appears and with brilliant appropriateness offers Pickwick the comfort of evasion: 'Why, I don't exactly know about perjury, my dear sir . . . Harsh word, my dear sir, very harsh word indeed. It's a legal fiction, my dear sir, nothing more' (XL). This is exactly the frame of mind Mr. Pickwick must renounce, but he seems at first attracted to it; for as he is led by the prisoners, he gazes into the rooms 'with great curiosity and interest', something close to his old scientific attitude. And, as a result of this evasion, he makes a callous observation, which prompts the sharpest rebuttal Sam makes in the novel: 'It strikes me, Sam, that imprisonment for debt is scarcely any punishment at all.' Sam points out quickly that the law fails to make any distinctions between those who are really worthless and those who are victimized and that while victims are damaged heavily, the worthless enjoy it. The law's rigidity and impersonality thus result in awful cruelty:

"'It's unekal,'" as my father used to say wen his grog warn't made half-and-half: "It's unekal, and that's the fault on it."'
'I think you're right, Sam,' said Mr. Pickwick, after a few moments' reflection, 'quite right.' (XLI)

For the first time, Pickwick does not dismiss Sam's point 'hastily'.

Sam also promotes the reader's education by arranging, through his own arrest, an exact parody of Mr. Pickwick's rigid principle, his confrontation with the law, and his defiant determination. The instrument of this parody, Mr. Solomon Pell, suggests not only the quantity of arms Dickens uses to force us to his side, but also the brilliance of his means. Pell is himself an unconscious parody of law and order and allows us to release aggressions at those same agencies. He is, ironically, most proud that he is a 'regular' man of the law and a true 'professional'. The fact is, of course, that he is sustained by drinking and by playing the elaborate role of the confidant of the Lord Chancellor. We see, though, that his true place is at the side of Tony Weller, not a judge, and the aggressive humour, therefore, is directed not at his hypocrisy but at the legal order he imitates. Mr. Weller and Sam both slide smoothly into the parody roles, even to playing with the conventional terms of reproach: 'you unnat'ral wagabone', 'a reg'lar prodigy son!' (XLIII).

Mr. Pickwick, of course, tries to persuade his servant to pay off his creditor, giving Sam the opportunity to make the parody's application very sharply clear:

'Wy, I'd rayther not let myself down to ask a favour o' this here unremorseful enemy.'

'But it is no favour asking him to take his money, Sam,' reasoned Mr. Pickwick.

'Beg your pardon, sir,' rejoined Sam; 'but it 'ud be a wery great favour to pay it, and he don't deserve none; there's where it is, sir.' (XLIV)

He objects, very clearly, to the unreal and egoistic background to such false principle, to the self-deception which makes impossible a life of real principle or joy. Sam makes this objection even more explicit: 'I takes my determination on principle, sir . . . and you takes yours on the same ground; wich puts me in mind o' the man as killed his-self on principle, wich o' course you've heerd on, sir.' An exemplum follows concerning the man who died rather than abandon his crumpet-eating principle. The story embodies the major protest against sterile abstractions: they are opposed to life and resiliency and lay an invalid foundation for a true identity.

Pickwick's test then proceeds, and he learns in it the true blackness of social reality, the identity of the real villain (both Jingle and Mrs. Bardell are prisoners), and the limits to his easy benevolence (there is little he can do for many there). The pressure of these multiple realizations is almost too much for him, and he retires to his room, announcing, 'My head aches with these scenes, and my heart too. Henceforth I will be a prisoner in my own room' (XLV).

Sam's role here is partly to protect Pickwick from just this kind of despair or the even more dangerous reaction of evasion by showing him a third and healthier response to pain: Freudian humour. For instance, Sam interrupts the gloomy sniffling of the disheartened Tupman, Snodgrass, and Winkle with: 'Avay vith melincholly, as the little boy said ven his

school-missis died. Velcome to the College, gen'l'm'n' (XLIV).
He plays a double part here, really, both protecting and
exposing Mr. Pickwick.

There are, in fact, limits to the awfulness of existence Pickwick can face, and Sam must and does find the balance. When
he arranges for Perker to come and persuade his master to
leave, the humanizing process has been completed. Mr. Pickwick sees the results of his principle: the imprisonment of
Mrs. Bardell. He sees that he must submit to Dodson and
Fogg, that they represent a condition of life he must acknowledge. He sees, as Perker argues, that he will be justified only
'in the eyes of reasonable men' (XLVII). Finally, when leaving,
he learns from Sam the melancholy truth that even his benevolence can be neutralized by this black reality: 'He bust out
a cryin', sir, and said you wos wery gen'rous and thoughtful,
and he only wished you could have him innokilated for a
gallopin' consumption, for his old friend as had lived here so
long, wos dead, and he'd noweres to look for another' (XLVII).
The lesson is one of limitation, served by humility. The result
is, paradoxically, a triumph.

It is true that the tone of the last section of the book is very
mellow, even occasionally sad, but it is all the more satisfactory
for that. The wheelbarrow vision has been retained, even in
the midst of the darkest reality. Mr. Pickwick has given up
the easy comfort maintained by detachment. Even the last
of the interpolated tales,[7] the Bagman's Uncle's Story, echoes
the mood. The story is a reminiscence of the environment
Pickwick had once inhabited, the old coaching days. Significantly, the story is a happy fairy tale, followed not by a

---

[7] Though sometimes dismissed as disastrous, they have recently been
vigorously defended by Robert L. Patten, 'The Art of *Pickwick*'s Interpolated
Tales', *ELH*, xxxiv (1967), 349–66. In terms of the education theme, it should
be noted that these stories, however crude, do have a thematic relevance which
parallels one of Sam Weller's functions: they introduce to Mr. Pickwick a dark
reality he is trying to ignore. The first story, Dismal Jemmy's 'Stroller's Tale',
explicitly makes the point that only illusion makes life bearable; the second
story, 'The Convict's Return', is the antithesis of the familial bliss celebrated
at the Wardles' party, at which it is told; the third, 'The Madman's Manuscript', presents such bleak reality that Mr. Pickwick dives into bed to escape
from it; and so on. It is true that the 'reality' in these stories is often ludicrously
exaggerated, but so are Sam's bleak similes. The exaggeration functions as a
corrective to Mr. Pickwick's illusory view of a world of roses and grateful
beneficiaries.

sleepless night but by a few puns. It represents a mellow farewell to the world that Pickwick has lost.

But he has gained something much more real and important, a realization of the limits of existence and a resiliency in the face of death which make him all the more human and triumphant. He has learned from the Wellers the major lesson of sensitive and responsive existence, a life force they most pointedly illustrate at the death of Mrs. Weller. Tony's letter to his son, one of the first of Dickens's great humorous letters, is also perhaps the most moving; for in the midst of the comic misspellings and the uncharacteristic struggle with euphemism evidenced by Mr. Weller's amanuensis, we suddenly come upon the authentic voice of Tony and of his real grief: 'by the vay your father says that if you vill come and see me Sammy he vill take it as a wery great favor for I am wery lonely Samivel' (LII). Our laughter is used against us for one of the few times in this novel (though in later novels this is one of Dickens's favourite devices), and we are forced to acknowledge the reality of this death. Dickens's subversion is not emphatically aggressive, though, for our possible guilt is immediately relieved by Sam's response to this letter, a response which typifies the humane, realistic, and resilient attitude he has transmitted to his master:

'And so the poor creatur's dead! I'm sorry for it. She warn't a bad-disposed 'ooman, if them shepherds had let her alone. I'm wery sorry for it.'

Mr. Weller uttered these words in so serious a manner, that the pretty housemaid cast down her eyes and looked very grave.

'Hows'ever,' said Sam, putting the letter in his pocket with a gentle sigh, 'it wos to be—and wos, as the old lady said arter she'd married the footman. Can't be helped now, can it, Mary ?' (LII)

The Wellers' flexibility and strength, then, are finally merged with the tempered but firm optimism of Mr. Pickwick. The reader is urged to join this coalition by being subjected, like Pickwick, to a view of the full blackness of social reality. We are invited to share Mr. Pickwick's initiation, his cleansing, and, most emphatically, his triumph. In any case, the fact that the novel faces so resolutely both individual and social cruelty makes the final victory both more real and more resounding.

We can now join Mr. Weller in the wonderfully appropriate investment in 'the funs'.

Mr. Pickwick has moved from the illusory world of the Bagman's Uncle into the black world we all recognize, and by becoming fully human, he has preserved and made real the most important values. He has also been initiated into a world of childhood miraculously adapted to adulthood and shown, in fact, to be in opposition to the evasive and illusory ordinary world of the adult: Dingley Dell is more solid, finally, than the Fleet. And life is made a game by engaging in it resolutely and childishly. To participate fully in the game, Mr. Pickwick has been transformed from the Old Man to the Young Man (a version of the principal comic mode of resurrection, in which the Old Year becomes the New).[8] Sam sees how essentially young Mr. Pickwick's heart is, and Mr. Pickwick sums up his existence by saying, 'The happiness of young people . . . has ever been the chief pleasure of my life' (LVII).

The hero has built an Eden not at Dulwich but within, which is one reason the society at the end radiates outward and includes the reader. The persuasiveness of the psychological change has been long ago guaranteed by our laughter. We have really had nowhere else to go but to Dulwich and Pickwick; the other roads have been blocked and the invitation here has been so insistent. In fact, the compelling nature of the invitation and the fully realized joy of the party displayed supports in its way Chesterton's verdict, 'To the level of "The Pickwick Papers" it is doubtful if he ever afterwards rose.'[9] At least, one can say that all his faculties were never again so unanimous in supporting such a full affirmation.

[8] For a full discussion of this point see Cornford, *The Origin of Attic Comedy*, pp. 171–4.
[9] *Charles Dickens* (New York, 1965), p. 79.

3 *Oliver Twist*

LAUGHTER AND THE
RHETORIC OF ATTACK

'It was a nice sickly season just at this time. In commercial phrase, coffins were looking up.' (VI)

The Pickwick Papers begins with some highly facetious banter about clubs and debates; *Oliver Twist* with some highly facetious banter about death and nothingness. In place of the gently subversive Pickwickian humour we have the vicious and barbed black humour of the first official spokesman for the *Oliver Twist* world, Mrs. Thingummy, as she presides over the death of Oliver's mother:

'Lor bless her heart, no! [she must not talk about dying]' interposed the nurse, hastily depositing in her pocket a green glass bottle, the contents of which she had been tasting in a corner with evident satisfaction. 'Lor bless her dear heart, when she has lived as long as I have, sir, and had thirteen children of her own, and all on 'em dead except two, and them in the wurkus with me, she'll know better than to take on in that way, bless her dear heart! Think what it is to be a mother, there's a dear lamb, do.' (I)

This is nearly all this novel has to offer as comfort: a perverse and bitter sarcasm. The magic milk punch has become gin and water, and the joyous vision from the wheelbarrow has become a workhouse nightmare.

One thing the novel makes abundantly clear is that, compared with the two children now with Mrs. Thingummy in the workhouse, the eleven dead ones are lucky. In fact, some of the bitterest humour in the novel is based exactly on the notion of Malthusian redundancy, and time and again we are asked to laugh at the horrible concept that, in the face of the continually demonstrated fact that life is cheap, any importance placed on a single life or a single personality is ludicrous. Certainly the novel's officialdom is highly amused by this notion:

> 'The prices allowed by the board are very small, Mr. Bumble.'
> 'So are the coffins,' replied the beadle: with precisely as near an approach to a laugh as a great official ought to indulge in.
> Mr. Sowerberry was much tickled at this: as of course he ought to be; and laughed a long time without cessation. (IV)

And Sowerberry and Bumble are not, in the moral scheme of the novel, really very bad men. Coffins are seen as rather happy means of escape. The fact is that this novel comes about as close as is possible to building its final society literally in heaven. If *Pickwick* suggested that the Kingdom of God was available on earth, *Oliver Twist* exactly reverses that suggestion: here there is not even sanctity, only loneliness, brutality, and, above all, the pervasive and threatening institutions. The morally approved people in the novel, including Oliver when he is with them, exist on the edge of the grave.[1] There is simply no opening here for permanent joy. Dulwich cannot exist when the whole world has become the Fleet.

One of the major questions, then, is how such a dark novel can be so funny. It is probable that most critics often laugh while reading it; it is certain that when they are finished they write essays on its bleak effects. And they are right—in both cases. The reason for the paradoxical reaction is, I think, that Dickens uses laughter here to subvert our conventional reactions and to emphasize more dramatically the isolation of his young hero, indeed, the essential isolation of all men. In denying the possibility of a comic society and yet provoking laughter, the novel continually thwarts and frustrates the reader; for our laughter continues to search for a social basis, even when there is no longer any support for it in the novel. In other words, laughter is stirred, but the impulses aroused behind it are not allowed to collect and settle. Unlike the

---

[1] Dickens explicitly says of Rose Maylie that she was 'so mild and gentle; so pure and beautiful; that earth seemed not her element' (XXIX). Similarly, Oliver's joy when he is rescued for the second time is expressed in terms of a yearning for death: 'he felt calm and happy; and could have died without a murmur' (XXX).

convivial atmosphere of *Pickwick Papers*, where our laughter finally provides us a place with Sam and with Mr. Pickwick, here there is no possibility of escape to a society sanctified by the expulsion of all the villains. Instead, laughter is used primarily as a weapon, to suggest that we are the villains. The selfishness and unfeeling cruelty which are a subconscious part of much laughter are here brought to the surface and used to intensify our reaction and our involvement. Laughter is a necessary part of the proper reaction to the novel, but in the end it is used against us, undercutting the comfortable aloofness we had originally maintained and forcing us into conjunction with the lonely and terrified orphan. This suggests that, just as in *Pickwick*, the basic attack is on detachment. But the comparison doesn't go very far. There are no comparable rewards for submitting to the attack in *Oliver Twist* and no comfortably stable scheme of values to which we can attach ourselves. We are left alone in a rootless and threatening world.

There is, of course, an apparently brighter world in *Oliver Twist*, and the plot of the novel seems to point us towards it. Even before the narrative reaches midpoint, Dickens has rescued his hero and placed him firmly in the protection of the Maylie group; the last half of the novel simply reinforces Oliver's 'safe' position, on the one hand, by methodically hunting down the threats to his safety and eliminating them (Fagin and Sikes) or converting them (Charlie Bates and Nancy), and, on the other hand, by securing the prospects of wealth for the hero (through Monks's will) and eternal bliss for the rest of the good people (the marriage between Rose and Harry Maylie). Yet most commentators have found themselves untouched by this arrangement of events and have emphasized the novel's predominantly grim effect.[2] This paradox has generally been explained by the argument that Dickens portrayed Fagin and his group with great vividness, that a part of him identified very closely with them, that he treated them with great 'sympathy'. In contrast, even Forster admitted that the Maylie–Brownlow group were so poorly

[2] Edmund Wilson ('The Two Scrooges', p. 17) calls it a 'somber book'. For a fuller discussion of this aspect see Arnold Kettle, *Oliver Twist*, in *An Introduction to the English Novel*, i (London, 1951), 123–38.

realized, so completely unbelievable as to constitute 'the weak part of the story'.[3] Graham Greene has merged these two contrasting impressions by describing the controlling view of the novel as 'Manichaean'; he argues that the power of the book comes from 'the eternal and alluring trait of the Manichee, with its simple and terrible explanation of our plight, how the world was made by Satan and not by God, lulling us with the music of despair'.[4]

But the problem really goes much deeper, and the novel really does not make such simple distinctions as are implied by these views. The fact is that there are two separate and conflicting dualisms: one social, between the individual and the institution, the second moral, between the respectable and the criminal. Arnold Kettle has described this conflict as that between the pattern and the plot of the novel.[5] For the first eleven chapters the basic pattern of the novel is developed: the evocation of the dark world of the poor and the engagement of our sympathy with them in their struggle against institutions. This pattern, he argues, is most deeply felt and continues throughout, though in the second half of the novel it tends to lose ground to the plot, a relatively superficial and conventionally formulated moralistic conflict. The basic problem, though, is not in the superficiality of the moral theme, but in its conflict with the more deeply-felt theme of institutional oppression. The 'good' people in the second half of the novel sometimes use the hated institution of the first half to fight not only the persecutors but the victims as well.

Laughter leads us to Oliver's side, but Oliver soon leaves us and heads for the enemy. As a result we are likely to be stranded. Our laughter has exposed us and isolated us along with Oliver, and it then deprives us of even his alliance. It is

---

[3] Forster's *Life*, i. 91. For an enthusiastic but, I think, unconvincing defence of the role of Brownlow, see Joseph M. Duffy, Jr., 'Another Version of Pastoral: *Oliver Twist*', *ELH*, xxxv (1968), 416–19.

[4] 'The Young Dickens', in *The Lost Childhood and Other Essays* (London, 1951), pp. 56–7.

[5] Though many will think Kettle's articulation of the central theme as 'the struggle of the poor against the bourgeois state' (*Introduction to the English Novel*, i. 132) rather over-specific, I believe his essay is the most sensitive to the important issues in the novel, and I am heavily indebted to it. For a vigorous dissent from Kettle's position see Kathleen Tillotson, '*Oliver Twist*', *Essays and Studies*, xii (1959), 87–105.

our response to this desolation, pushed on us by our laughter, that is at the core of the novel's one undoubted effect: discomfort. We not only have an uneasy aesthetic response to a thematically fractured novel, but an uneasy emotional response at being forced into the same isolation the novel portrays. In the end, *Oliver Twist* comes near to making orphans of us all by dislocating us from the world we are comfortable in, and displaying the full force of Mrs. Thingummy's bitter mockery of consolation.

1

The most obvious cause of this dislocation is the lack of consistency in the narrative personality. It is impossible to define the characteristics or moral positions of the narrator in this novel, for they are continually shifting. It is true that, as in most Dickens novels, the narrative voice provides a counterpoint to the story and gives oblique directions to the reader. But here the directions are generally misleading. We expect those obtrusive narrative commentaries at least to provide accurate signposts to a comfortable position we can take, but here Dickens exploits this very expectation to attack such smug confidence.

For instance, the narrator is often—though certainly not always—as detached as in *Pickwick Papers*, and this detachment and the 'tendency toward abstraction'[6] sometimes work together as a negative object lesson, 'an ironic rhetorical device to generate by negation the outraged sympathy of the reader'.[7] But moral outrage of this sort is rather a comfortable thing, and *Oliver Twist* never allows us to be comfortable for long; nor does it allow the stability which would come from consistent and obvious irony. The writing with which Dickens begins the novel, for example, certainly does not flatter the reader's sense of moral superiority or reinforce his moral certainty:

---

[6] Steven Marcus (*From Pickwick to Dombey*, pp. 63–7) has an extremely interesting discussion of the style. He argues that this impulse to generalize suggests an underlying dread that Malthus is right after all.

[7] J. Hillis Miller, *The Form of Victorian Fiction* (South Bend, Ind., 1968), p. 76. Actually, this quotation represents a distortion of Miller's view; for the most part, he argues, the style insulates Oliver and his experiences from the reader and the narrator.

Among other public buildings in a certain town, which for many reasons it will be prudent to refrain from mentioning, and to which I will assign no fictitious name, there is one anciently common to most towns, great or small: to wit, a workhouse; and in this workhouse was born: on a day and date which I need not trouble myself to repeat, inasmuch as it can be of no possible consequence to the reader, in this stage of the business at all events: the item of mortality whose name is prefixed to the head of this chapter.

Certainly there is more than a 'tendency toward abstraction' here; this seems to have been written by the head of the Circumlocution Office. Leisurely, presumably gentle and facetious, the passage throws out humorous barbs in a dozen directions: at authorial egotism ('I' is introduced gratuitously twice), at the reader's concern for trivia ('day and date'), at prudence and care, and so on. Perhaps most obvious, and certainly most important, though, is the attack on the mincing-genteel tone of many novels and, by implication, on the mincing-genteel expectations of many readers. The author parodies our refined concerns by offering mock assurance that he will keep in mind our delicate sensitivies (and the demands on our time) by maintaining an elevated tone. We can be assured, in fact, that no concrete hero will be introduced, simply an 'item of mortality'. The facetiousness of the tone, then, hides the bitterest sarcasm, not an irony which invites our participation in righteous indignation but a covert attack on a trait the narrator caustically assumes we all share: callousness. The narrator simply does not want our company; in fact, he does not allow us any single position. This opening attack dramatically upsets our normally stable position in reference to fiction and tears from us the accustomed comforting shield of a narrative friend and guide.

We might, of course, get used to this sort of attack and gradually assume a defensive but at least constant position. Dickens does not allow even this sort of masochistic stability, however. The appeals of the narrative tone are constantly shifting. Sometimes, in fact, we are invited to share in an easy and removed irony: 'What a noble illustration of the tender laws of England! They let the paupers go to sleep!' (ii). Occasionally, the narrator is even chummy in his appeals: Oliver 'was alone in a strange place; and we all know how

chilled and desolate the best of us will sometimes feel in such
a situation' (v). Even here, though, we are invited to share not
the narrator's detachment but Oliver's desolation—but at
least we have company. The point is that we can never count
on being in any single relationship with the narrative voice
for long. Just as we relax in the chumminess or in the comfort
of indignation, we are pushed away by an attack on us or by
an unsettling sick joke of the kind which heads this chapter—
'coffins were looking up'. The end result of the sick joke and
of this shifting point of view is that we are made to disavow
our accustomed positions in relation to fiction. No novel could
be more honest, at least in its rhetorical terms, than is *Oliver
Twist*: the reader is never flattered, never comforted. He is
pressed to renounce detachment and to enter more completely
into the action of the novel, simply because all other outlets
are closed. There are no buffers between us and the desolation
presented. On the contrary, the rhetoric of attack, based on
this radically uncertain narrative tone and on a subversive
humour, forces us to share in that desolation. It is an effective,
if somewhat vicious, alliance.

Laughter and point of view are, indeed, allied in viciousness,
and though the obtrusive narrative passages never help the
reader to orient himself, they do reveal an underlying
maliciousness which is central to the novel's humour. For
instance, early in the novel Dickens comments:

> I wish some well-fed philosopher, whose meat and drink turn
> to gall within him; whose blood is ice, whose heart is iron; could
> have seen Oliver Twist clutching at the dainty viands that the dog
> had neglected. I wish he could have witnessed the horrible avidity
> with which Oliver tore the bits asunder with all the ferocity of
> famine. There is only one thing I should like better; and that
> would be to see the Philosopher making the same sort of meal
> himself, with the same relish (IV).

This paragraph embodies the central attack on abstractions,
on treating people from such a distance that they become, like
Oliver, philosophically 'badged and ticketed' (I). But this
passage is more than simply an attack; it is an exercise in
malevolence. Since this is by no means a funny passage and
since there are no disguises for the appeals to vindictiveness,

we are very likely to resist its aggressive suggestions. Yet this same unvarnished desire for sadistic revenge is at the core of much of the humour in the novel; the very fact that the novel is not satisfied with piercing Bumble's folly, for instance, in the manner of Fielding or Meredith, but pursues him to the end, defeats him, degrades him, and rubs him in the mud, alerts us to the cruelty and barbarousness of this humorous process. We delight in Bumble's fall, but we are revolted at the extended details of his degradation. Dickens's subversive humour calls up in us, and presents all too clearly, the egoistic base from which we had probably been chuckling. We are likely to resist such exposure, of course, even to imagine that we didn't laugh at all, and the book is all the darker for having exposed the potential darkness within us.

2

The same subversive technique illustrated by the author's comments and the point of view is utilized more fully and more subtly in the narrative itself. Though there are other important humorous appeals, particularly later in the novel, it is the dominant humour of the first half, focusing on the conflict between the novel's outcasts and its established society, which is most functional. The laughter called up by these situations to a large extent determines our reaction to the general world of the novel and to the social assumptions on which that world is built.

The humour attending these conflicts between the institution and the individual almost invariably calls for an ambiguous response. For example, in the second chapter, Oliver is told that 'the board had said he was to appear before it forthwith'. Oliver is confused by this report, 'not having a very clearly defined notion of what a live board was', and when he is ushered into the august presence of 'eight or ten fat gentlemen' and told to 'bow to the board', 'seeing no board but the table, [he] fortunately bowed to that'. This is both tactful and pointed; it could be very funny. Dickens manages to use Oliver's ignorance to make the point that his confusion is, after all, not so meaningless: the board does have all the flexibility and feeling of a thick plank. Given only these details and this perspective, the humour could well be successful. There are, however, other factors which work against laughter. First of all, the situation is under the control of Bumble, who at this point is an almost unrelieved villain. Second, we are disturbed by Oliver's reaction: he 'was not quite certain whether he ought to laugh or cry'. Finally, however, the boy's conflict is resolved; Bumble gives him so many 'taps' behind that he cries. The scene seems to be devised in such a way as to undercut the aloofness we have originally assumed in order to laugh and to force us into a closer identification with Oliver, adding by the way a penetrating glance into the underlying viciousness of such laughter. In order to laugh in the first place, the reader must remove himself slightly from the situation: he knows what a board is, Oliver does not. Oliver's ambiguous reaction, however, recalls the novel's earlier remarks about institutions, workhouse institutions in particular; and the reference to the possibility of crying similarly recalls us to a position of sympathy for him. When he is finally forced by Bumble to decide against laughing in favour of crying, we too must decide. In order to laugh, we must identify ourselves with the board, and this is clearly impossible. Our probable laughter at the beginning of the scene is cut off, perhaps denied, but we are not likely to escape a recognition of the fact that, for a brief instant, we had allowed ourselves to be members of the board, regarding Oliver as an 'it'. The shock of recognition urges us closer to Oliver and denies us the easy sanctuary of laughter.

This same subversive process is used periodically in the novel both to reinforce the reader's feelings for Oliver and to undermine the social assumptions on which laughter is built. In Chapter iii, for instance, we are introduced to 'Mr. Gamfield, chimney-sweep', who 'in a species of arithmetical desperation' was 'alternately cudgelling his brains and his donkey'. The zeugma in the last phrase is a witty disguise for the hidden aggression, allowing both the speed and the conciseness necessary to all jokes. Again, we are very likely to laugh. Two paragraphs later, however, we are told that Gamfield gave the donkey's jaw 'a sharp wrench' and that he 'gave him another blow on the head, just to stun him till he came back again'. What happens here is that the wittily disguised 'cudgelling' at

which we had been asked to laugh is made repulsively explicit
in an entire paragraph devoted to the maltreatment of the
donkey. The disguise is removed and the aggression nakedly
exposed. When Gamfield then applies to the board in answer
to the advertisement offering Oliver as an apprentice, we again
sense how perilous is the boy's situation; we are dangerously
close to being Gamfields ourselves. In the scene between Gamfield and the board, then, it is hard to miss the point that
laughter is being used as a weapon:

'Boys is wery obstinit, and wery lazy, gen'lmen, and there's
nothink like a good hot blaze to make 'em come down vith a run.
It's humane too, gen'lmen, acause, even if they're stuck in the
chimbley, roastin' their feet makes 'em struggle to hextricate
theirselves.'
The gentleman in the white waistcoat appeared very much
amused by this explanation. (III)

Gamfield talks very much like Sam Weller here, but surely
his remarks are not funny. Not only is he a brutal man, but he
wants to subject Oliver to horrible tortures. We were tempted
to laugh at him once before and we certainly won't be
victimized again. In case there is any temptation, we are
immediately given a picture of the sort of person who is
amused: 'the gentleman in the white waistcoat', heartless,
stupid, and vicious.

Finally, there is the brilliant scene, perhaps the symbolic
centre of the novel, in which Oliver stands for a brief instant
against all the institutionalized cruelty and demands that he
be allowed to survive. One reason this scene is so memorable
is that Dickens controls the humour so as to make us stand
with Oliver as he asks for more.

Dickens first, however, tempts us to take a step back from
the 'slow starvation' he is discussing by focusing on a threat of
cannibalism made to his fellow victims by a cook's son, who
'hadn't been used to that sort of thing'. 'He had a wild, hungry
eye; and they implicitly believed him' (II). Notice the traps
Dickens sets here for the reader: we are urged to laugh, first,
by the camouflage put over the starvation, which becomes
'that sort of thing', second, by the substitution of mock killing
for the real institutional murder, and third, by the appeal to
our superior experience: the boys may believe him, but we

don't. He allows us, by our laughter, to shift our attention and thereby our concern. But, as I said, this shift is a trap meant to expose our callousness. Dickens is fattening us for the kill:

'Please, sir, I want some more.'
The master was a fat, healthy man; but he turned very pale. He gazed in stupefied astonishment on the small rebel for some seconds, and then clung for support to the copper. The assistants were paralysed with wonder; the boys with fear. (II)[8]

The reaction of the master is, in one sense, very funny. In one dazzling flash we are told that he is fat and healthy and that he clung to the pot for support. This appeal to our superiority in the absurd causal relationship, a cataclysmic reaction to a trivial event, would certainly satisfy our humorous demands, were it not for the peculiar situation, emphasized by the last sentence. What seems to be a supporting, funny detail, 'The assistants were paralysed with wonder', turns out to be a false lead, for the second part of the sentence, 'the boys with fear', jars us pointedly with the unexpected word 'fear'. We laugh only at the peril of ignoring this fear, and if we do ignore it, we implicitly share in the guilt for the brutality which comes to Oliver as a result of his daring.

These three episodes, similar in effect if not in execution, are all taken from the early sections of the novel. Throughout, however, Dickens subtly reverses even the most conventional humorous situations. For instance, the explosive coughing after drinking liquor is one of the most recurrent pieces of equipment in slapstick comedies. But in the novel Oliver's coughing is almost a threat or a dare, and it is very likely that by the time it takes place we know enough to avoid the trap. At any rate, just before the attempted robbery of the Maylies', the thieves are—rather happily—drinking 'Success to the crack!' Toby Crackit proposes 'A drain for the boy', and Oliver, 'frightened by the menacing gestures of the two men ... hastily swallowed the contents of the glass, and immediately fell into a violent fit of coughing: which delighted Toby Crackit and Barney, and even drew a smile from the surly Mr. Sikes' (XXII). By this time, we know instinctively not to be amused

[8] Jonathan Bishop, 'The Hero-Villain of *Oliver Twist*', *VN*, no. 15 (1959), p. 14, also discusses the humour in this scene, but suggests that our amusement may distract us from the important issues it contains.

by anyone who is 'frightened', and we identify too strongly with Oliver here to laugh at him. He is alone and is faced with an adventure which almost kills him. We can't even smile, lest we be associated with 'the surly Mr. Sikes'.

There are, however, times when we *are* associated with Sikes, or with any other victim, any other man who is hunted, frightened, or alone. Dickens uses the technique of subversion so consistently and subtly that, by the end of the novel, we are asked to react with the same combination of guilt, insight, and intense association with the victims, even when there is no 'gentleman in the white waistcoat' to nullify our temptation to laughter and even when the victim is an equivocal character at best. For instance, during Sikes's flight through the countryside, he draws near two mail-coach guards to hear them talk of the murder:

'Corn's up a little. I heerd talk of a murder, too, down Spitalfields way, but I don't reckon much upon it.'

'Oh, that's quite true,' said a gentleman inside, who was looking out of the window. 'And a dreadful murder it was.'

'Was it, sir?' rejoined the guard, touching his hat. 'Man or woman, pray, sir?'

'A woman,' replied the gentleman. 'It is supposed—'

'Now, Ben,' replied the coachman impatiently.

'Damn that 'ere bag,' said the guard; 'are you gone to sleep in there?'

'Coming!' cried the office keeper, running out.

'Coming,' growled the guard. 'Ah, and so's the young 'ooman of property that's going to take a fancy to me, but I don't know when. Here, give hold. All ri—ight!'

The horn sounded a few cheerful notes, and the coach was gone. (XLVIII)

The joke clashes strongly with an atmosphere which is so controlled and intense it allows us no real interest outside Sikes; the brilliant juxtaposition of the guard's slight and impersonal interest in the sensational aspects of the crime with Sikes's obsession with the eyes that won't shut is capped by the final unconsciously brutal witticism about 'the young 'ooman of property'. Since the focus has shifted only very briefly from the killer, the only woman on our minds at the moment is the mangled corpse of Nancy, who has been killed precisely because her 'fancy' for Bill would not allow her to desert him. Two orders of reality, connected only by a startling and accidental relevance of referents, are violently contrasted here: the order which contains the social world, easy jokes and thoughtlessness, and the horribly intense and torturous world of Sikes. By this point, the reader is most likely conditioned by Dickens's technique and has no real choice but to enter into the latter; the social world has consistently been shown to be cruel with the special cruelty of comfortable aloofness. The notes of the horn certainly are cheerful only to those who regard the fact that 'Corn's up a little' as equal in interest to the murder. The continual and subtle rhetorical insistence is that crimes of passion, no matter how brutal, are not nearly so pervasive as crimes of indifference.

The final goal of this technique is to pry us away from the normal identification we make with an aloof society and to force us to enter much more fully into the world of the terrified and alienated individual, who at various times is Oliver, Fagin, Sikes, Bumble, and the Artful Dodger. Laughter, the strongest expression of social identification, is brilliantly used as a weapon against our own safety, quietly urging us to assume, for the moment, the perilous position of the hunted and the trapped. Instead of providing for a comic society, our laughter is meant to deny society altogether and to force us to be as alone as the novel's victims. The novel's humour, in other words, maintains that the real conflict is between the outcasts and the establishment, even after the plot itself has introduced a new theme which seems to provide a sanctified society and which turns against the outcasts.

The ironic humour of the second half of the novel is generally either ignored or passed off as 'comic relief'. Dickens himself half-seriously suggested, in Chapter xvii, that he was merely alternating 'the tragic and the comic scenes'. There isn't much point in attacking these obviously inadequate formulations, but they do point towards some of the novel's most interesting humour, which centres on two outlaws, in and out of the establishment, Mr. Bumble and the Artful Dodger.

First of all, one should notice that, despite all his maliciousness, Bumble sometimes sounds very much like the narrator: 'And I only wish we'd a jury of the independent sort, in the house for a week or two . . . the rules and regulations of the board would soon bring their spirit down for 'em' (IV). Though the object is different from that in the narrator's attack on 'philosophers' two pages later, not only is the desire for revenge similar, but the means of accomplishing that revenge as well. Bumble and the narrator both want to subject the aloof commentators to practical experience and concrete reality. The point is that abstract pity is nearly as bad as abstract cruelty; both commit the central sin of remaining untouched. It may seem odd that Dickens is using Bumble here as his partial surrogate, but it does prepare us for the very complex treatment which follows.

Probably the most basic thing to be said about Bumble is that his humour is based on the role of the henpecked husband. He makes other appeals, but this one is at the root of his 'funny' position. But there is a great difference between Bumble and the array of traditional henpecked husbands in *Pickwick*. Mr. Pott, for instance, is not effectually vicious, nor does his condition inspire great pity; in fact, he, Mr. Nupkins, even Mr. Raddle we suppose, richly deserve the treatment they receive. These figures are also like the traditional figure in that ordinarily they are not physically mistreated by their spouses, or, if they are, they have some crafty resources to combat brutality. The traditional figure is, above all, resilient; he does not degenerate into a complete buffoon; he does not wholly sacrifice his identity. Bumble evades all these qualifications.

Bumble's marital relationship is further complicated by a kind of doubling, which functions as an ominous foreshadowing. The relationship between Mr. and Mrs. Sowerberry, early in the novel, is in its main outlines just like that which Mr. and Mrs. Bumble will later assume. Sowerberry is completely dominated by his wife:

'My dear—' He was going to say more; but Mrs. Sowerberry looking up, with a peculiarly unpropitious aspect, he stopped short.
'Well,' said Mrs. Sowerberry, sharply.
'Nothing, my dear, nothing,' said Mr. Sowerberry.
'Ugh, you brute!' said Mrs. Sowerberry.
'Not at all, my dear!' said Mr. Sowerberry humbly. 'I thought you didn't want to hear, my dear. I was only going to say—'

'Oh, don't tell me what you were going to say,' interposed Mrs. Sowerberry. 'I am nobody; don't consult me, pray.' (v)

This is the normal breakfast conversation between the henpecked husband and his wife. Mrs. Sowerberry cleverly manages to deny his manhood, and her claim that she is 'nobody' clearly is an assertion that it is her undertaking husband who is really a cipher. As with Mr. Nupkins, we are very likely happy to see officialdom deflated. But our amusement here ignores the relationship of these two to their victim, Oliver. It turns out that Sowerberry's subordinate position is exactly what leads to Oliver's cruel punishment, which, in turn, leads him to London and Fagin. Sowerberry, Dickens says, is 'kindly disposed' towards Oliver, but his wife demands that the boy be whipped and, when Mr. Sowerberry resists, she bursts into tears. The narrator then comments, 'The flood of tears . . . left him no resource; so he at once gave him [Oliver] a drubbing, which satisfied even Mrs. Sowerberry herself' (vii). This situation not only upsets the comic relationship but also contains a veiled warning against laughing at henpecked husbands; they can, it seems, turn out to be very dangerous.

Deepening this early shadow on the Bumbles' potentially comic relationship is the fact that Bumble is not the sort of Bergsonian automaton we can laugh at easily. In the first place, he is in Oliver's view an exceptionally vicious man; at one point the child is described as 'shaking from head to foot at the mere recollection of the sound of Mr. Bumble's voice' (v). But, alone among the characters associated with the workhouse, Bumble shows himself capable of sympathy for Oliver's plight. After the orphan utters his central complaint that he is 'so lonely, sir! So very lonely', the narrator says, 'Mr. Bumble regarded Oliver's piteous and helpless look, with some astonishment, for a few seconds; hemmed three or four times in a husky manner; and, after muttering something about "that troublesome cough", bade Oliver dry his eyes and be a good boy. Then once more taking his hand, he walked on with him in silence' (iv). 'That troublesome cough' makes all the difference. Bumble simply calls up far too many complex associations; he is too complex a human being to allow for easy laughter. Insofar as we identify with Oliver—and surely in the early

parts of the novel that identification is complete—we are required to hate the Bumble who is physically cruel, but we must
also feel gratitude for the Bumble who alone can sympathize
with Oliver's intense loneliness. And these two Bumbles are
decidedly part of one man. While it is true that the first
is dominant, to some extent Bumble's cruelty blends with
the background of almost unrelieved indifference and sadism
which Oliver faces and thus is unremarkable. It is the beadle's
sympathy which is unexpected, for his feelings mark the first
and only chink in the 'porochial' armour, and we sense that he
is somehow different from the hated institution, somehow a
more complete human being.

Though I do not mean to distort Bumble into a tragic figure,
this hint of disorientation from the institution he represents
is an integral part of his character. It makes it more difficult
for us to laugh at him, and, despite Dickens's deceptive insistence that we regard him as a villain, we are bound to reserve
some measure of respect for the only person in Oliver's youth
who managed even to have a 'troublesome cough'.

We are expected to approach the scene of Bumble's degradation, then, with somewhat mixed feelings. Dickens proceeds,
however, to cast the beadle in a slightly different role when he
comes in contact with Mrs. Corney and Mrs. Mann, two indistinguishably vicious workhouse matrons. He is slightly
more pompous and much more rigid, and in this mechanical,
Bergsonian pose he blunders on to Mrs. Mann, ' "A porochial
life, ma'am," continued Mr. Bumble, striking the table with
his cane, "is a life of worrit, and vexation, and hardihood; but
all public characters, as I may say, must suffer prosecution" '
(XVII). This, of course, engenders a stock response. The important detail, 'striking the table with his cane', alerts us to
the conscious role-playing,[9] as does the exceedingly formal
and self-important manner of address. Bumble has been subtly
altered. It is true that at times like this Mr. Bumble is, in more
ways than one, 'quite a literary character' indeed (II). From
the curiously full human significance he suggested earlier, he

---

[9] The element of self-dramatization in Dickens's comic characters is discussed by Douglas Bush, 'A Note on Dickens' Humor', in *From Jane Austen
to Joseph Conrad*, eds. Robert C. Rathburn and Martin Steinmann, Jr.
(Minneapolis, Minn., 1958), pp. 82–91.

has become an emblem of self-importance, an overblown and self-righteous balloon, making us yearn for the needle of the Comic Spirit.

Yet there are still elements, even here in the early stages of his bitter introduction to women, which cloud this simple view of him. For one thing, we can hardly help noticing that Mrs. Mann and her double, Mrs. Corney, are much more vicious characters than Bumble. They have about them a frightening competence which is born of deep cynicism; they are far more rigid than Bumble; they are both frozen into the role of a monster. For instance, when the dying little Dick speaks to Mr. Bumble, the narrator adds that 'the earnest and wan aspect of the child had made some impression [on him]: accustomed as he was to such things' (xvii). Mrs. Mann is equally 'accustomed to such things', we can be sure, but it is absolutely certain that little Dick makes no similar impression on her. The contrast is significant, for Bumble, we sense, is being cast out of his depths, entering, at least in part, into the ranks of the victims of oppression. Upon seeing Bumble, Mrs. Mann reacts as follows:

'Drat that beadle!' said Mrs. Mann, hearing the well-known shaking at the garden-gate. 'If it isn't him at this time in the morning! Lauk, Mr. Bumble, only think of its being you! Well, dear me, it *is* a pleasure, this is! Come into the parlour, sir, please.'

The first sentence was addressed to Susan; and the exclamations of delight were uttered to Mr. Bumble: as the good lady unlocked the garden-gate, and showed him, with great attention and respect, into the house. (xvii)

This is precisely the sort of smooth double-dealing Bumble could not possibly manage. His inability to see through Mrs. Mann is caused in part by his blinding ego, and in this regard he is funny, but part of his blindness comes also from the fact that he is simply a better human being, and in this sense he evokes not laughter but compassion.

Even during his hilarious proposal to Mrs. Corney, this contrast is subtly reinforced, and Bumble is shown to be more human and, surprisingly, less official. His ludicrous misuse of conventional terms is itself partly a parody of convention: 'I mean to say this, ma'am; that any cat, or kitten, that could

live with you, ma'am, and *not* be fond of its home, must be a
ass, ma'am' (XXIII). In his way, Bumble is an innocent here.
He is even capable of dancing around the table, which violates
what the narrator says we expect from beadles: that they '(as
is well known) should be the sternest and most inflexible' of
all 'public functionaries' (XXIII).

Dickens has again led us toward a comparatively false
reaction. If we laugh at Bumble, we are associating with the
society outside, from which he deviates. It is a part of Dickens's
subtlety that he often disguises that society, making it appear
safe, humane, conventional. By the time he is through with
Bumble, however, he demonstrates that the outcast beadle
has deviated mainly from the standards of Mrs. Mann, Mrs.
Corney, and the parochial board. Again we are likely to find
ourselves uncomfortably playing the part of 'the gentleman
in the white waistcoat'.

This reversal is caused primarily by the fact that Dickens
pushes Bumble's fall past the humorous point. There is no
question that we would rejoice in his deflation, but, in the end,
he has lost his identity, and his famous protest against the
law, 'the law is a ass—a idiot', recalls Oliver against Mr. Fang
and aligns Bumble with the victimized. What makes this
reversal all the more effective is that it seems so sudden.
Chapter XXXVII opens with a passage which begins by com-
paring Bumble to an insect in a trap and which leads to the
climactic announcement, 'Mr. Bumble was no longer a beadle'.
Now Mr. Bumble's egoistic involvement with his earlier role
had been complete; he was, very simply, a beadle. At his
height 'he was in the full bloom and pride of beadlehood; his
cocked hat and coat were dazzling in the morning sun', and
Mr. Grimwig identified him as 'a beadle all over' (XVII). When
Oliver first saw Mr. Bumble and was told to 'bow to the
gentleman', his bow was 'divided between the beadle on the
chair, and the cocked hat on the table' (II). The comic equation
is clear: Bumble = beadle = cocked hat. But with his marriage Bumble loses this identity, and in the attending symbolic
castration, the narrator says, 'The mighty cocked hat was
replaced by a modest round one' (XXXVII). Mr. Bumble has
been virtually annihilated.

Bumble's only comic alternative is to switch directly to the

submissive role of Mr. Leo Hunter, but this he refuses to do.
He first tries inordinate self-pity:

'I sold myself,' said Mr. Bumble . . . 'for six teaspoons, a pair of
sugar-tongs, and a milk-pot; with a small quantity of second-
hand furniture, and twenty pound in money. I went very reasonable. Cheap, dirt cheap!'

'Cheap!' cried a shrill voice in Mr. Bumble's ear; 'you would have
been dear at any price; and dear enough I paid for you, Lord above
knows that!' (XXXVII)

Bumble's treating himself as a thing might be funny; even in
his misery, we find, he has not lost his powers of ludicrous
exaggeration, but Mrs. Corney picks up the theme, without
contradiction, and leads us to believe that Bumble is not ex-
aggerating at all.[10]

Bumble then, with a modest kind of heroism, tries to recapture his old position with 'an exceedingly small expansion
of eye', an 'eagle glance', but Mrs. Corney (the narrator does
not often call her Mrs. Bumble, for very good reason), far from
being 'overpowered', as he had intended, laughs at him. The
shift is now complete; Bumble has changed from a persecutor
to a victim. Our memory of his earlier cruelty perhaps limits
our sympathy, but it is now perfectly clear that Bumble can
no longer be laughed at so easily. At the centre of the novel is
this polarization between masters and victims, and our understanding and sympathy are constantly directed toward the
latter.

Thus Dickens again undermines any comfortable laughter
and forces us beyond the rigid moral categories in which we
may have taken refuge. The laughter is once more used as a
weapon against our social assumptions, forcing us closer into
the novel and into a closer identification not only with Oliver
but also with Bumble, Fagin, and Sikes. By the end of this
chapter, Bumble has been beaten, humiliated in front of the
paupers, and driven to drink. But Dickens doesn't even allow

---

[10] Bergson says, '*We laugh every time a person gives us the impression of being
a thing*' ('Laughter', p. 97). He does, however, point out that this imitation of
the inanimate must not be self-conscious (p. 71). We can laugh here, then, only
if we can overlook Bumble's motives for self-dramatization and the reaction
of Mrs. Corney. Certainly such elaborate evasion of the implications contained
in the situation is difficult, and it is the virtue of Dickens's art that he makes
us start laughing and then recalls that laughter abruptly, making us look
closely at the uncomfortable truth we were trying to avoid.

him the traditional alcoholic solace of the henpecked; for in
the bar he meets Monks, and in the later interview between
Monks and the Bumbles, the former beadle is forced into the
role of the pathetic, self-conscious buffoon:

> [Mrs. Bumble:] 'But I may ask you two questions, may I?'
> 'You may ask,' said Monks, with some show of surprise; 'but
> whether I answer or not is another question.'
> '—Which makes three,' observed Mr. Bumble, essaying a stroke
> of facetiousness. (xxxviii)

His degradation is indeed complete.

While the Artful Dodger is not degraded, Dickens uses our
laughter at him in much the same way. The Dodger is the best
reflection we have in this novel of Sam Weller. At his first
appearance, his openness and friendliness even suggest that
he will champion the innocent Oliver much as Sam champions
Mr. Pickwick. At any rate, what is fundamentally important
here in the Dodger—as in Sam—is the consistent and effective
use of Freudian humour. His whole life is a kind of brilliant
parody of social convention and dull, regularized conduct.
This parody is most clearly illustrated by his trial.

His offence, first of all, amounts to a witty and insolent
defiance of social demands for pretentiousness. A policeman
testifies that he 'had seen the prisoner attempt the pocket of
an unknown gentleman in a crowd, and indeed take a handkerchief therefrom, which, being a very old one, he deliberately
put back again, after trying it on his own countenance' (xliii).
The handkerchief is the perfect symbol of social hollowness
(surpassed only by the silver snuff-box discovered on the
Dodger), and it indicates perfectly that the Dodger is not a
social threat but a kind of social medicine. His clever refusal
to take this monstrous society seriously is the best defence of
the human spirit and the closest thing to a possible alternative
to the system we have in this novel. But the Dodger is a
criminal, by society's definition, and is about to be imprisoned.
The charges against him are both trivial and serious, trivial
in fact but serious in the view of the law. The Dodger, however,
refuses to adopt the view of the law and insists on parodying
it. Thus he deals with the threat by ignoring it, and he allows
us to economize our sympathy by releasing it in laughter.

But Dickens is again deceptive; he again interrupts any laughter. As Arnold Kettle points out, the Dodger finally makes clear what had been implicit all along—that this trial is a symbolic restatement of the novel's central conflict between the individual and the threatening institutions.[11] As the Dodger says, 'this ain't the shop for justice' (XLIII), and our laughter has suggested that we may be no more just or merciful than the court.

Dickens further undercuts our amusement by allowing just a glimpse of the Dodger's courage. After he has been sentenced, he throws one more witty barb at the bench:

'Oh ah! I'll come on,' replied the Dodger, brushing his hat with the palm of his hand. 'Ah! (to the Bench) it's no use your looking frightened; I won't show you no mercy, not a ha'porth of it. *You'll* pay for this, my fine fellers. I wouldn't be you for something! I wouldn't go free, now, if you was to fall down on your knees and ask me. Here, carry me off to prison! Take me away!'

With these last words, the Dodger suffered himself to be led off by the collar; threatening, till he got into the yard, to make a parliamentary business of it; and then grinning in the officer's face, with great glee and self-approval. (XLIII)

The 'self-approval' is tantamount to self-consciousness, and, as Bergson points out, 'A comic character is generally comic in proportion to his ignorance of himself. The comic person is unconscious' ('Laughter', p. 71). As the Dodger is being led away, we are left with the haunting suspicion that his defiance was not, after all, so easy, and that his own wit was not so much a mechanical reaction as a rather desperate defence. All the talk of punishment, we see, is largely an expression of fear after all. Unlike Bumble, he does not lose his identity, but the hint that he has been able to retain it only with great courage is enough to cut off laughter and encourage us to identify with the victimized Dodger.

The humour in the novel, then, seems to me to be consistently and brilliantly directed to these ends: to make us see how incomplete and hostile a reaction our laughter is, to force us by this recognition briefly to see in ourselves the shadow of Fang,

---

[11] This is a paraphrase of Kettle's argument (*Introduction to the English Novel*, i. 134). He sees the trial as illustrating the novel's main concern: 'What are the poor to do against the oppressive state?'

Mrs. Corney, and the gentleman in the white waistcoat, and to direct us through this insight into a participation in the vital action of the novel which is, at once, more complete and much more intense.

3

But the 'vital action' of the novel supported by the rhetoric of laughter is not, as has been noted, coincident with the plot of the last half of the novel. The novel shifts its grounds to a concern with the simplistically defined good and bad, but we are already committed to a position which refuses to be so easily upset. In comparison with the problems suggested by Fagin and Mr. Bumble, the pivotal concern in the Maylie–Brownlow plot about 'stains' on one's honour, noble sacrifices of 'station', and recovered wills seems incredibly trivial. This means that when the novel switches to the conflict between the Fagin world and the Brownlow world, our laughter tends to tie us to the former, even when Oliver changes sides. Oliver may no longer be a victim (he almost, in fact, disappears from the novel), but there are plenty of victims around, and, in so far as the Maylies, Brownlows, Losbernes, and the like are relevant to this vital world of the thieves at all, they are enemies. The novel thus pushes us towards a position which it finally refuses to countenance; for all the concern with good societies at the end, when the thieves' society decays, the reader is left with no social possibilities. He is, in fact, as isolated as the young hero was at the beginning. This is one major reason why we react very intensely to *Oliver Twist* but still are likely to say that it is a bad novel. It lacks entirely the congruence of plot, theme, and emotion which was so marked in *Pickwick Papers*. But it accomplishes something perhaps as rare: it makes us live for a time with Fagin—and like it.

The opposition between the worlds of Fagin and Rose Maylie has often been discussed, and it seems clear that no one really likes, believes in, or remembers Rose and that everyone is somehow attracted to Fagin. Part of the reason for this has already been discussed: the rhetoric of laughter, which provides for a sympathetic alignment with the victims. But the social implications of these two worlds, the kinds of homes they provide for the reader, need to be investigated further.

As it is first introduced, Fagin's world is, in almost every way, a distinctly positive contrast to the one Oliver had known. It provides a release from misery, starvation, and, most important, loneliness. When the Artful Dodger crosses the street to say, 'Hullo! my covey, what's the row?' (VIII), there is no question that this is a new world, friendlier, freer, warmer. All sinister motives aside, the Dodger is the first person to express spontaneous and real concern for Oliver. He is the first to provide an alternative to the most horrifying part of the orphan's early life: its desolation. It is certainly better to be a thief than to be alone: the whole emotional force of the novel has made that clear. The Dodger's simple announcement, then, 'This is him, Fagin . . . my friend, Oliver Twist' (VIII), introduces us to a new and welcome environment. It hardly even matters that it is sinister.

More often than 'sinister' even, the words 'gentle' and 'soft' are associated with Fagin, and the over-emphasized and obvious satanic connections should not obscure the fact that there is something maternal as well about the recurring image of Fagin bending over the fire and about his favourite phrase, 'my dear'. Of course, these images are partly ironic, but, I think, only partly. In context, they are seen as relief from the workhouse and as an alternative to rigid system. Dickens makes the contrast pointedly. There is, first of all, no hint of starvation here; the thieves are constantly eating. Second, the thieves' life has a profusion and, paradoxically, an openness completely lacking in the pinched material and emotional life the workhouse allowed. The point is made by a characteristic Dickens symbol and with a characteristic—for this novel— sick joke:

It appears, at first sight, not unreasonable to suppose, that, if [Oliver] had entertained a becoming feeling of respect for the prediction of the gentleman in the white waistcoat, he would have established that sage individual's prophetic character, once and for ever, by tying one end of his pocket-handkerchief to a hook in the wall, and attaching himself to the other. To the performance of this feat, however, there was one obstacle: namely, that pocket-handkerchiefs being decided articles of luxury, had been, for all future times and ages, removed from the noses of paupers by the express order of the board, in council assembled. (III)

At Fagin's, pocket-handkerchiefs are everywhere. But the real contrast is of meagreness and openness, ultimately of life and death. The handkerchiefs are used by Fagin's group to maintain a lively and exuberant life; there is certainly no thought of suicide.

The one vigorous and persuasive life-force in the novel, in fact, is centred in Fagin. Both the workhouse and the Maylie group are associated with, if not dedicated to, death. The life celebrated at Fagin's is, in addition, of the kind that we associate particularly with a comic society. Like the Dodger, all Fagin's gang are adept at parody and speak a language which constantly makes fun of the petrified, respectable world. They are, further, extremely resilient and flexible, and they create a warm kind of conviviality through a life of the imagination[12] conspicuously absent at the Maylies'. Rose and Oliver, we gather, sit around for hours weeping at mental pictures of 'the friends whom they had so sadly lost' (liii). This gruesome faculty might be called the tombstone imagination. But the thieves' imagination is one of joy, of recapturing laughter from pain. For example, when Charley Bates is despondent over the Dodger's arrest, Fagin helps him to create an imaginative— and, as it turns out, accurate—picture of the trial. The vision of this 'regular game' allows Charley to escape from pain; he is transported by the humorous imagination:

'I think I see him now,' cried the Jew, bending his eyes upon his pupil.
'So do I,' cried Charley Bates. 'Ha! ha! ha! so do I. I see it all afore me, upon my soul I do, Fagin. What a game! What a regular game! All the big-wigs trying to look solemn, and Jack Dawkins addressing of 'em as intimate and comfortable as if he was the judge's own son making a speech arter dinner—ha! ha! ha!' (XLIII)

He sees that the Dodger's essential witty challenge is to society's (and the reader's) lack of compassion. He acts exactly as if he were our 'own son'. But it is perhaps the imaginative warmth generated by Charley and his fellow thieves that is most important. It is the only joy we find in the novel, defensive and often dark though it may be. It is the closest thing to Dulwich that *Oliver Twist* offers.

[12] See Mark Spilka, *Dickens and Kafka*, p. 73, for the best discussion of Fagin's imaginative powers.

Even Oliver is affected by this joy and significantly laughs at Fagin's 'droll and curious' stories 'in spite of all his better feelings' (xviii). Perhaps this phrasing suggests the real problem with this novel; the plot wants Oliver to drop the laughter in favour of his 'better feelings', but the central pattern, confirmed by the rhetoric, is all for ignoring these imbecilic and deathly 'better feelings' for ever. There is nothing more reminiscent of the freedom of *Pickwick Papers* than the wonderful parody games Fagin plays with his young charges, which make Oliver laugh 'till the tears ran down his face' (ix).

But Oliver deserts this life and us for games at the Brownlows' played 'with great interest and gravity' (xiv), and it is just this contrast which informs the emotional life of the last half of the book. The whole Maylie–Brownlow camp swim in a virtual bath of tears. Taking their lead from Rose, who cries at happiness, sorrow, disappointment, and hope, everyone, down to Brownlow, expresses himself with tears, and not the tears engendered by helpless laughter at a versatile and witty Fagin. Even 'delight', the central emotion of comedy, causes the dismals here: Mrs. Bedwin, 'being in a state of considerable delight at seeing [Oliver] so much better, forthwith began to cry most violently' (xii). It is perhaps perverse, but not ultimately inaccurate, to suggest that Mrs. Bedwin is really crying because Oliver did not, in fact, die. The Maylie–Brownlow group are in every way the antithesis of the comic dedication to life. Even Dickens seems hard pressed to imagine them doing anything (i.e. living), and we long for a touch of those 'continental frivolities' (xlix) to which Monks's mother had apparently so abandoned herself. We want them even more because Mr. Brownlow is so ridiculously stolid and pompous in denouncing them.

But Mr. Brownlow is not unique. The only real laughter to be found among the good people is the malicious chortling of Grimwig, who finds his one source of perverse pleasure in the fact that, after all, Oliver did not come back from the errand. When Grimwig meets Oliver, he reacts in the unfeeling, selfish way usual for him but far from the usual manner of Dickens's comic eccentrics; it is, rather, a blunt foreshadowing of Miss Murdstone, with a touch of Mrs. Raddles:

'That's the boy, is it?' said Mr. Grimwig, at length.

'That is the boy,' replied Mr. Brownlow.
'How are you, boy?' said Mr. Grimwig.

    .   .   .

'He is a nice-looking boy, is he not?' inquired Mr. Brownlow.
'I don't know,' replied Mr. Grimwig, pettishly.
'Don't know?'
'No. I don't know. I never see any difference in boys. I only know two sorts of boys. Mealy boys, and beef-faced boys.' (xiv)

We must, it seems, take Grimwig's good heart mostly on trust. It is clear, though, that his aloof posture is a defensive reaction. He chooses not to cry and is allowed, apparently, only this recourse. All the rest in the camp of the good is tears.

The subversion, then, is complete and fundamental. The laughter of the reader and the characters is used as a weapon of self-exposure, and we are pulled toward the one isolated pocket of spontaneity in the novel, Fagin's den. When, with Fagin's execution, the last echo of unmalicious laughter dies away, we almost certainly feel a sense of regret. By this point, we have been encouraged to cast aside altogether our normal social identification by means of the most solid of all social gestures, laughter, and we are left without a society. Dickens has here used the technique of attack through our laughter with great intensity but without complete control. The experience of isolation is insisted upon and made real by our laughter, but this experience works against that 'little society' of nearly 'perfect happiness' which the entire second half of the novel has been somewhat desperately trying to establish. The novelist does work out a tactic here he will use in later novels, perhaps never with more startling effect but more in consonance with major themes and patterns. Here the novel remains fractured. Most readers have some tendency, encouraged by their laughter, to rewrite it in their minds, though, and when Charley Bates says of Oliver, 'What a pity it is he isn't a prig!' (xviii), we are tempted to respond, using the term without the thieves' irony, 'What a pity he *is*!'

4 *The Old Curiosity Shop*
LAUGHTER AND PATHOS

'I hate your virtuous people!' said the dwarf,
throwing off a bumper of brandy, and smacking
his lips, 'ah! I hate 'em every one!' (XLVIII)

DICK SWIVELLER steps into the Old Curiosity Shop for the
first time in order to introduce the logic of Mr. Wardle: 'Why
should a grandson and grandfather peg away at each other
with mutual wiolence when all might be bliss and concord?
Why not jine hands and forget it?' (II). Why not indeed? It is
just this argument which could settle for ever the friendly
differences in *Pickwick Papers*; it is a sane argument and ought
to have great force in a sane world. But it has no relevance at
all to the madhouse world of *The Old Curiosity Shop*, and Dick
Swiveller is funny precisely because he is so incongruously
sane. He sees, for instance, that Nell's grandfather is really
'the jolly old grandfather' and Fred 'the wild young grandson'
of the comic theatre and that everything ought to come out
'all right and comfortable'. But no one will play these reasonable roles; 'the old dotard', as Quilp not unfairly calls him,
becomes a type of demonic selfishness, and Fred sinks in lurid
degradation. Dick suggests that they all pack up and go to
Dingley Dell. But there is no room for the bright simplicity
of Dingley Dell in this novel; it is both too dark and too
complex. There is, for instance, an awful and subtle irony in
the narrative structure. For all the travelling and frantic rushing about that goes on, no one really moves anywhere or
finally escapes from the pursuers.[1] This irony is also present in

[1] Both Miller, *Charles Dickens*, pp. 95–6, and Larry Kirkpatrick, 'The Gothic
Flame of Charles Dickens', *VN*, no. 31 (1967), p. 20, argue that the ironic
identification of rural 'escape' with death functions as a criticism of the ending
of *Oliver Twist*.

the narrative tone. For all the 'quietness'[2] Dickens worked for—and achieved—in the atmosphere, there is an underlying bitterness and a dominant motif of retribution which makes this quietness much more sinister and dark than soft and sad.

But soft and sad we continue to think it, and complexity is about the last quality ordinarily granted to *The Old Curiosity Shop*. More than any other Dickens novel, this one has tended to be rewritten in critical mythology and has become grossly oversimplified in the process. For many, in fact, the novel has been distilled into the climactic page and a half, of which the following is a fair example: 'She was dead. Dear, gentle, patient, noble Nell was dead. Her little bird—a poor slight thing the pressure of a finger would have crushed—was stirring nimbly in its cage; and the strong heart of its child-mistress was mute and motionless for ever' (LXXI). Perhaps even this is not representative, for the bitterness reflected in this passage, the rather ugly vindictiveness suggested by the reference to the bird, and the strange urge to wallow not with Nell but with the worms are not part of the popular myth. *The Old Curiosity Shop* has often become 'The Death of Nell', and even that episode has been simplified in this century to the image of 'ineptitude and vulgar sentimentality'[3] attending the awful iambs with which the two-headed monster[4] is slaughtered. The contrasts between the Victorian response to Nell and our own have been often described and variously explained.[5] Obviously more is involved in this change than can be dis-

[2] To Thomas Latimer, *Nonesuch Letters*, i. 305. 13 Mar. 1841.

[3] The phrase is Aldous Huxley's in *Vulgarity in Literature* (London, 1930), p. 57.

[4] This one is Swinburne's in 'Charles Dickens', *The Quarterly Review*, cxcvi (1902), 22.

[5] The standard historical argument is given by Edgar Johnson, *Charles Dickens*, i. 323–4. He argues that 'we live in a different emotional climate from theirs' and that 'our response is the deviation'. Our general fear of sentiment, in other words, is far more unnatural than the presumed attraction many Victorians felt to it. The editors of the second volume of the Pilgrim Edition of the *Letters* (Oxford: Clarendon Press, 1969), however, argue that the evidence suggests a much more moderate response to Nell on the part of the Victorians than critics like Johnson have supposed. The assumptions of such arguments as his may therefore be based on a vision of a weeping audience that is, if not entirely mythical, at least inaccurate.

Justifications of Nell on artistic grounds ordinarily emphasize the ironies which attend her and deny sentimentality altogether; see A. E. Dyson, '*The Old Curiosity Shop*: Innocence and the Grotesque', *CritQ*, viii (1966), 112.

cussed here, but one thing, at least, seems to me clear. Our rather hysterical rejection of Nell is at least as much a rejection of those crowds on the docks in America, waiting for the ships from England and calling out, 'Is Nell dead ?', as it is of the novel itself. We strongly resist identifying ourselves with that group and that society, partly, I suppose, out of the snobbery which, assuming the progress of taste, allows us to sneer at the Victorians; but surely more important is the inability to respond to or even admit the existence of the extraordinarily intimate appeals in that novel. We may laugh at the boorishness of those who could admire such unsophisticated art, but there is something challenging and therefore frightening about the openness with which they invested so much of themselves in Nell.

There is the same threat and challenge in the novel itself. When Dickens speaks in the Preface of 'the many friends it won me, and the many hearts it turned to me when they were full of private sorrow', he is talking about something more than a novel, and he is asking for something more than a conventional response. *The Old Curiosity Shop*, for all its hatred of Little Bethel, uses evangelical rhetoric and clearly expects something like a religious conversion to Nellyism. In this expectation, then, the novel is clearly antagonistic, implying that a failure of response is not an aesthetic but a spiritual failure.

And the proof of responsiveness is very simple and very extreme—tears. *The Old Curiosity Shop* is alone among Dickens's novels in being so emphatically centred on the dominant emotion of pathos, the most horrifying and deceptive of appeals. As Northrop Frye says, 'Pathos, though it seems a gentler and more relaxed mood than tragedy, is even more terrifying. Its basis is the exclusion of an individual from a group, hence it attacks the deepest fear in ourselves that we possess.'[6] The intimacy demanded by the novel, then, is an intimacy with desolation and death. We tend to escape these extremities, paradoxically, by concentrating on Nell alone; for even though she is the central figure of the pathos, the weight of the rhetorical burden is carried by other figures. While it is certainly true that Nell can, by herself, support

[6] *Anatomy of Criticism*, p. 217.

very little meaning or emotion, she does receive enormous reflexive strength from her surroundings. Dickens's decision to surround Nell with the 'grotesque and wild' (Preface, p. xii) was made not simply to gain picturesqueness but also to provide complexity and strength to the central figure and the central emotion. To a very large extent, Nell is made possible by Quilp and by Dick Swiveller, and the pathos is guaranteed by the humour.

For it was laughter that moved those dock crowds as well as tears, and laughter is primarily important in fixing our relationship to the central figure. In fact, for all its celebration of the grave, *The Old Curiosity Shop* is rooted in a comic impulse. Certainly the impulse is perverted and narrow, but it is there none the less. Since Dick cannot carry everyone off to Dingley Dell, we all go to the churchyard; Nell is fed to the worms in lieu of a Christmas festival. The unconscious logic of this movement towards death is comic in the sense that it is so strongly dedicated to youth and so violently opposed to age: if youth and its attendant values can no longer win in this world, then they will turn to the greater victory in death, thereby defying the aged, who want them to adopt their corruption. The grave becomes almost sanctified. In the child's defiance of the parent and the protection of the pleasure principle through suicide, the novel suggests the last desperately ingenious defence of the comic spirit.

But this description puts too grossly what is in the novel a subtle and submerged tendency. It is also true that this suicidal tendency is disguised by the existence of its opposite: the glorification of the grave is matched by a repulsion from it. At one point Dickens says that to mourn the death of children is to forget the 'bright and happy existence [to which] those who die young are borne, and how in death they lose the pain of seeing others die around them' (xxvi). This, it must be admitted, is not an indication of subtlety or complexity; it is mere confusion. Death is seen both as a victory and as an escape from the pain which somehow comes from seeing others attain that victory. Dickens's ambivalence towards death neutralizes any meaning. The ambivalence is understandable, of course, but it does tend to weaken the novel by dissolving many of its ironies. The perverse comedy of Nell cannot ultimately be sustained because the grave cannot be sanctified for the young. The old die too.

But because of the conflicting attitudes toward death, the comedy can be maintained for long periods, primarily through a relentless underground attack on the old. At the funeral of Nell, the narrator makes this attack explicit by arguing that these old horrors are more dead than Nell: 'Old men were there, whose eyes were dim and senses failing—grandmothers, who might have died ten years ago, and still been old—the deaf, the blind, the lame, the palsied, the living dead in many shapes and forms, to see the closing of that early grave. What was the death it would shut in, to that which still could crawl and creep above it!' (LXXII). Notice that these ancient vermin 'crawl and creep', quite a change from old Wardle and old Pickwick. Usually, however, Dickens's attack is much more subtle and uses the mask of humour. Even Dick Swiveller contributes to this warfare: '. . . these old people—there's no trusting 'em, Fred. There's an aunt of mine down in Dorset-shire that was going to die when I was eight years old, and hasn't kept her word yet. They're so aggravating, so un-principled, so spiteful—unless there's apoplexy in the family, Fred, you can't calculate upon 'em, and even then they deceive you just as often as not' (VII). The light tone and the physical absence of Dick's aunt provide the disguise for the aggression, but the tendency of the joke is serious indeed.

The central symbol for this attack is, of course, Nell's grand-father. Directly responsible for her death by removing her from every point of safety and kindness, he, it is clear, is much closer even than Quilp to being the chief villain. He serves as the archetypal parental butt, the object of the comic if vicious revenge of the child on the adult. He is allowed none of the conventional superiorities of age; he is simply a 'hollow mockery' of 'childishness', an adult ludicrously attempting to be a child, but justly (according to the comic logic) denied 'the gaiety', 'the light and life', 'the hope', and 'the joys' of child-hood. Instead, he is to childhood what 'death is [to] sleep' (XII). The key joke against him is, significantly, made by children who run along beside Mrs. Jarley's caravan, 'fully impressed with the belief that [Nell's] grandfather was a cunning device in wax' (XXVIII). The point of the joke is certainly clear, and it coalesces with many others to reinforce the secret dream wish: that the old might be annihilated.

Our laughter here, as in *Pickwick Papers*, is asked to reject the pompous and stuffy formulas of the old for the freshness of youth. The rejection in *The Old Curiosity Shop*, however, is much more desperately violent, and the alternative turns out not to be freshness but youthful death. In this basic way, then, laughter pushes us toward the ultimate terror of pathos invested in the solitary child.

And it is certainly the pathetic Nell who is at the centre of the novel and who makes the primary demands for our responsiveness. But the dominant critical error is to separate Nell from her surroundings. Despite her central importance, she is defined and made effective by the figures around her. I think we can, therefore, best understand Nell and the pathos she represents by dealing with the major forces exterior to her, primarily those represented by Dick Swiveller and by Daniel Quilp. In this most dreamlike of novels, the connection of the important motifs exists almost entirely beneath the conscious level of the narrative. The major figures and attitudes are logically involved with one another, but the involvement is scarcely explained at all by the logic of the plot. Instead, we have a conflict of very basic tendencies, or, as Gabriel Pearson says, 'fields of force',[7] arranged in patterns of opposition and contrast often tangential to the plot itself. On one hand, there is the movement of Nell, her grandfather, Kit and the Garlands, Witherden the Notary, and those associated with this group towards peace, sanctity, the expected, acquiescence, and stasis. Diametrically opposed is the force of Quilp, mostly isolated, but echoed to some extent in Sally Brass and Tom Scott, toward energy, violence, surprise, rebellion, and motion. Paradoxically, the mutual repulsion of these extreme forces tends to push them so far apart from each other that they meet in common self-extermination. Despite Quilp's continual and brilliant parody of the Nelly-group, he ends in the same position

[7] I am very much indebted to Pearson's article in *Dickens and the Twentieth Century*, pp. 77–90, particularly to his conception of the novel as being defined by the three forces of Nell, Quilp, and Dick. Though I do not agree that Dick's humour is a 'subversive commentary' (p. 87) on the other two forces, I think his general view of Dick's relation to Nell and Quilp is accurate, and I have used it here.

exactly. As Pearson points out (p. 90), this opposition of forces creates a more and more apparent vacuum in the centre, which becomes filled, more and more adequately, by Dick Swiveller and the Marchioness. Dick is not, I think, primarily a parody on either group but a sane alternative made possible by their extreme and self-destructive antipathy. One can easily see this pattern as a simple extension of the one which existed only in potential in *Oliver Twist*. Rose Maylie (as Nell) is pushed happily into the grave where she belongs and Fagin (as Quilp) is made specifically subterranean. By carrying these tendencies to their logical conclusions, one could argue, there is room for a middle position in Dick, not possible when the split is as tenuous as in *Oliver Twist*. At any rate, the unity of *The Old Curiosity Shop* and its elemental force are determined by these three groups and the ways in which they reflect on one another.

The novel is not, however, really kaleidoscopic, nor is the pattern quite this neat. The determining reflections come from outside into Nell, and there is relatively little interplay in the other direction. The main problems, then, have to do with Nell and with the pathos she is meant to generate. In my opinion, the laughter which is exterior but thematically relevant to Nell makes that pathos possible and effective. Providing for the pathetic is one of the two main rhetorical functions of laughter in this novel; the other is to provide for the final comic solution centred in Dick and the Marchioness. Dickens, by our laughter, leads us to the grave and back again, provides us with tears and with joy. But the tears are unquestionably dominant for a large part of the novel and even help make possible by reaction the final joy. The first and main issue, then, is the relationship in the novel between laughter and pathos.

Laughter provides for pathos primarily through its aggressive component. Like the humour of direct attack, it awakens the aggression necessary for laughter and then exposes that aggression by removing the original disguise. Both types of humour also utilize the guilt made possible by this exposure of the reader's callousness. The differences are mainly of intensity and distance. In *Oliver Twist* the backlash is immediate and the laughter immediately turns round on us; in *The Old Curiosity Shop* there is vital distance between the laughter and the serious reversal, so that the guilt is less felt and less insisted on, and may therefore be transferred to pity or tears. In the latter case, the guilt is a medium, not a final goal, and we are not so much attacked as softened up. Another way to explain this is to use the notion of vulnerability discussed in the first chapter. According to this idea, we release the energies of aggression or hostility only when we are assured by the disguise that it is safe to do so. Once these energies are expended, we are firmly committed and also defenceless, since there is no protection for the exposed impulse. We can, then, be made to react much more intensely to pathetic appeals. To be more specific, in this novel laughter at the Quilp and Swiveller forces, and at the people Nell and her grandfather meet in their travels, is used to heighten the response to Nell's sorrows and trials. A few examples should make this relationship of laughter and pathos clearer.

Probably the most basic relationship is rooted in the fact that in Little Nell the novel dedicates itself to all the feminine virtues, whilst at the same time it is inviting us to participate in hostile laughter at all women. The softness, humility, and gentle subservience of women is both staunchly supported and ridiculed. For instance, there is the brilliant humorous triumph of Daniel Quilp over all the neighbourhood women, gathered to sympathize with Mrs. Quilp. Now Betsy Quilp is very nearly Nell's double, but we are by no means invited to share in the cackling neighbours' sympathy for her. We are, in fact, invited to laugh, first, at the cowardice, blind egoism, and petty spitefulness of the neighbours:

'Ah! . . . I wish you'd give her a little of your advice, Mrs. Jiniwin . . . nobody knows better than you, ma'am, what us women owe to ourselves.'

'Owe indeed, ma'am!' replied Mrs. Jiniwin. 'When my poor husband, her dear father, was alive, if he had ever ventur'd a cross word to *me*, I'd have—' the good old lady did not finish the sentence, but she twisted off the head of a shrimp with a vindictiveness which seemed to imply that the action was in some degree a substitute for words. (IV)

Mrs. Quilp is urged to stand up for her superficial 'rights' as a woman, but she cuts through the chorus of self-deception with an admission that substantiates our aggressive laughter: 'It's

very easy to talk, but I say again that I know—that I'm sure—
Quilp has such a way with him when he likes, that the best-
looking woman here couldn't refuse him if I was dead, and she
was free, and he chose to make love to her. Come!' This provides the perfect comic reversal and the perfect justification
for our hostile amusement. Women, we are assured, are
ludicrous, and their pretences to power are absurd simply
because they are sexually inferior. Their hilarious, snarling
reactions to Betsy's truth amount to confessions of impotence:
'Before I'd consent to stand in awe of a man as she does of him,
I'd—I'd kill myself, and write a letter first to say he did it!'
So when Quilp, the representative of pure male energy, scatters
the women merely by entering and inviting them to supper,
the comic triumph is complete. It is capped only by the once-
proud Mrs. Jiniwin being forced to go to bed (of all things)
against her will. Mothers, wives, and daughters are all routed
here in this vigorous humour of expulsion.

Much less harsh but certainly parallel is Dick Swiveller's
victory over the Wackles gaggle four chapters later. Dick
invades the 'Ladies' Seminary' ostensibly to escape from his
entanglement, but really to demonstrate again the hideousness
of the female and to allow Miss Sophy to foil her own predatory
plot to catch him by making him jealous of the market-
gardener, Cheggs. Even Sophy's sister and fellow-conspirator,
young Jane, is described as 'prematurely shrill and shrewish',
though only sixteen. In this world all women are hags; little
girls are hags-in-training. Dick's famous verbal triumph, then,
is made more wonderful by being coincident with the general
triumph over women:

'I am sure I don't know what you mean, Mr. Swiveller,' said
Miss Sophy with downcast eyes. 'I'm very sorry if—'
'Sorry, ma'am!' said Dick, 'sorry in the possession of a Cheggs!'
(VIII)

Dick's phrasing is masterful; Sophy now 'possesses'—and the
commercial diction is intentional—*a* Cheggs, as if it were *a*
handbag or *a* curlpaper. Dick's sarcasm is very pointed here;
since she is a woman, what right has she to want anything
more? She has, after all, received just 'what us women owe
to ourselves'.

Examples of humorous assaults on women could be extended

indefinitely: Miss Monflathers and Sally Brass are flayed alive, and even Mrs. Nubbles comes in for attack on account of her religious stupidity. The existence of this recurrent impulse to attack women would seem to subvert the values associated with Nell and invest that figure with a strong irony, but I think not. There is a long distance between these attacks and Nell, and the very rejection of the feminine makes us all the more ready to respond to it when it is presented seriously. Again, this is a matter of distance and great tact; if Dickens brings the attack and the celebration close together, the result undoubtedly would be parody. But it seems clear that few have ever reacted to Nell as a parody figure, and it must be remembered that while the defence of Nell's virtues is overt and explicit, the attack comes through laughter, which by its very nature hides its source. Thus, since the reader is given a breathing spell, the laughter is preparatory to pathos; our aggression against the feminine is activated again and again, but we are never forced to admit this aggression consciously. The hostility is therefore drained rather than focused and is redirected to a more intense pity for the threatened femininity of Nell.

Perhaps an even clearer example of the comic–pathetic interrelationship is provided by the use made of jokes on loneliness to heighten our feeling for Nell's desolation. There are, for example, many jokes specifically involving the confusion of friend and foe. First, there is the fixed notion of the business manager of the travelling Punch show: 'Recollect the friend. Codlin's the friend, not Short. Short's very well as far as he goes, but the real friend is Codlin—not Short' (xix). The dark point of this humour is that neither is friendly and that both are willing to sell out Nell for the proper sum. The distinctions we are asked to make between the gruff and grim misanthrope, Codlin, and the jolly Short Trotters break down; there is no play on the appearance-reality theme here, except that under all appearances is the uniform bleak selfishness which causes everyone to be completely alone and friendless. This same point is made through humour several times by Quilp. A good deal of his success rides on just this confusion of friend and enemy, with the same awful point about human desolation being made. He traps Fred Trent, for instance, with just this ruse: 'You little knew who was your friend, and who your foe: now did you ?' (xxiii). Ironically, Quilp is at least an enemy, and the existence of feeling, even of negative feeling, is better than the black indifference of Codlin and Short. Finally, in the case of the Marchioness, we have the most extensive humorous treatment of this theme of loneliness, and a completion of the three-sided humorous pattern which reflects on Nell from each of the fields of force. The Marchioness is desperately lonely but combats this, at least partially, through the resources available to her through the keyhole. Though a very complex figure, she has a fund of protective Freudian humour at her disposal which makes it possible for us, at least at first, to conserve our pity and laugh at her. The Brasses treat her purely as a thing, a noise-maker: 'We have been moving chests of drawers over [the lodger's] head, we have knocked double knocks at the street-door, we have made the servant-girl fall down stairs several times, (she's a light weight, and it don't hurt her much,) but nothing wakes him' (xxxv).

The laughter in all three areas of the novel prepares us for the pathos attending the dominant emotion, the awful isolation caused by the individual pursuit of selfish concerns. At the centre of the novel is this vision of alienation, of man lost in a purely atomistic society, 'an atom, here, in a mountain-heap of misery' (xliv). Our previous laughter at the failure of human concern, at the absence of human friendship, prepares us for the heart of the pathos:

the two poor strangers, stunned and bewildered by the hurry they beheld but had no part in, looked mournfully on; feeling, amidst the crowd, a solitude which has no parallel but in the thirst of the shipwrecked mariner, who, tost to and fro upon the billows of a mighty ocean, his red eyes blinded by looking on the water which hems him in on every side, has not one drop to cool his burning tongue. (xliv)

Even the parallel to Coleridge's poem is ironic, for the loneliness here is the more awful loneliness 'amidst the crowd', a crowd which emphatically does not hold out the possibility of grace or redemption, even if the commercial water-snakes are blessed. The jokes have been used as preparatory notes to establish in the reader a readiness for, really a susceptibility to, this appeal.

The most important support for this pathetic and serious appeal comes from the humour associated with the three basic sections of the novel: the Nelly-group; its polar opposite, the Quilp-group; finally, the resultant Swiveller-group.

1

The approved goals of the Nell group are peace, serenity, sameness, and acquiescence—finally, of course, death. Nell is not alone in having these negative aspirations; she shares them with associated characters, such as the Nubbleses and the Garlands. The Garlands, when hiring Kit, explain their extreme carefulness on the ground that they are 'very quiet regular folks'. Because of this, they say, 'it would be a sad thing if we made any kind of mistake, and found things different from what we hoped and expected' (xxi). The direction of this force is characterized very aptly by the sort of life described here: quiet and regular, without surprises. The whole group really distrusts change and excitement so much that its members are even unable to resist feeling guilty after the night at Astley's (xl). All their energy and rebelliousness seem to have been transferred to the pony; the rest huddle desperately together in a pathetic search for safety.

It is this same search for safety which motivates the travels of Nell and her grandfather, an attempt above all to elude the nightmare enemies, those who are 'searching for me everywhere, and may come here, and steal upon us, even while we're talking' (xxiv). The awful irony is that they are running from their avowed friends.[8] More horribly ironic still is the suggestion that they really don't go anywhere, that they simply move from death to death. Dickens makes this literally vicious circle symbolically clear by connecting the original Old Curiosity Shop with their final home provided by the schoolmaster. Both, of course, are associated with death, decay, and disuse, but the tie is made even more explicit. The shop contains 'fantastic carvings brought from monkish cloisters' (i),

[8] G. K. Chesterton has the best and most evocative description of this irony: 'All the good fairies and all the kind magicians, all the just kings and all the gallant princes, with chariots and flying dragons and armies and navies go after one little child who has strayed into a wood, and find her dead' (*Appreciations and Criticisms*, pp. 53–4).

and the final home 'a pile of fragments of rich carving from
old monkish stalls' (LII), and they both have 'strange furniture'. Even the old church where Nell is so attracted to the
dead contains rusty armour corresponding to the 'rusty
weapons' of the original shop. Finally, Nell's grandfather is
described as simply returning home; at the original shop,
Master Humphrey says, 'The haggard aspect of the little old
man was wonderfully suited to the place; he might have groped
among old churches, and tombs, and deserted houses, and
gathered all the spoils with his own hands. There was nothing
in the whole collection but was in keeping with himself;
nothing that looked older or more worn than he' (I). And just
before his death the same association is made: 'He, and the
failing light and dying fire, the time-worn room, the solitude,
the wasted life, and gloom, were all in fellowship. Ashes, and
dust, and ruin!' (LXXI). The circular structure insists that they
have run desperately hard only to remain stationary—in the
tomb where they began. And behind this structural circle of
futility is a similar thematic one: Quilp is chasing the old man
for the non-existent gold the old man is also chasing; the dog
is, indeed, chasing its tail and driving itself mad. The delusive
and frustrating search for security in a commercial world ends
in death.

For underneath all are those satanic mills and the system
of life they have created. When Nell persuades her grandfather
to leave London, she is clearly thinking of an escape from the
industrial present. But it is equally clear that he cannot
loosen himself from the premises of industrialism:

'If we are beggars—!'
'What if we are?' said the child boldly. 'Let us be beggars, and
be happy.'
'Beggars—and happy!' said the old man. 'Poor child!' (IX)

At the heart of their problem is the fact that they are unable
to be happy outside the commercial system. This suggests an
imaginative failure (Dick Swiveller is certainly an alternative
in this regard) but partly an inescapable fact. The most intensely imagined scene in the novel shows Nell and her grandfather alone in the midst of a seething business crowd:

The throng of people hurried by, in two opposite streams, with no symptom of cessation or exhaustion; intent upon their own affairs; and undisturbed in their business speculations, by the roar of carts and waggons laden with clashing wares, the slipping of horses' feet upon the wet and greasy pavement, the rattling of the rain on windows and umbrella-tops, the jostling of the more impatient passengers, and all the noise and tumult of a crowded street in the high tide of its occupation. (XLIV)

Here is the root cause of the central isolation, the separation of man from man by the cash nexus.[9] Dickens's attack on the mercantile organization of life in this novel is more indirect than in the later novels, but it is none the less powerful. The novel is more than a 'failed idyll';[10] it is an exploration of the defeat of the Romantic imagination, the disjunction of man from nature and from his fellows. Even the divine child of the Romantics and of the parable is distorted: 'It was plain that she was thenceforth his guide and leader. The child felt it, but had no doubts or misgivings, and putting her hand in his, led him gently away' (XII). And she leads him to loneliness, defeat, and death.

It is against this background that Dickens introduces the 'grotesque and wild, but not impossible, companions' he intended as a counterpoint to 'the lonely figure of the child' (Preface, p. xii). And it is through these companions that Dickens begins the humorous juxtaposition that controls the form of this novel and makes effective its pathos.

Codlin and Short, the first of these contrasts, act as an awful parody of comic existence and of warm affection. At the 'Jolly Sandboys' they are joined by Mr. Grinder and his weird company, Vuffin and his Giant, the dogs—in short, a kind of circus of feasting and revelry. The economic attack, however, becomes more and more insistent as the talk turns to the marketability (Short would use this sort of jargon if he knew it) of giants. 'Once get a giant shaky on his legs, and the public

---

[9] Edgar Johnson (*Charles Dickens*, i. 326–37) is one of the few critics to take seriously the commercial and economic implications of the novel's theme; he argues that behind all is the 'acquistive greed callous to the suffering it caused'. J. C. Reid, *The Hidden World of Charles Dickens* (Auckland, 1962), pp. 34–47, does offer a similar reading, but it seems to me somewhat weakened by being so self-consciously 'archetypal' in approach.

[10] This descriptive term is used by Steven Marcus and discussed at some length (*From Pickwick to Dombey*, pp. 135–42).

cares no more about him than they do for a dead cabbage-stalk' (xix), says the experienced Mr. Vuffin. Economically obsolete giants, he explains, are protected, not on account of kindness, but because they must be kept scarce: 'Once make a giant common and giants will never draw again. Look at wooden legs. If there was only one man with a wooden leg what a property *he*'d be!' (xix). The alternative to protection is suggested by the case of the giant 'who took to carrying coach-bills about London, making himself as cheap as crossing-sweepers'. 'He died', Vuffin ominously continues; 'I make no insinuation against anybody in particular . . . but he was ruin-ing the trade;—and he died.' Laughter is used to reject this system and this cruelty. In case we were inattentive, Dickens suddenly reminds us that Nell has never laughed at this group but has, in fact, been wearily trying to urge her grandfather to leave. We realize, perhaps with some guilt, that she has been utterly alone in this company of economic freaks, unamused and unhelped. The presumed friends, Codlin and Short, then complete the reversal and turn the laughter back on us. It becomes finally clear that they are also protecting Nell and her grandfather for economic reasons, and when Short calls through the keyhole, then, we see how sinister the note of friendship is and how deceptive the circus joy has been: 'I only wanted to say that we must be off early to-morrow morning, my dear, because unless we get the start of the dogs and the conjurer, the villages won't be worth a penny' (xix). The perfect burlesque of this sort of cruel economic life is surely the picture of an enterprise which is determined to 'get the start of the dogs'.

Nell and her grandfather escape, however, and after a brief stop with the lugubrious schoolmaster, come on 'a Christian lady, stout and comfortable to look on' (xxvi), Mrs. Jarley, a figure paralleled to Dick Swiveller in her imaginative powers and her humorous strength. 'Unquestionably Mrs. Jarley had an inventive genius' (xxix), the narrator says, and that genius offers a potential solution to all the problems Nell faces; it is, in fact, a foreshadowing of Mr. Sleary's circus in *Hard Times* and is an early alternative to the devastatingly rigid political economy. With Mrs. Jarley, even the taking of tea becomes a time for joy, and her use of the 'suspicious bottle' is exactly

like Mr. Pickwick's: to make everything and everyone comfortable. Comfort is, in fact, just what Mrs. Jarley exists for—
in a sense what she is; she has 'not only a peculiar relish for
being comfortable herself, but for making everybody about
her comfortable also' (xxix). Notice that this comfort is not,
as with Codlin and Short, either delusive or menacing, nor is
it associated with the rest and escape Nell seeks. It offers not
safety but joy, not escape but active and continual combat
with all the deadening economic forces. Mrs. Jarley is, most
centrally, a figure who is associated with comic and comfortable life at war with death. She actively parodies calmness,
low spirits, the commercial world, and, most of all, death:

> 'I never saw any wax-work, ma'am,' said Nell. 'Is it funnier than
> Punch?'
> 'Funnier!' said Mrs. Jarley in a shrill voice. 'It is not funny
> at all.'
> 'Oh!' said Nell, with all possible humility.
> 'It isn't funny at all,' repeated Mrs. Jarley. 'It's calm and—
> what's that word again—critical?—no—classical, that's it—it is
> calm and classical. No low beatings and knockings about, no
> jokings and squeakings like your precious Punches, but always the
> same, with a constantly unchanging air of coldness and gentility;
> and so like life, that if wax-work only spoke and walked about,
> you'd hardly know the difference. I won't go so far as to say that,
> as it is, I've seen wax-work quite like life, but I've certainly seen
> some life that was exactly like wax-work.' (xxvii)

She hates Punch for being 'low', 'wulgar', but most significantly, 'practical' (xxvi). The perversion of all joy to ugly
economic ends is suggested by this last adjective, and Mrs.
Jarley's proper distaste for the practical is consonant with her
parody of the deadly cold genteel. Her description of gentility
contrasts so directly with her own existence that our laughter
is made to reject precisely what she pretends to promote: the
death that imitates life. The waxworks themselves function
as a kind of portable burlesque of 'life that [is] exactly like
wax-work'.

This abundant life-force is terribly impatient with the
querulous old man—'I should have thought you were old
enough to take care of yourself, if you ever will be', she
says 'sharply' (xxvii)—and suggests the real alternative to

economic captivation: a comic transcendance of the economic system and its accompanying retributive morality. Even her waxworks burlesque the suffocating maxims; probably the best is the cautionary one of 'the old lady who died of dancing at a hundred and thirty-two' (XXVIII). Her methods of warfare are made explicit in her confrontation with that pillar of commercial life, Miss Monflathers. Grimaldi the clown simply becomes by pronouncement the grammarian Mr. Murray, and a murderess of great renown is made to do for Mrs. Hannah More. No wonder Miss Monflathers is repulsed; only an absolute fool could miss the parody.

Miss Monflathers is, in fact, another softener for the concerted pathos to come. Her very gate, clearly an extension of herself, is a joke on security: 'More obdurate than gate of adamant or brass, this gate of Miss Monflathers's frowned on all mankind. The very butcher respected it as a mystery, and left off whistling when he rang the bell' (XXXI). And her economic assault on Nell makes it clear that the central pursuer of innocence and purity is really the system of profit and loss:

'Don't you feel how naughty it is of you . . . to be a wax-work child, when you might have the proud consciousness of assisting, to the extent of your infant powers, the manufactures of your country; of improving your mind by the constant contemplation of the steam-engine; and of earning a comfortable and independent subsistence of from two-and ninepence to three shillings per week? Don't you know that the harder you work, the happier you are?' (XXXI)

This doctrine is anathema to comedy, and it is no wonder she—or her equally hard-working gate—cuts off the butcher's whistling. Even Mrs. Jarley needs a double dose of alcohol to relieve her mind of Miss Monflathers, who almost makes her 'turn atheist' (XXXII). But the alcohol does the trick, and she finds the right solution; Miss Monflathers gradually changes from 'an object of dire vexation' to 'one of sheer ridicule and absurdity', and it is finally decided that whenever Miss Monflathers is thought of, 'she would do nothing but laugh at her, all the days of her life' (XXXII). She persuades Nell to try the same cure, the application of Freudian humour.

But Nell's infuriating grandfather is far too deeply infected with getting and spending to be touched by this medicine, and he forces Nell to take him away. The symbolic battle between joy and economic despair has resulted in the defeat of joy, and from this point on the travellers have no chance. The recognition of their doomed state adds a special poignancy to Mrs. Jarley; she was much more than a grotesque counterpoint or a funny distraction; she was the last hope, now subsumed by the general commercial death. It is necessary to insist on the generality of the villain, for there is a tendency merely to blame everything on the old man. The inescapable temptation one feels to use vituperative adjectives for him expresses this evasion, but the dodge will not ultimately work. The narrator demands that we regard him as a purified economic dupe, not interested in personal gain and, despite his hysterical statements to the contrary, certainly not interested in Nell. In the midst of gambling, 'the anxious child was quite forgotten' (xx). It is the system that has caught him in its hypnotic power, and, by allowing that system to operate through 'games', Dickens suggests how sinister and insidious the infection is.

From this point on, the route to death is unimpeded, and our laughter no longer strives for alternatives. The jokes are by now clearly preparatory for death. When Nell faints and is carried to an inn, 'everybody called for his or her favourite remedy, which nobody brought; each cried for more air, at the same time carefully excluding what air there was, by closing round the object of sympathy; and all wondered why somebody else didn't do what it never appeared to occur to them might be done by themselves' (xlvi). How loaded the term 'object of sympathy' is! The joke about the narrow limits of sympathy clashes with the real and pervasive indifference and makes the pathos possible. By the time Nell is ready to die, our laughter, oddly enough, moves us towards an acceptance, almost a welcoming, of death and of the impossibility of any escape for her. The old sexton, for instance, who is so resistant to death that he practises the most ludicrous evasions, stirs the darkest laughter in the novel. It is a laughter which, for once, yearns for the grave. The sexton avoids the reminder of death brought on by a woman who died at the early age of seventy-nine by deciding that she, like all women, lied about her age:

'Call to mind how old she looked for many a long, long year, and say if she could be but seventy-nine at last—only our age,' said the sexton.
'Five year older at the very least!' cried the other.
'Five!' retorted the sexton. 'Ten. Good eighty-nine. I call to mind the time her daughter died. She was eighty-nine if she was a day, and tries to pass upon us now, for ten year younger. Oh! human vanity!' (LIV)

He and his helper, David, 'seemed but boys to her'. By the time they leave, David chuckling to himself over the notion that the sexton is 'failing very fast', our laughter has likely rejected this absurd self-preservation and has moved to an instinctive support of the appropriateness of the grave for the limited humanity of this extreme age. As a result, we are prepared for the climactic and inevitable pathos attendant on the ironic reversal: the preservation of the sexton and the death of Nell.

2

At the opposite pole is Daniel Quilp,[11] dedicated to life literally with a vengeance. Sensitive to all personal attacks, he makes his existence over into a brilliant retaliation in order to attack the dehumanizing enemy and protect his own being. An expert parodist, he has enormous capacity for delight in 'the rich field of enjoyment and reprisal' (XXIII) he creates around him. He is really a more elemental Alfred Jingle, whose wit was also hostile and defensive and who was likewise caught in the system by the continual necessity of defence. The system, in other words, is so powerful that it absorbs all reactions to it that use its weapons; Quilp, like Jingle, is trapped by his very anger. Fighting bitterly against every-thing Nell suggests—the passive, the calm, and the dead— he meets the same end. Like Jingle he fails to see that it is the economic weapons which are really at fault, and he is finally destroyed by them.

[11] Marcus also sees Quilp as the polar opposite of Nell and notes that he is her 'other half' (p. 151), though he does not pursue this suggestion.

Before his death, however, he provides an important parody of the main plot. The humour of this parody, however, is qualified locally by Quilp's viciousness and finally by his death. That is, our laughter is often made difficult in individual instances by Quilp's own demonic laughter, or by his cruelty,[12] and we finally recognize, as we see him caught in the same economic quagmire, that his parody has lacked the freedom and detachment for validity. His humour ultimately reinforces rather than undercuts the pathos of the main plot. Just as much as the old grandfather, he represents the brutal power of the economic mill, and nearly as much as Nell is he a victim of it. Our laughter at Quilp, then, is contributory to our tears for Nell.

He is, first of all, an outlet for much aggression, a safety-valve for our hostility against purity, women, and pathos itself. Among other things, he cleanses our reactions and makes possible an unqualified response to Nell. His witty sadism checks our possible impatience with gentleness and drains off our mischievous impulses: 'I don't eat babies; I don't like 'em. It will be as well to stop that young screamer though, in case I should be tempted to do him a mischief' (xxi). Quilp is the deadly enemy of the stock sentiment, of babies and all little, presumably helpless objects of easy tears. He hates the terrible meek and their grinding demands, and he loathes the falseness of the transference of sympathy to babies, little girls, or even dumb animals. When Kit finds Nell's little bird and tearfully asks, 'What's to be done with this?', Quilp responds immediately, 'Wring its neck' (xiii). There is surely a part of every reader that applauds the appropriateness of that response. Quilp allows our impulse to wring necks an outlet in laughter, so that the counter-impulse to protect and love the small and helpless might be expressed more fully. He is a very functional enemy of sentimentality.

But he is more than that. His sarcasm amounts to an insistence that life be met head-on, without paralysing precautions. When accused of being in the Little Bethel chapel for nefarious purposes, he answers with a wonderful burlesque of prudence:

'Yes, I was at chapel. What then? I've read in books that

[12] Dyson (pp. 114–17) discusses this point and other interesting aspects of Quilp.

pilgrims were used to go to chapel before they went on journeys, to put up petitions for their safe return. Wise men! journeys are very perilous—especially outside the coach. Wheels come off, horses take fright, coachmen drive too fast, coaches overturn. I always go to chapel before I start on journeys. It's the last thing I do on such occasions, indeed.' (XLVIII)

The exaggerated politeness of his tone also suggests his central attack on all insulating gentility and his affirmation of a primary relation between human beings.

The primary relation with Quilp is at times strongly sexual and always extraordinarily physical. His most constant threat, 'I'll bite you!', is both frightening and innocent in its purity; for we recognize it as, basically, a cry from the nursery, the insistence of the child that he be noticed. Quilp is the elemental naughty boy, protesting with his very life against indifference. And it is the positive nature of this rebellion and its attractiveness in this cold novel that draw laughter to this partly demonic figure.

But in this demon is still the sense of physical freedom and self-gratification of the child. What other demon would choose to assert his selfhood and power by something as childish as staying up all night and smoking, especially after the mother has been sent to bed? Surely this is a childhood fantasy of the tables turned, both attractive in its simplicity and pathetic in its limitations. Quilp further loves physical tricks that are both satanic and pure, that are, in fact, little more than an exaggerated 'showing off': 'he ate hard eggs, shell and all, devoured gigantic prawns with the heads and tails on, chewed tobacco and water-cresses at the same time and with extraordinary greediness, drank boiling tea without winking, bit his fork and spoon till they bent again' (V), and performed other variations of sandbox tricks. He delights further in practical jokes or, as Dickens calls them, 'childish pranks' (XI). At one point, he wrestles with Tom Scott over a stick and manœuvres Tom into 'tugging at it with his utmost power, when [Quilp] suddenly let it go and sent him reeling backwards, so that he fell violently upon his head'. His success so tickles Quilp that he laughs and stamps the ground (VI). Perhaps most central to Quilp's boyishness, however, is his extreme vulnerability to personal remarks. He obviously lives in dread of the

pointing fingers of playground mockery. One of his chief
reasons for tormenting his mother-in-law is that she has called
him names: 'I'm a little hunchy villain and a monster, am I,
Mrs. Jiniwin? Oh!' (v). Most important, his primary motivation
for revenge in the novel comes from Kit's remark that Quilp
is 'a uglier dwarf than can be seen anywheres for a penny' (vi).
And his greatest delight comes in reversing the terms: 'Kit a
thief! Kit a thief! Ha ha ha! Why, he's an uglier-looking thief
than can be seen anywhere for a penny. Eh Kit—eh? Ha ha
ha!' (lx). Quilp is extremely sensitive, with just the sensitivity
of a child, and he lives to avoid, anticipate, and reverse
insults.

   This sort of life traps him in defensiveness, of course, and
admittedly causes him to be extremely violent, but his sadism,
pure as it is, is often neutralized by the narrative tone. As he
strikes at the wrestling Kit and Tom Scott, for instance, the
narrator remarks that he causes them to stop fighting, 'this
being warmer work than they had calculated upon' (vi). The
brutality is disguised as warm work, and this disguise allows
us both to expend our own violent energies in laughter and to
regard Quilp as less frightening. In addition, his violence is
most often released in language only. It is, of course, in language
that he excels, and in the language of parody only can he break
out of the defensive trap he is in. He can find temporary
release in his great and aggressive creative instinct, displayed
nowhere so brilliantly as in his arrangement for Dick to enter
employment with the Brasses. He creates a complete parody
image of Dick's legal life: 'With Miss Sally . . . and the beautiful fictions of the law, his days will pass like minutes. Those
charming creations of the poet, John Doe and Richard Roe,
when they first dawn upon him, will open a new world for the
enlargement of his mind and the improvement of his heart'
(xxxiii).

   We can laugh at Quilp, then, because his hostility is necessary to allow for purity, his extreme energy for extreme
passiveness, but also because his 'evil' is often merely mis-
chievousness. He is not the real enemy but an actual victim.
Though apparently in opposition to Nell, he is really part of
her; they form a continuum, and together make up the child,
both aggressive and compliant, pure and vicious. Faced with

the adult world, both try desperately to live, one by hiding, the other by attacking; and neither is allowed to survive.

The parallels between the two are numerous. Most basic is the play of Nell's pathetic littleness against the pugnacious and grotesque littleness of Quilp. Nell asks for pity; pity Quilp and he punches you on the nose. They suggest alternate responses, but they are continuous with each other. Similarly, Nell's flight to the country is perversely echoed in Quilp's association with the truly primitive, the slop and the slime. Nell's prettified country becomes Quilp's 'Wilderness' (XXIII) and his 'summer-house' (XXI). On 'the slimy banks of a great river', Quilp insists on the parody of the natural: ' "You're fond of the beauties of nature", said Quilp with a grin. "Is this charming, Brass? Is it unusual, unsophisticated, primitive?" ' (LI). Primitive it is exactly, and Quilp provides the earthquake to Nell's rivulets and hills, the tiger to her lamb.

The most important connection between the two, however, involves Quilp's mock death and resurrection, the triumph of his belligerent life and honesty over the cold and artificial mourning of the Brasses. The situation here evokes laughter specifically at the important thematic issues of death, pretence, and cold indifference masking as love. The laughter is not really at the Brasses but at the abstract and unfeeling language they use and the death they mock: ' "Ah!" said Mr. Brass, breaking the silence, and raising his eyes to the ceiling with a sigh, "who knows but he may be looking down upon us now! Who knows but he may be surveying us from—from somewhere or another, and contemplating us with a watchful eye! Oh Lor!" ' (XLIX). The dramatic irony is heavy but appropriate; Quilp's reappearance is a victory over the ghouls. And he times his entrance, with true artistic instinct, so as to insist on his physical reality:

'Our faculties [said Mr. Brass] must not freeze with grief. I'll trouble you for a little more of that, ma'am. A question now arises, with relation to his nose.'

'Flat,' said Mrs. Jiniwin.

'Acquiline!' cried Quilp, thrusting in his head, and striking the feature with his fist. 'Acquiline, you hag. Do you see it? Do you call this flat? Do you? Eh?' (XLIX)

He dares us to ignore him, to think he could die and leave these

terrors victorious, for it is not Quilp but the falsity he fights
that is dangerous.

But his fight is doomed and he finally becomes more and
more elemental. As Nell moves to purity, he regresses. From
joyfully punishing Mrs. Jiniwin, he moves to kicking an idol,
suggesting his primitiveness, certainly, but also the horrible
frustration he must endure. He finally is forced to retreat
altogether from other humans and to adopt the last desperate
defence of the unwanted child, imposed isolation. He is, at the
last, 'convivial' only by himself and, most significantly, will
laugh only when he has no company in laughing (LXVII). Like
Nell, he is finally killed by shutting out help; he dies while his
rescuers are at hand. The opposites meet then in a willed death,
and the child, even in this divided state, has been crushed by a
hostile world.

3

But out of this death is born an adult, the regenerated
and transformed Dick Swiveller. In the midst of the trapped
and the frustrated there emerges the liberated comic spirit.
It may be that the triumph of Dick and the Marchioness cannot eradicate the pessimism of the novel, but it does present
a very movingly realized alternative. It is an alternative,
moreover, supported throughout by our laughter. For the
humour has had two main functions, as always: not only
the aggressive function which here heightened the pathos
of Nell, but a defensive protection of pleasure, a construction which serves as a refuge from darkness. Dick not only
creates our laughter, then, but is in a very real sense created
by it.

That Dick was Dickens's favourite character in this novel[13]
is not surprising, for he is a dramatic artist very much like his
creator, using Freudian humour to create appropriate roles
for himself. Pain itself means very little if he can arrange it
into a part for which he has apt quotations.[14] His hat, even, is
rather an emblem of his protective and liberating humour:
it is a 'very limp hat, worn with the wrong side foremost, to

[13] Forster's *Life*, i. 119.
[14] J. B. Priestley interestingly and wittily discusses Dick's reliance on phrases
and roles; see *The English Comic Characters* (London, 1925), pp. 227–40.

hide a hole in the brim' (II). He is flexible in exactly this way and has the freedom the others lack to try out different poses and directions in order to hide the holes.

But Dick is not primarily a defensive character but an open and expansive one. The pleasure that we protect through him is certainly not thin or starved. He lives over a tobacconist's shop, which provides him with a perpetual snuffbox, and he is as comfortable as Mrs. Jarley. And like Mrs. Jarley, whose comfort always included her companions, Dick's creative life of the imagination engenders by necessity a similar life in others:

> By a like pleasant fiction his single chamber was always men-tioned in the plural number. In its disengaged times, the tobacco-nist had announced it in his window as 'apartments' for a single gentleman, and Mr. Swiveller, following up the hint, never failed to speak of it as his rooms, his lodgings, or his chambers: conveying to his hearers a notion of indefinite space, and leaving their imaginations to wander through long suites of lofty halls, at pleasure. (VII)

'At pleasure' indeed! As the narrator says, 'to be the friend of Swiveller you must reject all circumstantial evidence' (VII). Perhaps it is more accurate to say that Dick's friendship *allows* one to transcend the trivially circumstantial and re-strictive and live in 'the rosy', here as in *Pickwick* a sure provider of joy and amiable conviviality—even if it is only gin.

But Dick never is as unconscious, even in the early stages of the novel, as is Mr. Pickwick. The fact is that in his humour there is a degree of self-awareness that is terribly disarming. He is often aware of exactly what he is doing and can enjoy even that awareness:

> 'May the present moment,' said Dick, sticking his fork into a large carbuncular potato, 'be the worst of our lives! I like this plan of sending 'em with the peel on; there's a charm in drawing a potato from its native element (if I may so express it) to which the rich and powerful are strangers. Ah! "Man wants but little here below, nor wants that little long!" How true that is!—after dinner!' (VIII)

This might be called a joke on jokes. At any rate, there is an important degree of self-mockery in him that prepares us for later changes. He is, from the first, a serious and complex character. But his seriousness is always gentle. Unlike Quilp, the novel's other important life force, Dick is never defensive or malicious. Dickens makes the contrast clear in an important scene where Quilp, rushing out of the Curiosity Shop, crashes into a man, whom he instantly begins pummelling. He almost immediately finds himself on his back in the middle of the street, 'with Mr. Richard Swiveller performing a kind of dance round him and requiring to know "whether he wanted any more?" ' (XIII). Dick's dance engenders a kind of joy, and he launches into a fine parody both of the retribution and of the commercial ethic which dominate the novel: ' "There's plenty more of it at the same shop," said Mr. Swiveller, by turns advancing and retreating in a threatening attitude, "a large and extensive assortment always on hand—country orders executed with promptitude and despatch—will you have a little more, sir?—don't say no, if you'd rather not" ' (XIII). The dance and the parody neutralize the violence, and our laughter rejects the entire basis of the main plot. We are left with gentleness and freedom, pure pleasure and pure play.

But Dick is, unfortunately, not strong enough to maintain this purity by himself. Even in this same scene we are given hints that he is somehow incomplete. Mrs. Quilp's screams and jerks resulting from her husband's pinches, for instance, do not bother him at all: 'he did not remark on these appearances, and soon forgot them'. There are areas of life, in other words, which he is not equipped to handle, and it is, ironically, Quilp who begins his moral education by sending him to the Brasses, who, in turn, bring him into contact with the Marchioness and to an eventual initiation into poverty, starvation, nothingness, and symbolic death—and, of course, his triumph over them.

Dick's initial comic position is, in fact, for all its freedom, too acquiescent. It smacks too much of the attitude of Nell:

'No man knocks himself down; if his destiny knocks him down, his destiny must pick him up again. Then I'm very glad that mine has brought all this upon itself, and I shall be as careless as I can, and make myself quite at home to spite it. So go on, my buck,' said Mr. Swiveller, taking his leave of the ceiling with a significant nod, 'and let us see which of us will be tired first!' (XXXIV)

There is an un-Nelly-like defiance here, certainly, and a welcome rejection of work, but it is still too passive and, more
important, too callous: it ignores those who 'have been at work
from [their] cradle' (xxxiv), specifically the Marchioness.
Carelessness, by itself, is not enough. It is not enough to sing
'Begone, dull care'; one must earn the right to dismiss it.
Dick's announcement, then, that the situation at the Brasses'
does not concern him is ironic; his decision to 'have nothing
whatever to do with it' backfires—to his great advantage.

He soon begins to worry very much about the Marchioness.
It bothers him that 'nobody ever came to see her, nobody
spoke of her, nobody cared about her' (xxxvi). He sees Sally
beat her and must abandon his reliance on destiny and test
himself in this lonely world of the Marchioness. His own
humour begins to parallel his movement to reality:

> 'Why, instead of my friend's bursting into tears when he knew
> who Fred was, embracing him kindly, and telling him that he was
> his grandfather, or his grandmother in disguise (which we fully
> expected), he flew into a tremendous passion; called him all manner
> of names; said it was in a great measure his fault that little Nell
> and the old gentleman had ever been brought to poverty; didn't
> hint at our taking anything to drink; and—and in short rather
> turned us out of the room than otherwise.' (L)

His expectation of theatrical behaviour collapses just as he
does in the bleak world of rejection. He must come face to face
with the nothingness symbolized by the Brasses' servant-
girl:

> 'Where do you come from?' [Quilp] said after a long pause,
> stroking his chin.
> 'I don't know.'
> 'What's your name?'
> 'Nothing.' (LI)

The catechism of the Marchioness is brilliant in its suggestive-
ness. All she can do is repeat her pathetic plea for contact,
'But please will you leave a card or message?'. Dick begins by
helping the small servant, of course, and the joyous cribbage
games they play are the most important symbolic contrast
to the sinister games for cash which alienate and kill Nell and
her grandfather. Dick learns that the Marchioness is reduced

to looking through the keyhole for company, and though he is temporarily self-conscious at the thought of his own absurd pastimes she must have witnessed, he leaves self-consciousness behind and instinctively responds to her extreme loneliness. He brings food, drink, and, most helpful, his free imaginative re-creation of reality: 'To make it seem more real and pleasant, I shall call you the Marchioness, do you hear ?' (LVII). It *is*, in fact, more real. The reality of the imagination is played off against the reality of the grave, and our laughter begins to build a world of real joy.

It is a world made much more valid by the Marchioness's presence, though it still must be painfully created. Even now Dick reacts with a new sensitivity to others. When the Marchioness uses a less-than-poetic idiom, Dick thinks about correcting her but decides against it when he considers that 'it was evident that her tongue was loosened by the purl, and her opportunities for conversation were not so frequent as to render a momentary check of little consequence' (LVIII). He responds to her absolute trust and to the demands she makes on him simply as a lonely and isolated human being. But his initiation demands something more extreme than sympathetic and imaginative identification with the Marchioness; it demands that he re-create her grievous experience through a symbolic death.

Though Dick does become something of a classic hero,[15] his illness is more than an archetypal purging; it is a symbolic rehearsal of death, a real brush with non-existence. And it is the Marchioness whom he has saved who must eventually save him. He must face death and come back from it somehow made triumphant by his honesty and simple trust. When he regains consciousness after his illness and asks his nurse if he has been quite ill, the Marchioness very simply explains his situation: 'Dead, all but. . . . I never thought you'd get better. Thank Heaven you have' (LXIV). After this Dick is 'silent for a long while'. His response to her presence and her love displays a new style, almost stark in its clarity and simplicity:

'This poor little Marchioness has been wearing herself to death!' cried Dick.

[15] Marcus (pp. 165–8) argues for Dick's role as a hero but sees him finally as 'too light and supple' for the 'dead weight of the novel's great theme'.

'No I haven't,' she returned, 'not a bit of it. Don't you mind about me. I like sitting up, and I've often had a sleep, bless you, in one of them chairs. But if you could have seen how you tried to jump out o' winder, and if you could have heard how you used to keep on singing and making speeches, you wouldn't have believed it—I'm so glad you're better, Mr. Liverer.'

'Liverer indeed!' said Dick thoughtfully. 'It's well I *am* a liverer. I strongly suspect I should have died, Marchioness, but for you.' (LXIV)

This is the heart of the rejuvenated comic centre, a 'liverer' born out of nothing and fully deserving the delight given to it at the end. Out of hunger and servitude and loneliness they recapture a bit of joy. Perhaps it is not enough to counterbalance the central gloom, but there is an enormous amount of strength, supported by our laughter, invested in those 'many hundred thousand games of cribbage' (LXXIII) they play together. In the midst of death there is still this small but powerful glimpse of immortality.

5 Barnaby Rudge

LAUGHTER AND STRUCTURE

'Better be mad than sane, here,' said Hugh. '*Go mad.*' (LXXVI)

A T the height of the great riots in *Barnaby Rudge* Dickens says, 'Every man went about his pleasure or business as if the city were in perfect order, and there were no half-smouldering embers in its secret places, which, on the approach of night, would kindle up again and scatter ruin and dismay abroad' (LIII). *Barnaby Rudge* is really a novel about this sort of delusory immunity[1] and about the 'ruin and dismay' the delusion causes. The progression from snugness to chaos is very clearly indicated: extreme selfishness leads one to imagine a world of absolute ego; this, in turn, leads to a competition of tyrannies, with everyone playing on everyone else's fantasies; in the process the whole structure of society moves further from the natural and, to protect itself, becomes more and more fiercely tyrannical, finally causing just what it wanted to prevent—the eruption of the most chaotic natural forces. The search for cosiness and safety thus leads to destruction, and Dickens here undertakes his subtlest examination, to this point, of the defects of Dingley Dell.

[1] In her Preface to the Oxford Illustrated edition of this novel, Kathleen Tillotson points out the way the arrangement of the novel 'conveys the irony of the common assumption that private lives are immune from public events' (p. xi). A similar thematic reading is advanced by Harold F. Folland, 'The Doer and the Deed: Theme and Pattern in *Barnaby Rudge*', *PMLA*, lxxiv (1959), 406–17. Folland sees the main ethical theme as 'the evil of action divorced from responsibility' (p. 408). Although the novel has not received very extensive or generally very interesting critical treatment, the following discussions are excellent: Jack Lindsay, '*Barnaby Rudge*', in *Dickens and the Twentieth Century*, pp. 91–106; A. E. Dyson, '*Barnaby Rudge*: The Genesis of Violence', *CritQ*, ix (1967), 142–60; and the chapter in Steven Marcus's *From Pickwick to Dombey*, pp. 169–212.

It is not only his most subtle treatment but also his most prophetic and most sternly confident[2]—one could almost say his most didactic. The opening scene of the novel, in which John Willet and his friends huddle in imagined security around a fire, pleasantly titillating themselves with ghost stories and asserting their power with taunts at Joe, the perpetual boy, is a brilliantly compact paradigm of most of the novel's themes. The oppression born out of the selfishness which deals with threats by transplanting them into a new and mad world (one, for instance, in which Joe is always a boy and will never threaten his father) is seen collected in a small hovel while the elemental forces are raging outside. The scene, a symbol of the precariousness of all enforced and callously maintained security, is filled with foreboding, even warning. As Kathleen Tillotson says, the novel is 'almost journalistic-ally apt' in its relation to the situation in the late 1830s (Preface, p. vii), and despite the fact that Dickens seems somewhat equivocal in relation to his great theme of authority and in his attitude towards the rioters, he is piercingly straight-forward in his warning: England must abandon delusions of safety or face destruction. In view of such an aim, in the long run it does not seem to be equivocal both to sympathize with the victimized rioters, even in their violence and love of plunder, and at the same time to react to the riots themselves with horror. In a way this reaction is the only intelligent one. When a nation is, in its maniacal desire to protect its isolated tyrannies, moving toward its own doom, what may be needed is not a quiet analysis of the proper balance of authority but a violent shock. The nation does not need gentle remodifica-

---

[2] Though the novel has been vigorously defended by a few recent critics, the general evaluation is fairly represented by Edgar Johnson: *Barnaby Rudge*, he says, 'is the least satisfactory of all Dickens's full-length books' (*Charles Dickens*, i. 330). Part of the reason for what seems to me an extreme under-valuation is the peculiar publishing history of the novel, traced both by Johnson and by Kathleen Tillotson (Preface, p. v), in which Dickens postponed writing the novel during five years of various fights with publishers. George Ford argues that this postponement suggests that 'Dickens himself had little love for *Barnaby*, the unwanted child among his early novels' (*Dickens and His Readers*, [Princeton, N.J., 1955], pp. 42–3). Kathleen Tillotson, on the other hand, says Dickens's persistence through difficulties 'is evidence of his tenacity of purpose and the grip of the original idea on his imagination; not, as has been suggested, of the grudging performance of a task' (Preface, p. v).

tion of its aims but a vigorous awakening from its deadly sleep; for Dickens clearly sees England's course as not only wrong but suicidal, and he evokes a vision of the riots as the final judgement on a nation which has lost touch with all sanity and decency in God and in Nature:

> . . . the reflections in every quarter of the sky, of deep, red, soaring flames, as though the last day had come and the whole universe were burning; the dust, and smoke, and drift of fiery particles, scorching and kindling all it fell upon; the hot unwholesome vapour, the blight on everything; the stars, and moon, and very sky, obliterated;—made up such a sum of dreariness and ruin, that it seemed as if the face of Heaven were blotted out, and night, in its rest and quiet, and softened light, never could look upon the earth again. (LXVIII)

Barnaby Rudge is intended partly as an indication of a way to avoid this God-forsaken end. But there is a severe limit to the didacticism; the attack is purely negative and, as a result, even touched by disillusionment. The root causes of the sickness are indicated, but not only is no programme developed to deal with them, there is even a slight sense that the illness is finally incurable, the nation really already lost. Just around the corner from the confident didacticism is always a hint of cynicism, which seems to grow more apparent as the novel nears its end.

But for the most part *Barnaby Rudge* is one of Dickens's most firmly organized and rhetorically effective novels. His larger attacks on the tyranny rooted in enforced fantasies are focused in a symbolic attack on the very desire for snugness. The novel attacks not only the characters' sense of immunity but our own as well. For although the central image of *Barnaby Rudge* is an invasion, a presumed sanctuary being broken into, just about one-half of the novel is spent assuring us that we are safe and, correspondingly, that our fantasies are supportable, our fears easily dismissible, and our tyranny certainly justifiable. It is a novel based on reversal; the second half reverses the tendencies of the first half and negates its assurances. Safe daylight becomes night, the fairy tale becomes a nightmare, the comic wooden inflexibility is engulfed in fire, and the assumption of immunity is cruelly exploded. It is a novel whose very heart is rhetorical and whose themes are defined by its structure.[3] Its structure, in turn, is made rhetorically effective by laughter.

As the themes, gently and comically presented in the first half of the novel, are placed in a wider arena and violently reconstructed and re-interpreted after the five-year lapse near the middle of the novel, our laughter tends to die as we realize, with its help, exactly what those themes are. By laughing at John Willet we have been supporting tyranny; by laughing at Sim Tappertit we have been at the same time dismissing its significance. We have, in other words, created with our laughter an assumed world of safety and comfort which is blown apart as violently as Newgate itself. England here becomes the reader and the awful warning becomes sharply personalized as Dickens seeks to make the hidden tendency of our laughter literal: the custard pie *did* contain sulphuric acid, and we are not only responsible for, but richly deserve, the retaliation which follows.

At the beginning of the second part of the novel Dickens discusses this very use of laughter in relation to Lord George Gordon, the central symbol of fantasy, both dangerous and funny: 'Although there was something very ludicrous in his vehement manner, taken in conjunction with his meagre aspect and ungraceful presence, it would scarcely have provoked a smile in any man of kindly feeling; or even if it had, he would have felt sorry and almost angry with himself next moment, for yielding to the impulse' (xxxvi). If we yield to the impulse to smile at this terrible danger, we will feel 'sorry and almost angry' indeed, for it is exactly the tendency to dismiss this threat at the core of our amusement which is responsible for the repressive tyranny and the chaos it finally causes. Dickens points out that although Gordon 'might have moved the sternest looker-on to laughter, and fully provoked the smiles and whispered jests which greeted his departure from

[3] *Barnaby Rudge* has generally been seen as a fractured novel whose coherence is wrecked by the five-year gap at its centre. This criticism is so entrenched that one could easily trace its tradition; Forster obviously started it (*Life*, i. 144) and, with one exception, it has not been broken until recently. The one early exception is George Gissing, who called the novel 'Dickens's best constructed story' (*The Immortal Dickens* [London, 1925], p. 171). Defences of the unity of the novel are offered by the critics mentioned in the first note and by James K. Gottshall, 'Devils Abroad: The Unity and Significance of *Barnaby Rudge*', *NCF*, xvi (1961), 133–46.

the Maypole inn', he was 'quite unconscious . . . of the effect he produced' (XXXVII). In a society ruled by fanaticism, laughter loses its powers of sane correction and becomes a shameful evasion. When all the world has gone mad, one can laugh only by maintaining a blindness to this fact and creating a separate sanity, so detached from what is real that it becomes equally mad and so egotistical it becomes despotic. Laughter is parallel to the central sin in the novel and follows the same regressive series: to security, fantasy, and tyranny. What makes this parallel all the more emphatic is that Dickens hides it for so long. We are, in fact, encouraged to ignore the effects of foreshadowing in the first half of the novel and assume that private lives, at least, are 'immune from public events' and that whatever may happen old John Willet and Sim Tappertit *are* absurd figures who will always be around for one more laugh. John will always be ludicrously slow; Sim will always be admiring his skinny legs. But Willet's slowness becomes pathetic mental paralysis and death, and Sim's legs are crushed to a pulp. It is as if Mrs. Micawber actually deserted her husband and absconded with the bill collector or as if Mr. Winkle actually shot and killed Mr. Tupman. The laughter echoes the reflexive structure, and the irony is directed at us. The theme *is* the structure, and the structure is built by our laughter.

It is, however, a commonplace of criticism that the humour in *Barnaby Rudge* is terribly weak, flat, or mechanical. It is true that the humour is very nasty; there is nothing to match the freedom and joy of Dick Swiveller. Here the defensive part of laughter, the protection of pleasure, is itself relentlessly attacked, and the aggressive part of laughter is exposed for just what it is. The laughter stirred by the novel is finally, therefore, the reverse of pleasant; there is no allowance for comic pleasure and no dispensation to enjoy aggression. It is understandable, then, that we accuse Dickens of being unfunny, but that accusation is no more just or accurate than the consistent under-rating of the novel's general quality. *Barnaby Rudge* is a very un-Dickensian novel in many ways; no one could *love* a novel which has such insight into things so truly ugly as the pig-like, roaring brother of the Lord Mayor, the ignorant John Bull Englishman, who distrusts even Barnaby's mother and yet is clearly a pillar of this society and a repository of its trust. For all our pride in modern existential awareness and in the disciplined and unblinking vision of contemporary literature, we are unprepared to find such qualities in Dickens. As a consequence, the reader is tempted to defend his reaction by saying that the novel is somehow unsatisfactory, its humour somehow flat. But this is surely an ironic defence; it is really the habitual stance of John Willet, and it collapses in face of the facts.

And one fact about this novel is that it is, in its way, very funny. By 'in its way' I really mean 'in the first half', for it is true that Dickens controls the humour so that it gradually decreases, until in the last pages of the novel there is absolutely no chance to laugh. But this decline is part of the plan. In the first half of the novel we are encouraged to laugh, and Dickens's humour here seems to me on a level with that of *Pickwick*. But in the second half of the novel the jokes become more and more explicit, and the disguises for the aggression become thinner and thinner as the original topics for laughter become subjects for attack. The humour is thus controlled for very serious effects and nowhere provides the sense of freedom and comfort we expected in earlier novels. But freedom and comfort, this novel says, are impossible in the world envisaged here, and any attempt to create them easily leads to madness, tyranny, and self-destruction. *Barnaby Rudge*, then, though very funny, is one of Dickens's least comic novels. It is a denial of the comic impulse.

But this is, of course, no reason to call its humour mechanical; it is anything but that. Better terms might be 'organic', or 'disciplined', or 'functional'. For instance, though the narrative personality in this novel is generally the flattest and least distinctive in any Dickens novel, very important effects can be produced from a contrast to this flat base. The most famous of these effects comes from the brilliant writing which describes the riots and the strongly projected feelings of both attraction and repulsion. Dickens can also produce quieter but no less important humorous effects through this process of contrast. He almost never uses the facetious tone customary to *Pickwick Papers* here, for example, so when that tone does appear, it is all the more striking. At the end of the first half of the novel, the narrator begins three of the last four chapters[4] by discussing various adages in a highly jocular manner. Most generally, this concentrated onslaught on these proverbial phrases, representing the conventional and approved methods of dealing with life, expresses the irrelevance and, underneath that, the instability of the orderly and the accepted. Our laughter thereby is enlisted in the over-all attack on the stable and conventional, and the technique reminds us of the one used so successfully in *Pickwick Papers*. But in *Pickwick* the laughter was preparatory to a world of childhood joy; here it prepares for fire and riot, and our laughter implicitly underlines the inevitability of the downfall which waits for a world resting on mad values. More specifically, the laughter directed at this collection of adages summarizes the intended rhetorical effect of the first half of the novel: to make us side with the comforting dismissal of all threats, an evasion which characterizes all of the novel's tyrants.[5]

At the start of Chapter xxxii, for instance, the narrator remarks:

Misfortunes, saith the adage, never come singly. There is little doubt that troubles are exceedingly gregarious in their nature, and flying in flocks, are apt to perch capriciously; crowding on the heads of some poor wights until there is not an inch of room left on their unlucky crowns, and taking no more notice of others who offer as good resting-places for the soles of their feet, than if they had no existence.

The passage most centrally misleads us by treating all the effects of oppression (here those acting on Joe Willet and Edward Chester) as harmless and even gay. Notice how effective the word 'gregarious' is as camouflage; it helps allow us to agree that there really is no danger at all and no personal threat. Even a clearer humorous summary is given at the beginning of Chapter xxx:

A homely proverb recognizes the existence of a troublesome class of persons who, having an inch conceded them, will take an ell. Not to quote the illustrious examples of those heroic scourges

[4] See Chapters xxix, xxx, and xxxii.
[5] Notice how even the worldly wise Chester practises the same evasion: 'Men who are thoroughly false and hollow, seldom try to hide those vices from themselves; and yet in the very act of avowing them, they lay claim to the virtues they feign most to despise' (xxiii).

of mankind, whose amiable path in life has been from birth to death through blood, and fire, and ruin, and who would seem to have existed for no better purpose than to teach mankind that as the absence of pain is pleasure, so the earth, purged of their presence, may be deemed a blessed place—not to quote such mighty instances, it will be sufficient to refer to old John Willet.

Here we are encouraged to laugh at tyranny, pointedly at the 'blood, and fire, and ruin' which will be spread over the second half of the novel. After the elaborate disguise of mighty warriors and despots, we are presented with the connection to John Willet and allowed to think it ludicrous. We are also allowed to develop a central, though deeply submerged, wish for old John's death. Our laughter allows us both alternatives at once: the assurance, on one level, that this sort of tyranny is not serious and, on the other, that it might be serious but that its practitioners can be eliminated.

But the second half of the novel shows us that tyranny is certainly not trivial and that laughing at it and at old John Willet expresses the same dodge which caused the 'blood, and fire, and ruin'. At the same time, however, when John finally does die, our laughter is not vindicated but again turned back on us. Old John is clearly victimized by a general social evasion, and the laughers are really much more guilty than he. Perhaps, it is hinted, we want him dead because he goes too far and threatens to give the game away. At any rate, the richness of this narrative humour suggests the pervasive richness of the humour throughout the novel and the way in which it acts to support the structural principle of contrasts. Nowhere, however, is the operation of this relationship between humour and structure better illustrated than in the functional humour connected with two of Dickens's symbols for violated sanctity: the Maypole Inn and the home of Gabriel Varden.

1

The action at the Maypole Inn presents the whole novel in miniature, as even the 'snuggest' and 'cosiest' of inns (XIX) is ripped apart by the fury of the riots. Though it is introduced as the scene of light domestic comedy, Dickens gradually reveals how the Maypole is a symbol for all social wrongs, and

exhibits a tyranny based on the assumption of inviolable
individual safety. Our laughter, it turns out, rests on the same
delusory assumption and must share in the same guilt. Time
and again throughout the first half of the novel we are invited
to laugh at, and thereby dismiss, the very foundations of the
terror of the second half. This dismissal is the central error
and crime, in fact, of John Willet. And any desire for his death
expressed in laughter insidiously doubles back as we are asked
to see him later not only as chief villain but as chief victim as
well and, most important, as ourselves. Even the Maypole
itself is made part of this ironic reversal. The traditional
symbol of potency, youth, and gaiety has become the actual
sign of sterility, old age, and repression. But the development
of this reversal is gradual, and we are, in the first scene,
encouraged to assume, along with the Maypole crowd, a snug
immunity from the wild storm outside, a storm which suggests
the raging elemental forces being artificially shut out.

The Maypole group are, in fact, enemies of all that is natural,
and John Willet in particular extends his egoism to the point
of twisting nature into something subordinate to or even part
of himself. His first words invite our laughter at this monstrous
despotism:

'It'll clear at eleven o'clock. No sooner and no later. Not before
and not arterwards.'

'How do you make out that?' said a little man in the opposite
corner. 'The moon is past the full, and she rises at nine.'

John looked sedately and solemnly at his questioner until he
had brought his mind to bear upon the whole of his observation,
and then made answer, in a tone which seemed to imply that the
moon was peculiarly his business and nobody else's:

'Never you mind about the moon. Don't you trouble yourself
about her. You let the moon alone, and I'll let you alone.'

'No offence I hope?' said the little man.

Again John waited leisurely until the observation had thoroughly
penetrated to his brain, and then replying, 'No offence *as yet*,'
applied a light to his pipe and smoked in placid silence. (1)

Willet, the antithesis of nature, sees himself as equal to the
moon, indeed sees the universe as compact in his tyrannical
self, and though the humour rejects this rapacious ego, it also
refuses to take it seriously, even though such egoism is at the

bottom of all the violence. The humorous warning John ends with, 'No offence *as yet*', is brilliant in its foreshadowing of the real offence and the real violence to come, and our laughter promotes a delusion of safety similar to John's own. John continually links himself to nature; his pugnacious powers of argument, he says, are 'a gift of Natur', and for a man to ignore those powers would be 'a turning of his back on Natur, a flouting of her, a slighting of her precious caskets, and a proving of one's self to be a swine that isn't worth her scattering pearls before' (1). Here again the disguises are masterly. John's misuse of clichés emphasizes his stupidity and allows aggressive laughter, but our laughter not only dismisses him; it ignores the degree to which he is unconsciously prophetic. Those who are tyrants are indeed turning their backs on nature. Our laughter generally, then, tempts us to brush aside the major thematic issues reflected in John, a symptom of the general and horrid perversion of nature by a tyranny which leaves actual nature no outlet but raging storms and fire.

At this early point, John's presumptions are not connected to a larger scheme, however, and can therefore be treated humorously. Even his central combat with his son is used for functional laughter:

> 'Silence, sir!' returned his father, 'what do you mean by talking, when you see people that are more than two or three times your age, sitting still and silent and not dreaming of saying a word?'
> 'Why that's the proper time for me to talk, isn't it?' said Joe rebelliously.
> 'The proper time, sir!' retorted his father, 'the proper time's no time.' (1)

The struggle between father and son, echoed many times throughout the novel,[6] receives its funniest and, at the same time, most elemental treatment in the relationship between these two. John Willet clearly wants to annihilate his son; in his drive for absolute authority he sees Joe as the chief threat to his position and reacts by treating him as frozen, dead, and impotent. Even Joe's mild rebellion here meets with a demand that he acknowledge his nothingness by continual silence, and dramatically admit his subservience. Dickens is very blunt

[6] Marcus (pp. 169–212) has a full treatment of the parental roles in the novel.

about his father's goals: he 'snipped off' Joe's liberty and kept 'trimming' and 'shearing away' (xxx) at him.

John's antipathy to his son really extends to all rebellious and threatening youth; even of Hugh he says, 'I wish that chap was dead, I do indeed' (x). The problem with all young people, he argues, is that they lack 'imagination'—clearly his euphemism for absolute submissiveness. 'Imagination', he says, is created either by drawing one's faculties out or by forcibly knocking the faculties in if they aren't naturally there (xxix). Either way it expresses a violence equivalent to silencing them for ever. When his son goes to London, escaping for the moment his father's immediate control, John still holds the reins as tight as possible: 'The other sixpence is to spend in the diversions of London; and the diversion I recommend is to go to the top of the Monument, and sitting there. There's no temptation there, sir—no drink—no young women—no bad characters of any sort—nothing but imagination. That's the way I enjoyed myself when I was your age, sir' (xiii).

'Nothing but imagination' is right; he wants particularly to shield his son from women, not in order to protect him but to keep him a boy, living proof of his own mastery and dominance. He is, above all, the antithesis of his Maypole and the deadly enemy of procreation, life, and sex: 'I know my duty. We want no love-making here, sir, unbeknown to parents' (xxix). Further than this, he sees all women as 'a kind of nonsensical mistake on the part of Nature' (xxi). As Nature himself, he would never make the same mistake; he would have no sex, growth, development, or challenge. His uniting with Chester, then, in a league of repression composed of all the impotent tyrants is certainly not surprising. John Willet is symbolically at the heart of the problem in the novel, and our early laughter at him prepares us for the shock when his position is revealed. We have been as callous as Tom Cobb in our laughter and equally deserve the punishment he receives at the hands of Joe. Perhaps Tom Cobb gets off easily though: he is only knocked into the spittoons; but if we respond to Dickens's rhetoric, we are forced to see in ourselves the cause of the riots and the hideous death.

Willet's ego and his desire for dominance are so enormous that he is capable of transforming reality in a grotesque way.

Not only is Joe always a boy, John's fifteen-year-old, short-winded horse is a potential cup-winner: 'There's a bit of horse-flesh, Hugh! . . . There's a comely creature! There's high mettle! There's bone!' (XIII). We are likely to laugh at these delusions, ignoring the fact that they reveal the same egoistic imagination at work that depresses all youth and vigour. Dickens, in fact, shows that Willet's desire for dominance is, like the riots, self-destructive. He is so anxious to freeze time that he is willing to see himself as dead rather than give in to his son. 'We know nothing about coaches here, sir' (XXV), he says, nor of anything else expressive of change and growth. In his desire for mastery, John has created a fantasy world which is ultimately a suicidal one. This cycle of death is Dickens's fore-cast and warning for England and is, in a sense, what *Barnaby Rudge* is. We laugh at it finally only if we are willing to be John Willets, frozen in the past and destroyed by our fantasies.

Dickens reinforces this early connection between the humour of John Willet and the later riots by the reactions of Joe to his father. Though constantly tempting us to see the boy as a figure in comic opera or light sex comedy, he later makes it clear that our laughter has been dismissing a very dangerous threat. Joe decides that 'the only congenial prospect left him, was to go for a soldier or a sailor, and get some obliging enemy to knock his brains out as soon as possible' (XIII). The light language masks the dark truth: the real attraction of warfare is, in fact, the possibility of violence, of indirect retaliation on the oppressors—including those who laugh at him. The reversal is completed when Joe reappears not with his brains knocked out, it is true, but with his arm blown off.

Joe has re-created a pattern parallel to that of the rioters, to that of Sim and Hugh and Barnaby. He says early to his father, 'I say, that before long I shall be driven to break such bounds, and that when I do, it won't be me that you'll have to blame, but your own self and no other' (III). This makes clear the connection between the tyranny and the eruption of goaded youth. Also clear is the parallel between the attraction of the military and that of the riots. Both mask their real attraction and motive force behind the blatant and shallow cynicism of a 'cause'. The recruiting sergeant easily explains away the fear of being killed in battle:

'Supposing you should be killed, sir?' said a timid voice in one corner. 'Well, sir, supposing you should be,' said the serjeant, 'what then? Your country loves you, sir; his Majesty King George the Third loves you; your memory is honoured, revered, respected; everybody's fond of you, and grateful to you; your name's wrote down at full length in a book in the War-office. Damme, gentlemen, we must all die some time, or another, eh?' (XXXI)

This is exactly the cynicism of Gashford, always just touching the edges of this novel and suggesting that, in his way, Chester is right. The 'glory' of military life which Joe had been discussing with the landlord does, in fact, amount to having one's name 'wrote down at full length in a book in the War-office'. The sergeant later exposes briefly but significantly the truth behind the cynical rhetoric: 'You'll go abroad—a country where it's all sunshine and plunder—the finest climate in the world' (XXXI). The key word, almost hidden here, is 'plunder'; the attraction of lawlessness, of simply breaking out, is clearly paramount both for Joe and for the rioters, and the first half of the novel has completed, in disguise of humour, what becomes explicit in the second half: a progressive and deadly pattern of ego which leads to tyranny which leads to evasive fantasy which leads to rebellion. Dickens has made this pattern seem humorous in order to duplicate in us the illusion of safety held by John Willet.

The second half of the novel opens with John apparently triumphant, sitting at the Maypole Inn in the midst of another tumultuous storm. There are similar jokes on John's delusions —he has advertised for Joe as a 'young boy'—but the jokes are now becoming more and more pointed and more fore-boding:

'Do you hear it? It blows great guns, indeed. There'll be many a crash in the Forest to-night, I reckon, and many a broken branch upon the ground to-morrow.'
'It won't break anything in the Maypole, I take it, sir,' returned old John. 'Let it try. I give it leave.' (XXXIII)

Our laughter prepares the way for the defeat of this ego by the real invasion of natural forces soon to come.

The figure of John Willet is now extended and his characteristics are reduplicated in other characters in order to draw the structural connections with the first half of the novel and make it clear just what our laughter has done.

First, there is the extension of John into the 'genuine John Bull', the country gentleman who is, like John, deeply attached to a frozen past for equally egotistical reasons. Like John's parental methods, his own despotism is felt by his friends to be slipping away, and because there 'were not more like him . . . the country was going to rack and ruin every day' (XLVII). Both are 'extremely patriotic' and extremely conservative. The difference, of course, is that the country gentleman is openly vicious, advocates 'flogging to cure that disorder' of Barnaby's, and later shows up to give evidence against him.

His brother, the Lord Mayor, similarly shows the nasty implications of John Willet's tyranny and also helps give force to the growing suggestion that the rioters are mainly victims. The Lord Mayor, we can easily see, is a comic opera tyrant transplanted to a violent world where his impotence can no longer be accepted as funny. He puts off Mr. Haredale's request for help by saying that 'these ain't business hours' (LXI), and he suggests that the Catholic vintner get an alderman to stand in his window in order 'to awe the crowd'. Like his ugly brother, the Lord Mayor makes us more aware of the dark aspect of John.

But it is also curiously true that John is not only a tyrant but a victim, much more complex than the original laughter would have him. Dickens makes this complexity clear by means of another extension, Dennis the hangman. John had earlier foreshadowed Dennis by mouthing exactly the hangman's creed: 'It's a blessed thing to think how many people are hung in batches every six weeks for that [passing bad notes], and such like offences, as showing how wide awake our government is' (XI). Dennis is also an egoistic supporter of repressive order, here carried to the extreme where, to preserve that order, he is willing to support even its very antithesis: ' "I mustn't have no biling, no roasting, no frying—nothing but hanging. My lord may well call me an earnest fellow. In support of the great Protestant principle of having plenty of that, I'll," and here he beat his club upon the ground, "burn, fight, kill—do anything you bid me, so that it's bold and devilish—though the end of it was, that I got hung myself"' (XXXVII). This rich speech invites laughter, but we laugh at our peril, for Dennis has evoked the central issues here: the self-destruction attendant on the old order's hysterical demands for power, the complete identification of self with that tyrannical order, and the absolute dedication to retributive justice. We laugh only if we can evade these issues, and they are becoming impossible to evade. Dennis makes it clear that the comic opera tyranny is prepared to do anything rather than relinquish its power; in its mad way it is willing to destroy its own self rather than capitulate and to destroy with itself everything around it: 'Down with everybody, down with everything! Hurrah for the Protestant religion!' (XXXVIII).

Dennis is interested, ultimately, in protecting only death. As a member of 'the good old school', he wants to uphold the one law that matters in this ultra-Protestant country: retribution. Therefore, he guards the Newgate prisoners destined for the gallows with the 'air of a pastor' (LXV) and screams at Hugh for not respecting 'the law—the constitootion' (LXV). He becomes, in short, the grotesque but true symbol of the old order, itself identified here with 'Protestantism', the law of orderly, regularized death. 'Let's have revenges and injuries, and all that, and we shall get on twice as fast' (LII), Dennis says, underlining the terrible sadism which guards the old society and which now assumes the protection, ironically, of the religion of mercy. Even Dennis, hanged by the society he so gallantly defended, is more victim than villain, and in the image of the hangman hanged we see not poetic justice but a resurgence of the old mad order.

By the time of John Willet's defeat, then, we can no longer accept him as merely a funny character, nor are we allowed to accept the possibility of retributive comedy. John too is a victim of the general delusion, and Dickens rubs our noses in the reversed comedy.[7] He first of all sets us up for John's defeat by tempting us to laugh at his sense of safety; John

---

[7] Kathleen Tillotson says we 'enjoy the nicely contrived nemesis by which "history" converts the innkeeper from invincible stupidity to imbecile stupor, and from petty tyranny to submissiveness' (Preface, p. xi). I find the verb 'enjoy' incredibly inappropriate to what Dickens is doing here.

puts all his considerable argumentative force into proving that
there are no riots at all: 'Don't I tell you that His blessed
Majesty King George the Third would no more stand a rioting
and rollicking in his streets, than he'd stand being crowed
over by his own Parliament?' (LIV). We are likely to laugh at
this delusion of immunity and implicitly ask thereby for its
puncture by reality. When the puncture comes, however, it is
so graphic and so extreme that we are not allowed to enjoy
our triumph; rather we are shown our own sadism and our
own 'protestant' desire for retribution.

John's habitual slowness is brought into contact with
a speed, not now of natural growth but of a whirlwind and
chaos all the more terribly violent for having been so long
repressed. Unable to deal with this nightmare, John turns it
into a fantasy: 'he . . . found himself, without any consciousness of having moved, in the bar; sitting down in an arm-
chair, and watching the destruction of his property, as if it
were some queer play or entertainment, of an astonishing and
stupefying nature, but having no reference to himself—that
he could make out—at all' (LIV). The fantasy this time, however, is pathetic. Even here, though, Dickens tempts us to
laugh at the invasion of sanctity: the rioters are described as
'smashing the glass, turning the taps, drinking liquor out of
China punchbowls, sitting astride of casks, smoking private
and personal pipes, cutting down the sacred grove of lemons,
hacking and hewing at the celebrated cheese' (LIV). But we
surely see by now just what is happening and resist the
temptation. Even Hugh protects John, knowing that despite
his tyranny he is not primarily the cause but only a small part
of a pervasive social ugliness. But despite this protection,
John is destroyed. The symbolic Maypole is cut down, and
its owner goes completely mad. His slowness has simply been
exaggerated into paralysis, and the image of snugness and the
arrest of time is grotesquely completed: 'He was perfectly
contented to sit there, staring at [the ruin of the inn], and felt
no more indignation or discomfort in his bonds than if they
had been robes of honour. So far as he was personally concerned, old Time lay snoring, and the world stood still' (LV).

Dickens then begins attacking us for our own aggression
towards John, asking that we not externalize the villainy but

see it in ourselves. The first indication of this attack is Solomon Daisy's pathetic cry, 'Oh dear old Johnny, here's a change!' (LVI), but even more emphatic is the brilliant slow focus on John and his glimpse of the truth:

> John knitted his brow; looked downwards, as if he were mentally engaged in some arithmetical calculation; then upwards, as if the total would not come at his call; then at Solomon Daisy, from his eyebrow to his shoe-buckle; then very slowly round the bar. And then a great, round, leaden-looking, and not at all transparent tear, came rolling out of each eye, and he said, as he shook his head:
>
> 'If they'd only had the goodness to murder me, I'd have thanked 'em kindly.' (LVI)

John senses that the old order is gone and that he has, really, been virtually murdered. Dickens makes us see that the weapon of retribution is tyrannical in both Protestants and laughers. John Willet's guilt is finally identified with the reader's:

> ... [he] walked round to Joe, felt his empty sleeve all the way up, from the cuff, to where the stump of his arm remained; shook his head; lighted his pipe at the fire, took a long whiff, walked to the door, turned round once when he had reached it, wiped his left eye with the back of his fore-finger, and said, in a faltering voice: 'My son's arm—was took off—at the defence of the—Salwanners—in America—where the war is'—with which words he withdrew, and returned no more that night. (LXXII)

2

The situation and the process of reversal are similar with the Varden household. Dickens, as he often does, doubles the effect, thereby insuring the force of his rhetoric. In the comedy attendant on this shrew-ridden home the same points in relation to egoism, tyranny, fantasy, and retribution are employed, and we are made to run a similar rhetorical gauntlet: our own egoism, evasive fantasy, tyranny, and desire for retribution are first reinforced and then exposed. But there is one basic difference here; in the Varden circle oppressions are multiplied and stacked on one another. Mrs. Varden tyrannizes over Miggs and together they tyrannize over Gabriel, who, in turn, tyrannizes over Sim.

Even the basically good-hearted Gabriel is turned into something of a hypocrite in this subjugation mill, and he involves himself in complicated fantasies in order to rationalize stoping at the Maypole Inn for a drink: 'The merciful man, Joe . . . is merciful to his beast. I'll get out for a little while' (II). Though mildly humorous, this fantasy ties him to the tyrants and suggests the extent of the general disease: it infects even the good. Gabriel's advice to the frustrated Joe Willet further underscores his corruption: 'Roving stones gather no moss, Joe' (III). This comment deserves Joe's contempt. The locksmith's proverbial wisdom, like all stale adages in this novel, is not only irrelevant but actually callous, and Gabriel unintentionally links himself to old Willet in his insensitivity to youth, his implicit opposition to 'all love-making'. He is further like Willet in living in a house symbolically 'detached from the world' in a particularly 'shady street' (IV). The suggestion of smug detachment here allies Gabriel with the easy immunity and easy tyranny of all the novel's fathers.

This alliance is most clearly suggested, however, in his relation to his daughter, Dolly. He is so blind to the possibility that anyone could be interested in her that we begin to see the blindness as a form of the general egoistic fantasy, with the same resultant cruelty. When Sim casts what he imagines to be seductive looks at Dolly, for instance, Gabriel spots him and reacts fiercely:

'Why, what the devil's the matter with the lad ?' cried the locksmith. 'Is he choking ?'

'Who ?' demanded Sim, with some disdain.

'Who ? why, you,' returned his master. 'What do you mean by making those horrible faces over your breakfast ?'

'Faces are a matter of taste, sir,' said Mr. Tappertit, rather discomfited ; not the less so because he saw the locksmith's daughter smiling.

'Sim,' rejoined Gabriel, laughing heartily. 'Don't be a fool, for I'd rather see you in your senses. These young fellows,' he added, turning to his daughter, 'are always committing some folly or another. There was a quarrel between Joe Willet and old John last night—though I can't say Joe was much in fault either.' (IV)

Gabriel's 'amazement' clearly masks a basic jealousy, and he reacts to Sim as a rival, refusing to let him off easily and taking full advantage of the opportunity to humiliate him in front of Dolly. His desire to see Sim in his 'senses' is like old John's desire for 'imagination' in the young. Both are euphemisms for subservience. Even his after-thought, conceding that Joe is not much at fault, does not erase his secret alliance with age and with tyranny. And the second half of the novel makes these connections so unmistakable that evasive and blind laughter is turned back on the reader. Gabriel's good-heartedness is deceptive, as is his amiable blindness to his daughter's suitors. He obviously wants Dolly for himself; he is well-intentioned but, for all that, a tyrant.

His dominance is further obscured by his co-ordinate role as a victim. He is controlled almost completely by his wife, perhaps the chief shrew in Dickens's extensive gallery of female despots and the absolute opposite of Mrs. Jarley: 'Mrs. Varden was a lady of what is commonly called an uncertain temper—a phrase which being interpreted signifies a temper tolerably certain to make everybody more or less uncomfortable' (vii). Mrs. Varden is an antidote for comedy; she literally spreads discomfort. The humour she evokes does more, however, than tempt us to laugh at another form of tyranny and thereby anticipate the reversal of that laughter when the seriousness of tyranny is exposed; it also introduces the complicating factor that the individual villains are also victims. The real trouble between Mrs. Varden and her husband, pretty clearly, is the Protestant Manual, and 'whenever [they] were at unusual variance, then the Protestant Manual was in high feather' (iv). This suggests that she is the victim of a more general malady, termed 'Protestantism', or more exactly a perversion of religion to fantastic egotistical ends.[8] The Manual provides Mrs. Varden with a variety of religious poses, appropriate for all occasions. Here, for instance, is the pose for submission: 'And so, with a mighty show of humility and forgiveness, she folded her hands, and looked round again, with a smile which plainly said "If you desire to see the first and foremost among female martyrs, here she is, on view!"' (xix). It is no accident that this versatile domestic

---

[8] Dickens makes it very clear in his Preface that one of his targets in this novel is the fact that 'what we falsely call a religious cry is easily raised by men who have no religion' (p. xxiv).

tyrant is one of the chief contributors to Lord George Gordon's fund, for that fund and that campaign are simply expressions for her of the more general egoistic fantasy. She sympathizes with and easily understands the desire to rule a nation with the same religious terror she has used so successfully to rule a home. Her desire to put herself on display as a female martyr suggests waxworks again, and our laughter no doubt expresses, under everything, a wish for her death. But again this sort of retributive comedy backfires, and Mrs. Varden is seen finally as a victim of a widespread delusion. Notice that she changes quite readily when she is able to see the real danger, and Gabriel is able to assert his power rather easily.

Curiously enough, it is the servant Miggs who continues to resist Gabriel, even when her mistress has capitulated. Miggs's unrealistically prolonged defiance suggests, I think, an even more subtle form of subjugation. Having served so long in the tricky role of deputy shrew, she and her fantasies seem to have solidified completely, and she is unable to regain touch with reality, even when it is thrust upon her. The first thing Dickens says about Miggs is that she is forced as a part of her duties to second her mistress; she is her 'chief aider and abettor, and at the same time her principal victim and object of wrath' (VII). Because of this demanding situation, Miggs is left with nowhere to turn when her mistress abandons her customary behaviour. Dickens's use of our laughter in this case is perhaps most deceptive of all, for Miggs's fantasy life is the most insidious and the most dangerous.

The humour generated by Miggs is most dangerous perhaps because it is most elemental and least rational. Miggs is funny simply because she is, on the one hand, both ugly and impotent and, on the other hand, very interested in sex. Her fantasies of sexual power are treated as hilarious. She seems at first to be just one more old maid to be subject to Dickens's often cruel comedy, but she is more functional than that and is much more complex, finally, than Rachael Wardle, whom she seems at first to resemble. To take just one example of her complexity, after Mrs. Varden finishes extolling the virtues of Lord George Gordon and of *The Thunderer*, his No-Popery publication, she turns to Miggs to receive her servant's expected confirmatory echo:

She appealed in support of this proposition to Miss Miggs, then in waiting, who said that indeed the peace of mind she derived from the perusal of that paper generally, but especially of one article of the very last week as ever was, entitled 'Great Britain drenched in gore,' exceeded all belief; the same composition, she added, had also wrought such a comforting effect on the mind of a married sister of hers, then resident at Golden Lion Court, number twenty-sivin, second bell-handle on the right-hand door-post, that, being in a delicate state of health, and in fact expecting an addition to her family, she had been seized with fits directly after its perusal, and had raved of the Inquisition ever since; to the great improvement of her husband and friends. Miss Miggs went on to say that she would recommend all those whose hearts were hardened to hear Lord George themselves, whom she commended first, in respect of his steady Protestantism, then of his oratory, then of his eyes, then of his nose, then of his legs, and lastly of his figure generally. (XLI)

It is astonishing how many relevant issues Dickens packs into this speech and how cleverly they are disguised. The 'peace of mind' Miggs parodies is equivalent to the delusory search for immunity so important to this novel's theme and to the reader as well; her jokes on 'gore' are intended to put us off our guard, to disarm us for the shock of the real gore; the connection of retribution with 'steady Protestantism' is a central one, which we must not ignore; finally, the grotesque suggestion of Miggs lusting after Gordon tempts us to laugh at her, thereby not only expressing a secret hostility but dismissing her very relevant comments as well.

We are also tempted to ignore the facts that a fantasy life is a necessity to her and that her parody of a 'sense of duty' is a very dark one. Dickens depends a great deal on dialect humour with her—'Ally Looyer, mim! there's Simmuns's knock!' (LI)—and urges us to think her ignorant and socially inferior as well as hilariously ugly. The real temptation, though, is to ignore the meanness growing beneath the surface and the fact that the meanness is at least partly caused by the tyranny Miggs is forced to live under, the same tyranny which encourages her to manufacture a fantasy life. Even when she is captured by the rioters, her actions suggest the desperate battle for survival and contact she is waging. She clearly is anxious, literally, for *any* man:

'You know he meant all along to carry off that one!' said Dennis, indicating Dolly by the slightest possible jerk of his head:—'And to hand you over to somebody else.'

Miss Miggs, who had fallen into a terrible state of grief when the first part of this sentence was spoken, recovered a little at the second, and seemed by the sudden check she put upon her tears, to intimate that possibly this arrangement might meet her views; and that it might, perhaps, remain an open question. (LXX)

It is this same desperation which makes her so vicious to Dolly, and Dickens finally uses this conventional and easy humour allied with the sex-starved spinster to indicate the great reach of the tyranny. The Vardens are not responsible for Miggs's unhappy sexual state, of course, but they provide a rigid pattern of power and fantasy in which she has been securely caught. In the end, she is anything but funny.

Miggs is completely trapped by her fantasy life. Though she has already exposed her deadly jealousy of Dolly, she automatically bounces back to the Vardens' late in the novel for another try at shrewdom, the only thing, we realize, she has been trained for and the only occupation this society has allowed her. When she senses that things have turned against her, she responds with an acid retaliation which is brilliantly apt and perfectly justified: ' "Times is changed, is they, mim!" cried Miggs, bridling; "you can spare me now, can you? You can keep 'em down without me? You're not in wants of any one to scold, or throw the blame upon, no longer, an't you, mim? I'm glad to find you've grown so independent. I wish you joy, I'm sure!" ' (LXXX). Her bitterness finally explodes in hysterical, uncontrolled hatred, doubly repulsive because it reveals so much of the causes of that hatred: the callousness, egoism, and smug detachment, which have likely been behind our earlier laughter: 'He he! I wouldn't have a husband with one arm, anyways. I would have two arms. I would have two arms, if it was me, though instead of hands they'd only got hooks at the ends, like our dustman!' (LXXX). This is exactly the same desperation we had earlier been allowed to laugh at so easily. The laughter has been turned back on us and finally is exposed and utterly extinguished by the 'honest locksmith', who says of the sobbing Miggs, 'It's a thing to laugh at, Martha, not to care for' (LXXX). Gabriel asks her—and us—

to ignore the whole lesson of the riots. To cap this callousness he adds, 'we'll be all the merrier for this interruption'. Back to the Maypole! Gabriel makes the ultimate evasion terribly pointed: Miggs's storm is to be welcomed, like the storm which opened both halves of the novel, not for what it teaches or portends, but for the sense of safety which it provides in its lulls. We might well have been 'merrier' along with Gabriel if he hadn't expressed the point so blatantly and exposed our own potential cruelty so openly.

But probably not even then, for there is still in the Varden subplot, to remind us of the danger of such evasion, the most fundamental example of this reversal, Sim Tappertit. More than any other character, Sim lives in complete delusion; not only his language but also his mannerisms are drawn from another, more acceptable age. He deals with his unbearable servitude by transforming it into the glamorous role of a squire: '"Sir," said Sim, looking up with amazing politeness, and a peculiar little bow cut short off at the neck. "I shall attend you immediately"'' (IV). Though we laugh at this habit, it later becomes obvious, first, that Sim is only mirroring the general social madness in a small and pathetic way and, second, that he has much more excuse for evading the present than most. He does so less from a desire for personal gain than from an instinctive retreat from an impossible repression. The fact that he serves the gentlest of masters shows us finally how insidious the repression is.

Sim, in fact, goes through something like a parody of the entire main plot, tempting us to the functional evasive laughter so important here. When sufficiently goaded, he turns to his ludicrous substitute for violence, the sharpening of weapons:

Whirr-r-r-r-r-r-r.
'Something will come of this!' said Mr. Tappertit, pausing as if in triumph, and wiping his heated face upon his sleeve. 'Something will come of this. I hope it mayn't be human gore!'
Whirr-r-r-r-r-r-r. (IV)

No matter how much we may be amused, his suggestion is, of course, accurate. Dickens makes it completely clear that Sim's pose of fierceness is the result of domestic tyranny. When he leaves Varden's house, for instance, the narrator says he lays aside 'his cautionary manner' necessary there and adopts the compensatory manner of a 'ruffling, swaggering, roving blade, who would rather kill a man than otherwise, and eat him too if needful' (VIII). Sim reflects the same reactionary violence and the same madness that controls the novel, but he is at the same time differentiated from it by being essentially harmless, almost innocent. He desires 'black crosses' (VIII) against a person's name, not real vengeance, and his later appeal to Chester (XXXIV) is only a parody of retribution, comic in its limitations. After a series of preparations so elaborate as to make even Chester joke about the 'cloak and dagger' silliness, Sim comes to 'THE point'. He wants Chester to deal with Joe, the 'villain', that 'monster in human shape, a vagabond of the deepest dye', not by killing him but by having him 'kidnapped and carried off at the very least'. The reason he gives Chester for engaging in this intrigue is that 'the pleasure of doing a bad action . . . to [Joe] is its own reward' (XXIV). The comparison of Sim's vision of Arabian Nights' kidnappings with Chester's real and ugly evil is, of course, funny, but it also reveals Sim's childlike and potentially pathetic innocence. There is, at least, clearly no danger to be feared from one who lives so completely in the world of melodrama. Sim is obviously most comfortable in his false world, the unconscious parody of the real madness. The blind and evil Stagg makes this point unmistakable in terming Sim's legs 'these twin invaders of domestic peace!' (VIII). We realize that an invasion is the last thing Sim could accomplish, and we realize too that Sim's fantasies, focused symbolically on his legs, are ludicrous. But by laughing we identify with Stagg's cynicism and overlook completely the degree to which Sim is finally a figure of horror and pity, not of fun.

He is really a small and potentially funny man who has been deeply corrupted and thereby victimized by his 'Protestant' society: 'My life's a burden to me. If it wasn't for wengeance, I'd play at pitch and toss with it on the losing hazard' (XXVII). His desire for vengeance, of course, backfires on him—but much more fully on us; for by laughing at him we are again localizing what is, in fact, general and ignoring what has very personal relevance.

Sim's central comments on illusion and reality are equally

pointed and relevant. When he hears Joe take leave of Dolly
before going away with the army, he comments:

'Have my ears deceived me . . . or do I dream! am I to thank
thee, Fortun', or cuss thee—which?'

He gravely descended from his elevation, took down his piece of
looking-glass, planted it against the wall upon the usual bench,
twisted his head round, and looked closely at his legs.

'If they're a dream,' said Sim, 'let sculptures have such wisions,
and chisel 'em out when they wake. This is reality. Sleep has no
such limbs as them. Tremble, Willet, and despair. She's mine!
She's mine!' (XXXI)

'This is reality' indeed to all who are captured by the tyranny
Sim lives under. And it becomes more and more clear that Sim
is completely victimized. He can't understand the riots, is
much more interested in appearance than in action, and is
always asking for 'order'. At the height of his defiance of
Varden's tyranny, he produces a tooth, of all things, and
screams, 'this was a bishop's. Beware, G. Varden!' (LI), and
when cornered by Miggs he threatens to 'pinch' her. We have,
it turns out, been laughing at the little boy playing grown-up,
overlooking both the pathos and the danger.

Dickens then proceeds to expose the results of this evasion,
of our own fantasy of immunity: Sim is pictured at the end
of the riots 'with a gun-shot wound in his body; and his legs,
his perfect legs, the pride and glory of his life, the comfort of
his existence—crushed into shapeless ugliness' (LXXI). At the
end of the novel, Dickens completes this reversal with the most
truly obscene image anywhere in his novels, the view of the
retaliation of Sim's wife by 'taking off his [wooden] legs, and
leaving him exposed to the derision of those urchins who delight in mischief' (LXXXII). The structural pattern of contrasts
has thus been completed and the didactic point made re-
soundingly: the dangers of egoistic evasion and tyranny have
been made applicable to the reader by the transformation of
the originally amusing into the grotesque.

3

But this is not quite all there is to the pattern. If Dickens left
it at this we might infer a new order, free of egoistic delusions

and of tyranny, but he adds a coda which gives just a hint of cynicism, of the beginning of a new cycle of tyranny. There is a sense here that the didacticism is, after all, useless, that the causes of oppression and the consequent riots cannot be cured with maxims, no matter how rhetorically effective.

What really succeeds the riots, Dickens intimates, is a new cowardice and a new tyranny:

> In Southwark, no fewer than three thousand of the inhabitants formed themselves into a watch, and patrolled the streets every hour. Nor were the citizens slow to follow so good an example: and it being the manner of peaceful men to be very bold when the danger is over, they were abundantly fierce and daring; not scrupling to question the stoutest passenger with great severity, and carrying it with a very high hand over all errand-boys, servant-girls, and 'prentices. (LXXIII)

Everything returns to the previous insane normality; the Lord Mayor is let off with a mild reprimand and assumes his old authority. Even Dennis's mad hopes to remain a part of the social order are, in their way, justified by that terrible order: 'he felt certain that the national gratitude *must* relieve him from the consequence of his late proceedings, and would certainly restore him to his old place in the happy social system' (LXXIV). Dickens explicitly says, in fact, that the new system is symbolized by a new repression:

> It is not the least evil attendant upon the frequent exhibition of this last dread punishment [hanging], of Death, that it hardens the minds of those who deal it out, and makes them, though they be amiable men in other respects, indifferent to, or unconscious of, their great responsibility. . . . Just then, too, when the law had been so flagrantly outraged, its dignity must be asserted. The symbol of its dignity,—stamped upon every page of the criminal statute-book,—was the gallows. (LXXVI)

All murder, this bitter passage suggests, is the same, and the real madness exists when murderers are officialized and approved. Hysterical violence has simply given way to placid violence; nothing has really changed.

The death of Dennis completes this cycle of tyranny. Though victimized by the same system he once served, he sees that he is truly a part of that system and would continue to serve it if he had the chance. 'I an't inconsistent', he screams; 'I'd talk so again, if I was hangman' (LXXVI). It is not only the grotesque or stupid who are unable to learn or to change; even Haredale admits that no lesson can really alter the deepest impulses which completely control one's existence: 'I find the unwelcome assurance that I should still be the same man, though I could cancel the past, and begin anew, with its experience to guide me' (LXXIX). And Dickens begins the last chapter with the bitter assurance that there were many people 'still, to whom those riots taught no lesson of reproof or moderation'. In a sense the novel is as cynical as Chester and just as unpleasant.

In the last scene, then, when Joe reopens the Maypole Inn, it is just as if he were reopening the novel. He symbolically changes places with his father, routing him just exactly as he earlier had been routed. Old John dies saying, 'I'm a-going, Joseph . . . to the Salwanners', and Joe assumes his father's old position: 'he inherited the whole' and 'became a man of great consequence in these parts'. He joins with Dolly, just another version of her mother,[9] to suggest a new tyranny, ripe for new exploits of self-delusion. The final harrowing didactic point is that didacticism may not be enough. Our laughter is not only turned back on us but is finally transformed to bitterness.

---

[9] That Dolly is very much like her mother has been pointed out by Gissing, *The Immortal Dickens*, p. 189, and by Folland, *PMLA*, lxxiv (1959), 414.

6 *Martin Chuzzlewit*

THE COMEDY OF ACCOMMO-DATION

'I wish I may die, if this isn't the queerest state of existence that we find ourselves forced into, without knowing why or wherefore, Mr. Pecksniff! Well, never mind! Moralise as we will, the world goes on.' (IV)

Martin Chuzzlewit is Dickens's funniest novel,[1] but it establishes itself as a comedy only on its own very special terms. It rejects, or at least treats with suspicion, many of the values the world of *The Pickwick Papers* depended upon: the naturally good heart, the acceptance of simplicity, the belief in youth, and the denial of artful dealing as the basis of the new society. It moves much further than *Pickwick* towards an accommodation with a sophisticated world of experience and comes very close to building a comic society out of that world. It is very nearly Dickens's last attempt to present a comic solution, and *Martin Chuzzlewit* could be called a nineteenth-century version of *The Alchemist*, with a similar broadly tolerant norm. There is a similar realism, even darkness, in this novel and a similar sense of mature acceptance. Its central tendency is expressed perfectly by its most important moral agent: '"Ah! what a wale of grief!" cried Mrs. Gamp, possessing herself of the bottle and glass' (XIX). The 'wale of grief' is fully realized here and used as a basis not for a removal to Dingley Dell, to Nell's tomb, or to anarchy, but for a

[1] The excellence of the novel's humour has usually been recognized. R. C. Churchill, for instance, maintains that it is 'not only Dickens's best comic novel but the greatest work of comic genius in the whole of English literature' ('Charles Dickens', *From Dickens to Hardy*, ed. Boris Ford [Baltimore, Md., 1964], p. 120).

realization of the joy of 'the bottle and glass'. But while Mrs. Gamp is the central moral figure in the novel, she is not the only one and her views are not unopposed. She represents, in fact, that important morality which is decidedly anti-moralistic. It is the same unmoralistic morality which controls the comic tendency of the novel and which makes us respond to the seriousness behind John Westlock's abrupt challenge to Tom Pinch:

'You haven't half enough of the devil in you. Half enough! You haven't any.'
'Well!' said Pinch, with a sigh, 'I don't know, I'm sure. It's a compliment to say so. If I haven't, I suppose, I'm all the better for it.'
'All the better!' repeated his companion tartly: 'all the worse, you mean to say.' (II)

Later Tom really does become slightly more devilish, even witty (i.e. aggressive), in response to his sister's pudding, but he often seems, particularly in the early parts of the novel, too traditionally good for the more sophisticated code, and he suggests thereby another and competing morality: a rigid and conventional system directly opposed to the worldly code of Mrs. Gamp.

What happens, it seems clear, is that Dickens's original didactic design 'to show, more or less by every person introduced, the number and variety of humours and vices that have their roots in selfishness'[2] becomes subsumed in a more subtle exploration of the development of personality[3] and the growth of that personality away from its natural egoistic rapacity toward social accommodation and civility. In the process a whole new morality grows up which makes the original view of selfishness seem hopelessly puerile and which makes old Martin Chuzzlewit, as the chief instrument in the development of the original design, the most unsatisfactory character in all of Dickens. There is, as a result, a split between

---

[2] Forster's *Life*, i. 274. For a reading of the novel in terms of selfishness, see Johnson, *Charles Dickens*, i. 469–70.
[3] That the novel is really about the development of selfhood rather than simply selfishness is argued at length by Miller, *Charles Dickens*, pp. 98–142. Interesting complementary readings are given by Marcus, *From Pickwick to Dombey*, pp. 213–68, and by E. A. Horsman, *Dickens and the Structure of the Novel* (Dunedin, N.Z., 1959), pp. 9–11.

the simple, didactic surface and the more complex sub-surface of the novel, keeping the comedy from being fully realized or satisfactorily completed. This split is most clearly apparent at the end of the novel, where both Pecksniff and Mrs. Gamp are denounced by old Martin and sent packing. It is rather like Grandfather Trent denouncing Dick Swiveller or Serjeant Buzfuz humiliating Sam Weller, and it is just about as convincingly realized; for by this point the novel belongs not to old Martin but to Sairey and Seth, not because they are more 'real' but because the morality they live by is much more humane and more adequate to the demands of the bleak world realized here than is Martin's simplistic copy-book code. As in *Oliver Twist*, then, the plot gets in the way of the pattern.

But there is a deeper reason for the ultimate incompleteness of the comic vision: it is never integrated or fully realized in a compact society. Though many characters find their way out of pure isolation, the result is still pictured as fragmented groups of two or three: Tom Pinch, Ruth, and John; Mr. Pecksniff and Charity; Martin and Mary; Mark and Mrs. Lupin; Bailey, Poll Sweedlepipe, Mrs. Gamp, and Mrs. Harris. There is no sense in which all of these people are bound together, and the novel ultimately fails as a comedy because its socially realistic values are never socially realized. The comic society is never finally born.

Still, it nearly is, and it is a common mistake to over-emphasize either the defects or the darkness of the novel.[4] The comic vision here is one of the most mature and moving in English literature and even in its incomplete state it suggests

---

[4] As usual, Forster begins a tradition of negative criticism, this time in relation to the novel's structure: 'In construction and conduct of story *Martin Chuzzlewit* is defective, character and description constituting the chief part of its strength' (*Life*, i. 292). The most recent continuation of this critical view is by Barbara Hardy, '*Martin Chuzzlewit*', *Dickens and the Twentieth Century*, pp. 107–20. The structure of the novel (in terms of a unity of plot and theme) is defended by Edwin B. Benjamin, 'The Structure of *Martin Chuzzlewit*', *PQ*, xxxiv (1955), 39–47.

The overemphasis of the novel's darkness, probably started by H. A. Taine, *History of English Literature*, ii. 351, is, I think, an obvious defect of J. Hillis Miller's chapter on the novel. The best single study of the novel, A. E. Dyson's '*Martin Chuzzlewit*: Howls the Sublime', *CritQ*, ix (1967), 234–53, addresses itself interestingly to the central issue of the curious combination of grimness and hilarity.

the outlines of a new society. These indications are far too strong to be ignored; they are too deeply implanted by our laughter. Dickens's humour had never so consistently touched such deep roots and had never been so effective.[5] It perhaps does help upset his original design and damage somewhat the unity of the novel, but who would trade the exciting imperfection we have for the mechanical and superficial perfection implicit in the sermonizing plan Forster talks about? The humour may be disruptive, but it disrupts the fatuous and moves toward the profound. It creates such convincing accommodation to a harsh world, in fact, that one can almost accept as final the philosophy of the artful Mr. Tigg:

'Moralise as we will, the world goes on. As Hamlet says, Hercules may lay about him with his club in every possible direction, but he can't prevent the cats from making a most intolerable row on the roofs of the houses, or the dogs from being shot in the hot weather if they run about the streets unmuzzled. Life's a riddle: a most infernally hard riddle to guess, Mr. Pecksniff. My own opinion is, that like that celebrated conundrum, "Why's a man in jail like a man out of jail?" there's no answer to it. Upon my soul and body, it's the queerest sort of thing altogether—but there's no use talking about it. Ha! ha!' (IV)

As the narrator says, this is indeed drawing a 'consolatory deduction' from 'gloomy premises'. The premises are, however, true, and the consolation is fully earned. Our laughter, like Mr. Tigg's, protects a world of joy founded on adult values not on Mr. Pickwick's 'delusions of our childish days', and *Martin Chuzzlewit* comes close to establishing a new kind of humour, not accounted for by Freud: one which finds laughter not in a denial of the pains of living but in an acceptance of them. Such complete and honest accommodation, however, is not ultimately possible; even the tough

---

[5] It must be added that Dickens's humour had also never been so continuous. There is simply far *more* humour in *Martin Chuzzlewit* than in any other novel, with the possible exception of *Pickwick*. The difference in quantity obviously makes a difference in our response, but I know of no way to account adequately for the quantity. One can only nod to it in passing, and perhaps offer as evidence of the overflowing abundance something like the following, a nameless butcher who appears in only two paragraphs to sell some meat to Tom Pinch: 'When he saw Tom putting the cabbage-leaf into his pocket awkwardly, he begged to be allowed to do it for him; "for meat," he said with some emotion, "must be humoured, not drove"' (XXXIX).

Mrs. Gamp needs the support of Mrs. Harris. It may be the failure of the book to achieve this final impossible transcendence that caused G. K. Chesterton, of all Dickens's critics the most responsive to his humour, to say that the novel is, in the end, 'sad'.[6] It seems to promise a salvation through Mrs. Gamp but comes close to dismissing her at the last minute, just as she is about to begin presiding over the new world.

Her departure and the more general fragmentariness of the ending society, then, withhold the final comic satisfaction, but it is only just at the very end that the novel turns from the basis of its humour. Long before that our laughter has in all probability created the values of that society and defined its outlines. The potential of that society is, in fact, so firmly developed that it may have enough momentum to complete itself, at least in the minds of many readers. At any rate, the major qualification can easily be overstressed, since the values which matter in the novel are those of its comic rather than its moralistic pattern. The first and most important value of this society, as in all comic societies, is freedom, but here the freedom is of a very special kind, captured in the midst of restraints and limitations. The novel steers a middle course between two extremes: America, on the one hand, where the anarchy visualized in *Barnaby Rudge* is made official in a country without restraints, tradition, or culture, and where consequently there is absolutely no freedom,[7] and, on the other hand, the restrictive, introverted morality suggested by old Martin's initial suspicions and Mark Tapley's initial masochism. The resultant mean is explicitly a social freedom, and our admiration is directed toward the versatile imagination which creates freedom for itself and for others out of extremely limited conditions, as, say, Mrs. Todgers does in the midst of the London maze. The anarchy of the uninhibited ego and the restrictions of selfish morality are equally repudiated here.

---

[6] *Appreciations and Criticisms*, p. 90.

[7] In a letter to Forster, Dickens said, 'I believe there is no country, on the face of the earth, where there is less freedom of opinion on any subject in reference to which there is a broad difference of opinion than in this' (*Life*, i. 194). Less direct but perhaps more expressive of Dickens's extreme dislike of America is a later sarcastic reference in a letter to Miss Coutts: 'Macready [in America] still continues as successful as it is possible to be. He is very well, and likes the people—which must be a great comfort to him' (*The Heart of Charles Dickens*, ed. Edgar Johnson [New York, 1952], p. 59).

Similarly, the incipient comic society rejects the whole doctrine of natural goodness, which was at the heart of *Pickwick*. There, it seemed, men would be good if they could only resist the awful corruption of institutions and return to the basic simplicity inherent within all and symbolized in nature. *Martin Chuzzlewit* overturns all this; innocence is replaced by experience, simplicity by sophistication, nature by art. Here, man must resist the basic impulses and restrain them with civility, tolerance, and consideration. In this comedy one does not escape to nature for revivification; one escapes to London for civilized training.

As corollaries to these main precepts of the comedy of accommodation, there are several secondary tendencies. First, there is a movement away from the youthful norm toward greater maturity, even age. Tom Pinch is, in some ways, at the centre of the novel, and he is a man of thirty-five who looks as if he were sixty (II). Even the archetypal battle played out tragically between Jonas Chuzzlewit and his father is finally won by the father through his deputy, Chuffey, surely the oldest old man in literature. Second, there is an insistence on an absolute openness to all experience, without regard to compensation of any sort, financial or moral, and without reliance on artificial systems to explain that experience. Mark Tapley errs by translating experience into his narrow masochistic wish for 'credit', old Martin by translating it into an egoistic, dark moral code, Tom Pinch (at first) by not curbing his joy in being patronized. Finally, the demand for openness presupposes perhaps the most basic aspect of this developing society: its elemental dedication to life. The novel touches on many possible reasons for despair but never relaxes its insistence on the supremacy of the reasons for living. Even the most peripheral characters maintain this constant theme; there is, for example, Mr. Bill Simmons, coach-driver, who tells young Martin the story of the musically talented Lummy Ned of the Light Salisbury and his trip to America. When Martin misunderstands and thinks Ned has died, the driver retorts quickly and with 'contemptuous emphasis', 'Dead! . . . Not he. You won't catch Ned a-dying easy. No, no. He knows better than that' (XIII). So do the readers who respond to this society; for through our laughter it promises a vigorous and creative life, which is so contemptuous of any evasion that it builds itself, as does Lummy Ned, on facing resolutely its ultimate enemy, which, in various disguises, appears as nature, the United States, or death.

But as this last triad suggests, one does not come to this sort of life easily. The central action of the novel is, in fact, a series of ritual initiations or purifications, undertaken partly in order to establish a more permanent selfhood but more importantly in order to qualify for the comic society, for the company of Mrs. Gamp and Poll Sweedlepipe. In different ways and with varying degrees of success, old Martin, young Martin, Mark Tapley, Tom Pinch, and through them Ruth Pinch and Mary Graham are all changed and learn the values acceptable to Mrs. Harris. In view of this mass initiation, it is not surprising if the reader is rhetorically initiated too, and the second function of our laughter, after first creating the society, is to provide us a place in it. Since similar rhetorical processes have already been discussed in earlier chapters, this positioning of the reader can be dealt with briefly, so that the primary function of laughter, the creation of the comic values listed above, can be investigated more fully.

1

The rhetorical pattern of the laughter in *Martin Chuzzlewit* is like that in *Barnaby Rudge* turned inside out; instead of moving from assurance to subversive attack, it moves from attack to assurance. The novel opens with bitterness and insults and moves gradually to include the reader; it is the one time in Dickens, outside *Pickwick*, when the rhetoric serves the purpose of relaxation. We are first sensitized to our own defects, urged to examine our own anti-comic tendencies, and then are allowed to be comfortable. Since, as we have said, the novel does not *quite* complete the comic pattern, the comfort is perhaps not absolute, but with this one major qualification (which I make now for the last time) *Martin Chuzzlewit* reverses the essential action of *Barnaby Rudge* and develops from anarchy to security. It is not so much *Barnaby Rudge* written backwards as *Barnaby Rudge* transcended.

But in order that the novel may accomplish this transcendence, the reader is first viciously attacked. Until Forster dissuaded him, Dickens had planned to emphasize this attack in a motto for the novel: 'Your homes the scene, yourselves the actors, here!'[8] Even without this obvious insult, the beginning lines of the book open a very wide gulf between narrator and reader: 'As no lady or gentleman, with any claims to polite breeding, can possibly sympathise with the Chuzzlewit Family without being first assured of the extreme antiquity of the race. . . .' The tone is unmistakably sarcastic and jeering; the reader is, in a sense, made responsible for the gruesome chapter which follows. Though an odd chapter in many ways, it does perform the brutal but necessary function of preparing us for the development of true selfhood by knocking out some ludicrously invalid props for self, specifically family pride and snobbery. At the end of the chapter the narrator sneeringly assumes that he has provided evidence of the Chuzzlewit pride 'to the full contentment of all . . . readers'.

The very next chapter begins with another interesting inversion, a comic episode turned inside out. Mr. Pecksniff is introduced being knocked on his back by his own front door. The pompous man, in other words, *begins* by being deflated, and Dickens continues in this chapter to paint him as a Bergsonian automaton who moves his jaws like 'a toy nut-cracker'. The presumed comic satisfaction in deflation, then, somehow precedes the comic antagonism, but Pecksniff is reduced to this state only to be enormously expanded, and we, very likely to our embarrassment, are forced to expand with him and to accept at least some of his values.

This sort of grim and embarrassing reversal occurs continuously throughout the first part of the novel. For example, old Chuffey is introduced as a comic figure, 'of a remote fashion, and dusty, like the rest of the furniture'. 'He looked', the narrator adds, 'as if he had been put away and forgotten half a century before, and somebody had just found him in a lumber closet' (xi). This extreme dehumanization is cleverly enough disguised to make laughter easy, but any laughter

---

[8] Quoted in Forster's *Life*, i. 296. Steven Marcus argues that 'the novel amounted to something in the way of an assault upon Dickens's audience' (p. 223) but misplaces the motive and result of this assault, I think, in emphasizing the 'separation between Dickens and his audience'.

rebounds sharply. Chuffey, first, so lights up when Anthony
Chuzzlewit talks to him that it is 'quite a moving sight to see';
second, Jonas says he brought old Chuffey out 'for the joke of
it', in order to 'amuse' the Pecksniff girls; in the next line,
finally, Dickens calls the old man 'poor old' Chuffey. We have
no chance against rhetoric of this sort.

Sometimes, however, the humour is not so pointed or so
clearly subversive. The harsh tone of the early part of the
novel comes in large measure simply from the bitterness of its
very aggressive humour. At the Chuzzlewit family gathering,
for instance, both the brilliant contest of insults and the
devastatingly contemptuous descriptions encourage hostile
reactions. Old Martin's grand nephew, for example, is attacked
so wittily that one is willing to accept the shallowness of a
man 'apparently born for no particular purpose but to save
looking-glasses the trouble of reflecting more than just the
first idea and sketchy notion of a face, which had never been
carried out' (IV). Pecksniff later allows himself an even more
fundamental joke on freedom and restraint: 'It is good to
know that we have no reserve before each other, but are
appearing freely in our own characters.' The sort of freedom
expressed by the Spottletoes and their amiable kin is, of
course, exactly the sort of freedom we later see in America,
the freedom from civilizing restraints. It is also the same
freedom expressed by our laughter, but the primary point
here is not to attack us with this identification but rather to
encourage the release of aggression. Just like the five snarling
female cousins, we too are likely to have 'a great amount of
steam to dispose of'. The early part of the novel urges us to
do just that. We can, as a matter of fact, find instances in
which Dickens simply divides the source of the laughter,
repeating a characteristic in different circumstances so that
the original strong aggression may be gradually weakened
and then dispelled and the originally weak pleasure and
approval strengthened. Mrs. Lupin, for example, is first
introduced as 'a widow, but [one who] years ago had passed
through her state of weeds, and burst into flower again' (III).
The aggression aroused here is simply removed as Mrs. Lupin's
resurrection is later identified as a form of the novel's central
comic symbol. She is joined by character after character—

Martin, Mark, Mrs. Gamp, Young Bailey, and others—in facing death and annihilation and returning 'in full bloom'. Mrs. Lupin's ability to blossom, we later see, is the ability we are asked to find in ourselves.

After the encouragement to let off aggressive steam and to recognize the falsity of a conventional outlook, the novel comforts the reader and provides him with a security all the firmer for our testing. This is not to say that this security is contrived or simple; as Tom Pinch says, 'You think of me, Ruth . . . as if I were a character in a book; and you make it a sort of poetical justice that I should, by some impossible means or other, come, at last, to marry the person I love. But there is a much higher justice than poetical justice, my dear, and it does not order events upon the same principle' (L). Tom is able to 'reconcile himself to life', a recurrent phrase made all the more suggestive by the novel's insistence that life is not necessarily easy. Tom still can be happy; for in a curious way he has, as he insists, gained a reality he did not have before and is no longer 'a character in a book', believing in perfect Pecksniffs, and gaining a secret and ugly pleasure from being patronized. His education was rough but, in every sense, worth it, and the accepting tone Tom uses is very much like the mellow tone which spreads over the last half of the novel.

Against this general pattern of attack-acceptance runs one counter-movement, however, one antithetical and cautionary development: the subplot involving Jonas Chuzzlewit and the Pecksniff daughters. This subplot tempers the mellowness of the final tone and warns us against accepting the comic solution too easily; for it deals with an always dangerous nature, manifested in murder, loneliness, and fear. The most terrifying figure here, Jonas, begins, surprisingly, as an absurd comic butt, caught in the middle of a thinly disguised sex battle between the Chuzzlewit girls: '"Mercy is a little giddy," said Miss Charity. "But she'll sober down in time"' (VIII). Merry responds in kind: '"What a relief it must be to you, my dear, to be so very comfortable in that respect, and not to be worried by those odious men! How *do* you do it, Cherry?"' (XI). It begins to look like Rachael Wardle and her nieces all over again, and we can express aggression at either girl easily. They are, after all, hypocritical and false.

But what is Jonas? From the country bumpkin he initially appeared to be, he becomes a complex and cunning parricide. We first notice this change as his jokes against his father become more and more literal: 'A fine old gentleman! . . . Ah! It's time he was thinking of being drawn out a little finer too. Why, he's eighty!' (XI). The tendency of this joke is coming closer to the surface all the time as we progress in this sub-plot, and is finally realized literally as Jonas completes the Oedipal pattern. The basis of the original conflict between youth and age is exposed and laughter is impossible. The Pecksniff girls, artificial and hypocritical as they are, are forced into contact with the much greater and more powerful evil: raw and natural cruelty. Jonas, exactly like the Americans, loses all restraints and becomes the elemental man—or beast—crafty and murderous. Merry early calls him, in play, a 'low savage' (XXIV), but the joke rebounds horribly as Jonas returns to the country to kill more terribly, Dickens says, than 'a wolf' (XLII). This pattern is created to make the contrast between Jonas and the Pecksniff girls most explicit. Jonas is the natural man, without curbs on his ego and therefore the apotheosis of revenge. Merry's good-hearted hypocrisy and mild selfishness are nothing compared to his evil, and the reversal of the humour makes more emphatic the danger of uncivilized naturalness. Mark Tapley may be able to brag that he has 'been among the patriots' (XLIII) and miraculously survived, but the rhetoric makes it clear that survival is by no means assured. Merry is sacrificed to make that grim point.

Developing along with this is the superficially lighter but, in its implications, really equally dark and bitter romance of Charity Pecksniff and Augustus Moddle. We laugh at Moddle, first of all, to economize pathos, I think, and to protect ourselves from the pain of those committed to trying for human contact and failing: 'I have seen him standing in a corner of our drawing-room, gazing at her, in such a lonely, melancholy state, that he was more like a Pump than a man, and might have drawed tears' (XXXII). Laughter hides the dark truth that Moddle suggests: that there are the failures, the unwanted, and the unloved to modify the joy of any actual society. Moddle's final letter comes very close to uncovering this truth: 'She is Another's. Everything appears to be somebody else's' (LIV). But perhaps this interpretation over-emphasizes the pathos of Moddle; for Dickens says that he is entering a kind of Eden (the American variety) with Charity, and we are, no doubt, happy for his escape. But, particularly in the final image of the doubly unwanted Charity, fainting away in dead earnest, this ludicrous romance does again temper the final society by insisting on the isolation of many and the great difficulty of escaping that isolation.

2

Even with these qualifications, and partly because of them, it is a robust and realistic comic society which this novel points towards and nearly completes. It is the primary—at least the most interesting—function of laughter to define that society and its values.

Though the society is created partly by a series of initiations, its values are there from the beginning, and are symbolized by a series of mainly static characters who, though we are not likely to realize it until very late, are all along conducting the initiation: Mrs. Todgers (and her boarders), Mr. Pecksniff, Montague Tigg, Mrs. Gamp, her associate Mr. Mould, and perhaps the gayest and sweetest comic pair in Dickens: Young Bailey and Poll Sweedlepipe. All these characters, in their various ways, help mainly to define, through our laughter, the positive values of this society. They do, of course, also serve some negative function, but the primary agent of the laughter of rejection and expulsion is the cast of non-characters populating the United States. Further, the American experience serves as the grand prototype for all the initiations; it is the Inferno of natural and unrestrained ego each of the heroes must pass through. By means of our primarily aggressive, negative laughter at the United States, then, and our primarily protective, positive laughter at the English artistic comedians named above, the comic world is created. The American and English chapters are, of course, intertwined in the novel, but it is much more convenient to deal with them separately, first with the great sideshow of freaks Dickens observed on the other side of the Atlantic.

It is no compliment to America to say that it is epitomized

by its own version of Eden or to say that Martin is journeying here through a symbolic extension of his old self. America is the primeval slime of self-love, the natural, unchecked ego which must be faced directly and conquered. Martin and Mark[9] are symbolically purified there by illness; we are meant to be purified by our laughter, which asks us to see what America is and, at the same time, violently reject it. Our laughter functions to awaken the proper aggressions and expel them in order to purify the latter part of the book and secure its particular comic values.

Probably the most important final value is kind civility founded on restraint, and, correspondingly, the most violent rejection in America is of the perverted manner in which the natives have developed the unrestrained, uncivil sense of the natural. As General Choke says, America offers a display of man 'in a more primeval state' (xxi), and it is not an appealing exhibit. These violent people live, the narrator says, by 'the first law of nature' (xvi), making even dinner a contest for survival and exposing themselves as a collection of egos and intestines. This country's 'na-tive raw material' is, as Elijah Pogram points out (xxxiv), splendidly represented by Mr. Hannibal Chollop, and Mr. Chollop is splendidly represented by his killing of the man 'in the State of Illinoy' who asserted 'that the ancient Athenians went a-head of the present Loco-foco Ticket' (xxxiii). There is, however, a greater danger in America than being killed by Mr. Hannibal Chollop, and that is becoming Mr. Hannibal Chollop; for America develops that sort of natural man. 'Some institutions develop human natur'; others re—tard it' (xvi), says Colonel Diver, and it is the primary terror of America that its notion of 'unre—tarded' human nature is contagious and that it does nothing to check the spread of its natural inclinations.

Rather, it accelerates a tendency to the bestial, and the

---

[9] Mark's need for purification is not so immediately apparent as is Martin's, but is just as intense. He must expel his masochistic tendency to 'hope for the worst' (vii) and his eternal desire for moral rewards, or 'credit'. In his selfishness he rejects comfort and the entire range of positive comic values we are encouraged to accept. When he returns to England after his initiation at Eden, he delights in parodying his old desire to see others miserable and finally repudiates his initial position entirely by opening a pub, 'The Jolly Tapley'. 'Jolly' has by this time, for Mark and for us, lost all its suggestions of sarcasm and perversion.

major warning of the book is that without the checks of tradition and culture, without the selfhood firmly nurtured on civility and restraint, men become beasts: 'And, oh! ye Pharisees of the nineteen-hundredth year of Christian Knowledge, who soundingly appeal to human nature, see first that it be human. Take heed it has not been transformed, during your slumber and the sleep of generations, into the nature of the Beasts' (XIII). The laughter evoked at the Americans expresses both a rejection of their condition and a shoring up of the restraining inhibitions that protect us from this animal state. The resulting ethic, surprisingly enough, is rather like that in a Jane Austen novel, and Dickens, for once, is solidly on the side of kindly tolerance and social accommodation. We are led towards accepting this norm by a brilliant evocation of America as a giant pigsty, a vision whose hilarity is muted by a note of terror. The tone in the American sections is often like that in Book II of *Gulliver's Travels*, combining amazement and disgust, but in *Martin Chuzzlewit* there is none of the irony which qualifies Gulliver's view of the Brobdingnagians; the narrator here must be accepted totally. The Americans *are* beasts.

The first thing that Martin hears when he lands is the American self-advertisement: the *New York Stabber* and the *New York Plunderer* with their news of the latest 'gouging case' and 'dooel with Bowie knives' (XVI). Dickens was obviously fascinated with the American use of 'gouge' and presents the term as particularly expressive of savagery. The basic lack of restraint extends further than physical brutality: the *Private Listener*, the *Family Spy*, the *Keyhole Reporter* all suggest not only the absence of privacy but also the absence of any feeling of delicacy and the consequent obliteration of the private life. As a result, all Americans exist as public beings only, more specifically as orators or freaks constantly on display. Laughter is used constantly to intensify the sense of the dangerousness and bestiality of these people. The description of the house of Major Pawkins, for instance, is masterful in its deceptive simplicity and its quiet evocation of the ugly: 'a rather mean-looking house with jalousie blinds to every window; a flight of steps before the green street-door; a shining white ornament on the rails on either side like a

petrified pine-apple, polished; a little oblong plate of the same
material over the knocker, whereon the name of "Pawkins"
was engraved; and four accidental pigs looking down the
area' (XVI). It is with some shock that we realize that the pigs
are real pigs, that they are 'accidental' only in not being
intended in the design. Their appropriateness, however, is
never called in question; they are typical citizens.

The Americans are paradigms of the most frightening social
type, the poor winner. They live continually in the jungle
howl of triumph and thereby violate the first code of civilization, reverting to something much worse than savagery. In
rejecting aristocracy, it seems, they have also rejected all
genuine stabilizing value:

'Oh! there *is* an aristocracy here, then?' said Martin, 'Of what
is it composed?'
'Of intelligence, sir,' replied the colonel; 'of intelligence and
virtue. And of their necessary consequence in this republic.
Dollars, sir.' (XVI)

This, the central commercial lie, leads to the ethic of 'smartness', a euphemism, as Martin makes clear, for 'forgery' (XVI)
or for any plundering immorality. The saints of this society
are its most competent scoundrels. Because of this perverted
ethic, it is not only consistent but brilliantly apt that they
should lionize Martin[10] after they find he has 'purchased a
"location" in the Valley of Eden' (XXII). Dickens is simply
showing their most natural urge: to collect in a pack and howl
over the victim of their smartness. It is really impossible to find
an analogy in nature for such gratuitous cruelty, and Mrs. Lupin
certainly has the last approved word on the Americans: 'How
could he ever go to America! Why didn't he go to some of
those countries where the savages eat each other fairly, and
give an equal chance to every one!' (XLIII).

This land of the free, as Mrs. Lupin sees, exists on denying

[10] Harry Stone argues that Martin's being lionized in this way is a principal
example of the fault of the American section: that Dickens is unable to maintain an adequate aesthetic distance because he is 'too emotionally involved
with his recent memories to modify and subdue them sufficiently for credibility'
(p. 472). Though Stone's article ('Dickens's Use of His American Experiences
in *Martin Chuzzlewit*', *PMLA*, lxxii [1957], 464–78) traces interesting patterns
in Dickens's use of his letters and notes in the novel, I think that in this case
he is dead wrong.

'an equal chance to every one', and Dickens uses the symbol of slavery over and over again to show, as Martin says, that for 'masters' this country has simply substituted 'owners' (XVI). But by cutting themselves off from the past completely —'darn your books' (XVI), says a representative citizen— Americans have lost touch with decency and value, and also with reality. The United States is, in fact, a pre-figuring of Lewis Carroll's Wonderland, with Humpty Dumpty in charge:

'I go back Toe my home, sir,' pursued the gentleman, 'by the return train, which starts immediate. Start is not a word you use in your country, sir.'
'Oh yes, it is,' said Martin.
'You air mistaken, sir,' returned the gentleman, with great decision: 'but we will not pursue the subject, lest it should awaken your prĕjŭ-dīce.' (XXII)

Our laughter rejects this potentially terrifying sense of certainty; for it is the certainty of the madhouse, and Americans are so dangerous and violent mainly because they are so completely unable to tolerate objection. Objection, or even mild correction, implies a doubt of their identity, it seems, and their identity is completely rooted in a wild and un-restrained language.

Their colourful vocabulary, constant use of inverted sentences, and general practice of speaking as they write, 'with all the indignation in capitals, and all the sarcasm in italics' (XXII) rob them of any sense of reality and expose their hysterical attempts to hide their emptiness. As Dickens says, 'wherever half a dozen people were collected together, there, in their looks, dress, morals, manners, habits, intellect, and conversation, were Mr. Jefferson Brick, Colonel Diver, Major Pawkins, General Choke, and Mr. La Fayette Kettle, over, and over, and over again. They did the same things; said the same things; judged all subjects by, and reduced all subjects to, the same standard' (XXI). There is a sense, of course, reinforced by the aggressive humour, in which the whole country is an empty balloon.[11] American speech has lost

[11] Edgar Johnson says these Americans are 'non-human beings' ('Dickens and the Spirit of the Age', *Victorian Essays: A Symposium*, eds. Warren D. Anderson and Thomas D. Clareson [Kent, Ohio, 1967], p. 39). Miller, similarly, says that 'America is an entire society which lives as pure surface, a surface which hides a profound void' (p. 130).

entirely its relation to the particular. The natives speak a true poetry, but they also believe that 'your true poetry can never stoop to details' (XXI), and it is details on which language and identity are established. The same sense of hollowness is behind the recurrent remark that virtually any person in question is 'one of the most remarkable men in our country, sir'. Everyone is remarkable, just as everyone speaks in italics, partly because no one is really remarkable at all, it is true, but also partly because America is a vast side show, a group of Yahoos, each superficially different but united in their repulsiveness. Our laughter emphasizes the nothingness, but it is surely a laughter so extremely negative as to include a large measure of disgust.

Only twice does Dickens allow us to move past this disgust and glimpse in a compassionate way the awful barrenness of these lives. The first glimpse comes at the end of a satiric discussion of the aggressively intellectual female and her diet of absurd lectures—'The Philosophy of Vegetables' on Fridays (XVII)—when Mr. Bevan explains that they only go 'as an escape from monotony' (XVII). The second time is in a letter from Mr. Putnam Smif, who writes to Martin asking for literary assistance in England. Smif, it turns out, is a brilliant parody-in-advance of Walt Whitman: 'I am young and ardent. For there is a poetry in wildness, and every alligator basking in the slime is in himself an Epic, self-contained. I aspirate for fame. It is my yearning and my thirst' (XXII). The humour is directed against both this 'wildness' and this egoistic 'thirst' for fame, but at the end of the uproarious letter Dickens again catches us up short with a potentially touching PS.: 'Address your answer to America Junior, Messrs. Hancock and Floby, Dry Goods Store, as above.'

But American naturalness is far too dangerous to allow for much of this, and Martin finally makes explicit the reason for disavowing this country: they lack 'that instinctive good breeding which admonishes one man not to offend and disgust another'. He explains, further, that 'from disregarding small obligations they come in regular course to disregard great ones' and that this creeping insensitivity to others forms 'a part of one great growth which is rotten at the root' (XXXIV). In the end, our laughter is used to aid in the destruction of all

that this country represents, and the final black joke is pro-
nounced by Mark Tapley: 'But they're like the cock that went
and hid himself to save his life, and was found out by the
noise he made. They can't help crowing. They was born to it,
and do it they must, whatever comes of it' (xxxiii). This
nation of proud cocks, similarly, is setting itself up for the
slaughter, and its symbolic elimination corresponds to an
elimination in us of the anarchic ego.

The final scene in America completes this elimination by
pushing the natural rapacity of this country out of sight and
into the total void of empty space. The two transcendentalist
ladies act as a climax and summary of this harsh laughter of
rejection. The first lady, in her philosophic way, raises the
question as to whether she and, 'oh gasping one!' the honourable Pogram and the honourable Hominy really do exist. The
second lady, in her equally philosophic way, unintentionally
gives a clear answer to the question and, at the same time,
pronounces the resounding negative verdict on all America:

'Mind and matter . . . glide swift into the vortex of immensity.
Howls the sublime, and softly sleeps the calm Ideal, in the whisper-
ing chambers of Imagination. To hear it, sweet it is. But then,
outlaughs the stern philosopher, and saith to the Grotesque, "What
ho! arrest for me that Agency. Go, bring it here!" And so the vision
fadeth.' (xxxiv)

And so fadeth America. The naked rapacious ego has been
conquered, and there is no more need for the natural. The
humour has done its job.

3

The contrast with England is the contrast between the
natural and the refined, between crudity and art, between
the Bowie knife and the soft word, between the death of the
Valley of Eden and the teeming life of Mrs. Todgers's boarding house. Mrs. Todgers's is the centre of the comic principle
of accommodation and is the most important agent in stirring
our more positive laughter. Just as America tells us what to
reject in our laughter, so we are able to learn what to accept
through this Commercial Boarding House and through those
who come in contact with it: Mr. Pecksniff, Mrs. Gamp and
Mr. Mould, Young Bailey and Poll Sweedlepipe.

'The parlour was wainscoted, and communicated to strangers a magnetic and instinctive consciousness of rats and mice. . . . It had not been papered or painted, hadn't Todgers's, within the memory of man. It was very black, begrimed, and mouldy' (VIII). And it is from this sordid place that the principle of the comic society springs. Mrs. Todgers's primary ability is a fully developed and versatile art of accommodation; 'I think I know how to arrange it' (VIII), she says when Mr. Pecksniff presents her with an un-looked-for problem, and indeed she does. She is not only versatile in this manner, however, but also kindly: though 'calculation' shines out of one eye, 'affection' beams in the other. She shows how one can face a black reality and live with it without the necessity of violence or madness.

She not only lives with it, of course; she triumphs over it. Her comments on gravy actually parody age and prudence, and display a kind of comic luxuriance:

'Presiding over an establishment like this makes sad havoc with the features, my dear Miss Pecksniffs,' said Mrs. Todgers. 'The gravy alone, is enough to add twenty years to one's age, I do assure you.'

'Lor!' cried the two Miss Pecksniffs.

'The anxiety of that one item, my dears,' said Mrs. Todgers, 'keeps the mind continually upon the stretch.' (IX)

Her mind is on the stretch, notice, not to survive but to provide a comfortable superfluity, a luxury for all. Her dinners are, in fact, exercises in comic gluttony reminiscent of those in *Pickwick,* and she manages an image of abundance from the most meagre pickings. She is an artist of comfort and luxury, and her house is the reverse of Commercial. Her lodgers, even, express their real 'turns' in her presence: a sporting turn, a theatrical turn, a speech-making turn, a literary turn, a vocal turn, a whist turn—in short, inclinations toward art, pleasure, and fun. This Commercial Boarding House is the antithesis of the commercial ethic and in its airy, joyful life stands as an indictment of American solemnity and death.

Mrs. Todgers's art is admittedly rather hard to distinguish sometimes from hypocrisy, but it is an indication of the comic norms of this novel that it is the arch-hypocrite, Mr. Pecksniff, who makes the charge of hypocrisy. The irony here does not, certainly, rebound on Mr. Pecksniff but on the whole rigid moral standard which is anxious to judge hypocrisy as evil. Mrs. Todgers's defence further helps dissolve the foolish conventional morality by economizing contempt through laughter and transforming it into approval: 'I am forced to keep things on the square if I can, sir. . . . I must preserve peace among them, and keep my connexion together, if possible, Mr. Pecksniff. The profit is very small' (x). She turns the search for profits not only into peacemaking but also into joy. In the end, Mrs. Todgers is presented as a kind and lovely person, to us as to Tom Pinch: 'She was growing beautiful so rapidly in Tom's eyes; for he saw that she was poor, and that this good had sprung up in her from among the sordid strivings of her life' (XXXVII). Her 'well-conditioned soul' (LIV) shows us the directions for a comic society: realism, kindness, restraint, and creative accommodation. Her house is not a boarding house at all, in these terms, but a sacred and mystic training centre for the education and protection of 'liverers'. It 'was in a labyrinth, whereof the mystery was known but to a chosen few' (IX).

One of those chosen few is the accomplished 'architect, artist, and man' (IX), Seth Pecksniff. While it is true that the plot of the novel casts Pecksniff as a villain, the comic pattern knows better and places him at the centre of our instructional experience. Though old Martin, in one of the few truly bungled scenes in Dickens, actually clubs Pecksniff, the real verdict on him is quietly suggested by a person much closer to the moral norm, Mrs. Lupin, who remains loyal to this 'noble-spoken gentleman' (XLIII).[12] In responding to Pecksniff's mastery of speech, Mrs. Lupin is, in fact, displaying the true sensitivity; for in this novel Mr. Pecksniff's hypocrisy is ultimately judged to be almost trifling; his style is his salvation. Pecksniff is an important contrast to America, and matters are arranged so that the first thing Martin and Mark see when they return is a result of one bit of Mr. Pecksniff's artful cunning: the ceremony attending his (actually Martin's) successful design for a grammar school. This scene presents some parallels, certainly, with American 'smartness', but any resemblance is

[12] Even Dickens confessed of Pecksniff and his daughters, 'I have a kind of liking for them myself', to C. C. Felton, *Nonesuch Letters*, i. 647, 31 Dec. 1842.

nearly obliterated by Mr. Pecksniff's great speech: 'My friends!
. . . My duty is to build, not speak; to act, not talk; to deal
with marble, stone, and brick: not language. I am very much
affected. God bless you!' (xxxv). No gore, no eagle's talons, no
Bowie knives, no gougings, just restrained and consummately
synthetic style.

Mr. Pecksniff suggests the great flowering of civilization,
over-ripe it is true, but still presenting a glorious blossom.
Even his horse creates the illusion of speed and grandeur from,
we gather, very unpromising raw materials. It is this ability
to manufacture joy and comfort from shabbiness and violence
that the comedy continually approves of, and no one is more
of a virtuoso in this regard than Mr. Pecksniff. He is properly
much more concerned with beauty than with morality, more
with sound than with sense. He chooses his words on this
principle (ii) and models his action on the grand single point
of style. Dickens brilliantly indicates his remarkable abilities
in an early conversation he has with Mrs. Lupin:

> 'A gentleman taken ill upon the road, has been so very bad up-
> stairs, sir,' said the tearful hostess.
> 'A gentleman taken ill upon the road, has been so very bad up-
> stairs, has he?' repeated Mr. Pecksniff. 'Well, well!' (iii)

'Anybody', Dickens continues, 'would have been, as Mrs.
Lupin was, comforted by the mere voice and presence of such
a man; and, though he had merely said, "a verb must agree
with its nominative case in number and person, my good
friend", or "eight times eight are sixty-four, my worthy soul",
must have felt deeply grateful to him for his humanity and
wisdom.' Mr. Pecksniff's genius transforms dullness and dreari-
ness into comfort. He later explains his comic triumph over
circumstances to Martin in relation to his delicate architec-
tural skills: 'For it really is, my dear Martin, it really is in
the finishing touches alone, that great experience, and long
study in these matters tell' (vi). This statement touches the
heart of this novel and suggests exactly what the Americans
lack: the finishing touches of restraint, gentility, courtesy, and
tradition, which allow for beauty, harmonious social existence,
and true identity. Mr. Pecksniff, just slightly overplaying his
artistic role, anticipates another decadent, not only in his

fatness and oiliness, but in his creed. It is the mighty voice of Pecksniff, surely, that we recognize in Wilde's play: 'In matters of grave importance, style, not sincerity, is the vital thing' (*The Importance of Being Earnest*, III. i). It is hypocritical, of course, but it does away with Bowie knives and allows for cucumber sandwiches. Mr. Pecksniff is, through it all, outrageously mendacious and self-serving, but the point is that we are not really asked to search for these labels. In the face of the kind of life he promises, 'liar' or 'thief' seem like vulgar and shrill headlines from the *New York Stabber*.

But Pecksniff does more than allow for a delicate and refined existence; he adds his immense weight to the rejection of nature. As Steven Marcus says, he is 'a monumental parody of the ideal of pastoral innocence',[13] and he does reinforce our negative and hostile laughter in this regard. Much more important, however, is his ability to provoke laughter which protects a pleasure in self-created joy: 'In a word, even his plain black suit, and state of widower, and dangling double eyeglass, all tended to the same purpose, and cried aloud, "Behold the moral Pecksniff!"' (II). Nature is defeated, it is true, but art is more impressively triumphant. He arranges not only his double eyeglass but also his daughters and furniture to create an effect, and he continually constructs brilliant stage-props from the commonest materials. Mr. Pecksniff is the stage-manager of hypocrisy, artful and joyous. After a particularly dazzling renunciation of the principle of personal gain, he and his daughters join in hilarious laughter and kiss each other affectionately in 'a kind of saintly waggishness' (II). If there were anything remotely like this enjoyment surrounding old Martin, perhaps Pecksniff would not steal the show and come so near the novel's normative position, but there is not and so he does.

He continually fights against restrictive morality, and harsh and masochistic inhibitions, protecting the possibility of lively and free pleasure:

'And eggs,' said Mr. Pecksniff, 'even they have their moral. See how they come and go! Every pleasure is transitory. We can't even eat, long. If we indulge in harmless fluids, we get the dropsy;

---

[13] *From Pickwick to Dombey*, p. 253.

if in exciting liquids, we get drunk. What a soothing reflection is that!'

'Don't say *we* get drunk, pa,' urged the eldest Miss Pecksniff.

'When I say we, my dear,' returned her father, 'I mean mankind in general; the human race, considered as a body, and not as individuals. There is nothing personal in morality, my love.' (II)

Our laughter, though probably mainly aggressive at this early point, becomes more and more protective as we sense the importance and profundity of his last statement. As well as giving himself a licence to practise hypocrisy, Mr. Pecksniff is offering us an alternative to the cold, death-like morality of old Martin or the profit-loss morality of Mark Tapley. Pecksniff's later attack, 'if every one were warm and well-fed, we should lose the satisfaction of admiring the fortitude with which certain conditions of men bear cold and hunger' (VIII), is a parody of a morality based on egoistic comparisons and rejects exactly what Mark Tapley will later reject in America. Ironically, Mark is initiated into the wisdom of Pecksniff and is allowed to come back and experience what the old hypocrite has known all along: the supreme importance of comfort. The 'Jolly Tapley' owes a great deal to Pecksniff and his values.

For it is Pecksniff's positive values and not his moral failings that are important. Pecksniff is very much like Falstaff in allowing us to economize contempt, not so much by showing his own awareness of it or by staring us out of countenance as by simply rendering contempt a trivial or irrelevant response to his dazzling display of artistic resiliency. Time and again he is confronted with impossible situations, and time and again he creates not only workable but triumphant responses. Even in his opening interview with old Martin, Pecksniff takes away the old misanthrope's weapons by arguing from the startling assumption of his own selfishness. Given that calculating selfishness, he argues, if he had wanted something from his kinsman he would never have addressed him warmly, knowing that Martin lives in such constant suspicion. All Martin's vicious pessimism, he says, is 'natural, very natural' (III), which is to say it is American and terrible. The old man is left speechless by this amazing artistry, and Pecksniff's victory is complete.

Even more classic is his handling of the wonderful comedy-of-manners situation in which Charity is 'in loud hysterics, Mercy in the utmost disorder, Jonas in the parlour, and Martin Chuzzlewit and his young charge upon the very door-steps' (xx). Though the situation is one of 'total hopelessness', Dickens says, Pecksniff manages another triumph. Popping Jonas and his daughters out of the way and appropriating from his wardrobe department a spade and garden hat, he begins 'warbling a rustic stave' and calmly opens the door:

'Mr. Chuzzlewit! Can I believe my eyes! My dear sir; my good sir! A joyful hour, a happy hour indeed. Pray, my dear sir, walk in. You find me in my garden-dress. You will excuse it, I know. It is an ancient pursuit, gardening. Primitive, my dear sir; for, if I am not mistaken, Adam was the first of our calling. *My* Eve, I grieve to say, is no more, sir; but:' here he pointed to his spade, and shook his head, as if he were not cheerful without an effort: 'but I do a little bit of Adam still.' (xxiv)

So much for the primitive, for old Martin, for grief, and for harsh morality. Mr. Pecksniff cannot be defeated. He even neutralizes the final renunciation by bouncing off the floor for one more witty rejoinder, piously forgiving old Martin and accusing him of mistreating his own gracious hospitality: 'Do I not know that in the silence and the solitude of night, a little voice will whisper in your ear, Mr. Chuzzlewit, "This was not well. This was not well, sir!"' (lii). Mr. Pecksniff has the last word here; he is infinitely resilient and creative, thereby assuring us of the final triumph of the life force.[14] He is, finally, a liverer: 'Mr. Pecksniff, being a father of a more sage and practical class [than stage fathers who die immediately after their daughters' marriages], appeared to think that his immediate business was to live' (xxx). Like Lummy Ned, he knows better than to die; better than that, even, he shares his secret with us.

Pecksniff's contagious life force is also supported by a double, Mr. Montague Tigg, a man so versatile that even his name can go either way. Tigg is an artist nearly as talented as Pecksniff, turning his unspeakable role of financial pimp for

---

[14] I acknowledge that this interpretation disregards Dickens's final mention of Pecksniff as a 'drunken, squalid, begging-letter-writing man' (liv), but I think no apologies are required. For a fuller discussion of Pecksniff's final position, see Michael Steig, '*Martin Chuzzlewit*: Pinch and Pecksniff', *Studies in the Novel*, i (1969), 186–7.

Chevy Slyme into a display of verbal genius: 'You will understand me when I say that I am accredited agent of Chevy
Slyme; that I am the ambassador from the court of Chiv?'
(VII). At one point Dickens even brings these decadent doubles
head-to-head for a brilliant example of an ornate discourse
competition:

'And pray,' asked Mr. Pecksniff, obviously not quite at his ease,
'what may be Mr. Slyme's business here, if I may be permitted to
inquire, who am compelled by a regard for my own character to
disavow all interest in his proceedings?'

'In the first place,' returned the gentleman, 'you will permit me
to say, that I object to that remark, and that I strongly and
indignantly protest against it on behalf of my friend Slyme. In the
next place, you will give me leave to introduce myself. My name,
sir, is Tigg. The name of Montague Tigg will perhaps be familiar
to you, in connexion with the most remarkable events of the
Peninsular War?' (IV)

Dickens passes up the rich comic possibilities of such battles of
the word artists, however, and generally keeps the two separated so that the Pecksniff image may be more widely spread,
and the comedy of restraint and accommodation more continuously supported. The refined comedy is everywhere.

It at first seems odd that the high priestess of this refined
comedy is the most elemental figure in Dickens's works,
Sairey Gamp. Mrs. Gamp exists in the midst of birth and death
and is mistress of the secrets of both. In fact, she is so little
ruffled by these startling events that they are alike pleasant to
her; 'she went to a lying-in or a laying-out with equal zest and
relish' (XIX). The key words are 'zest and relish'; she clearly
creates a world of joy out of pain and death and thereby
establishes the most elemental comedy and the most wonderful
reassurance. She shows us that no evasion is necessary; for she
is surely one of the greatest realists in literature, insisting
always on the immediate and the concrete: 'Ah, dear! When
Gamp was summoned to his long home, and I see him a-lying
in Guy's Hospital with a penny-piece on each eye, and his
wooden leg under his left arm, I thought I should have
fainted away. But I bore up' (XIX).

By providing a constant parody of moralistic depression,
she is a walking rebuke to those who do not bear up: 'One's

first ways is to find sich things a trial to the feelings, and so is one's lasting custom. If it wasn't for the nerve a little sip of liquor give me (I never was able to do more than taste it), I never could go through with what I sometimes has to do. . . . "Mrs. Harris," I says, "leave the bottle on the chimley-piece, and don't ask me to take none, but let me put my lips to it when I am so dispoged" ' (xix). This comment might easily stand as an epigraph for the entire novel. Mrs. Gamp is really a more primal version of Mrs. Todgers, simply a deeper extension of the comic centre of the novel. She wrests out of death a life of tolerance and humour: 'And as to husbands, there's a wooden leg gone likewise home to its account, which in its constancy of walkin' into wine vaults, and never comin' out again 'till fetched by force, was quite as weak as flesh, if not weaker' (xl). Colourful as this sort of autobiographical and moralistic humour is, though, she really prefers to exercise her artistry by moulding her speech into a cleverly contrived self-advertisement and an assertion of a fully realized self. Though purely selfish, she is never mean and, more important, directs our attention and our values far away from such narrow moral verdicts. Mrs. Gamp is selfish only from the perspective of a fool like old Martin; Dickens and his readers saw her as a triumphant expression of selfhood.

But she does more than economize contempt and transform laughter to joy; she is used to support most of the issues in the novel and is amazingly functional, particularly when she is supported by her extension, Mr. Mould the undertaker, who is to Mrs. Gamp what Mr. Tigg is to Pecksniff. At one point they discuss the interesting issue of why death attracts more money than birth. After Mrs. Gamp makes the professional joke that undertakers simply charge more than nurses, Mould suggests the real issue: 'Hearts want binding, and spirits want balming, when people die; not when people are born' (xix). He sees that binding and balming are necessary to cover over our guilt and fear. Here the reference is specifically to Jonas, and it unintentionally connects to the archetypal guilts and fears he raises. Mr. Mould and Mrs. Gamp give 'relief' and spread 'consolation' by healing these deep wounds, and by laughing at these two sordid and grand comic agents we are led to accept their own brand of honesty and accommodation.

Mrs. Gamp has, however, nothing to do with the sort of relief which might come through evasive comfort, and she continually satirizes the barbaric consolation offered to the poor by religion and its basic appeals to envy and vindictiveness: 'Rich folks may ride on camels, but it ain't so easy for 'em to see out of a needle's eye. That is my comfort, and I hope I knows it' (xxv). Mrs. Gamp's comfort, we already know, has nothing to do with such American savagery as this; it is found in cowcumbers, the omnipresent bottle, and, perhaps most of all, in words. There is a real sense in which Mrs. Gamp, in her happy economic flattery, actually defeats time with words, creating a world far beyond the mortal wale she is so cheerfully obsessed with:

'There are some happy creeturs,' Mrs. Gamp observed, 'as time runs back'ards with, and you are one, Mrs. Mould; not that he need do nothing except use you in his most owldacious way for years to come, I'm sure; for young you are and will be. I says to Mrs. Harris,' Mrs. Gamp continued, 'only t'other day; the last Monday evening fortnight as ever dawned upon this Piljian's Projiss of a mortal wale; I says to Mrs. Harris when she says to me, "Years and our trials, Mrs. Gamp, sets marks upon us all."—"Say not the words, Mrs. Harris, if you and me is to be continual friends, for sech is not the case. Mrs. Mould," I says, making so free, I will confess, as use the name,' (she curtseyed here,) ' "is one of them that goes agen the obserwation straight." ' (xxv)

The reference to Bunyan is exceptionally apt here in expressing what Sairey is not; she is the archetypal anti-Puritan, who would drink and laugh even in the Slough of Despond. She hates the prudential life which does nothing more than prepare for death, and she is dedicated to the happiness to be found in society and in the time-defeating perfection of compliments such as 'Young you are and will be.' Like Pecksniff, then, she functions to provide a way out of despair, through imagination, versatile artistry, and resiliency.

Resiliency comes a little more easily to Pecksniff, however. Mrs. Gamp shows several times that she really does have to worry about survival: 'My half a pint of porter fully satisfies; perwisin', Mrs. Harris, that it is brought reg'lar, and draw'd mild. Whether I sicks or monthlies, ma'am, I hope I does my duty, but I am but a poor woman, and I earns my living hard;

therefore I *do* require it, which I makes confession, to be brought reg'lar and draw'd mild' (xxv). This is not only an artful parody of puritanical restrictions in order to justify pure self-indulgence; there is, underneath, something darker, a momentary glimpse of something that goes much deeper than Pecksniffian experience. As she says, 'My earnins is not great, sir, but I will not be impoged upon. Bless the babe, and save the mother, is my mortar, sir; but I makes so free as add to that, Don't try no impogician with the Nuss, for she will not abear it' (xl). This indicates her real battle and her real appeal. She is not only continually advertising herself but, more subtly, exposing her loneliness and weakness in order to ask for tolerance.

In the end, Mrs. Gamp is a lonely and courageous woman; she touches our deepest fears and anxieties and still wins. It is for this reason that she is such a magnificent Freudian humour character. The parallels to Chaucer's Wife of Bath are surely not accidental; both she and Sairey are completely honest with themselves, audacious, outrageous, and, for the briefest moments, pathetic: 'Likeways, a few rounds o' buttered toast, first cuttin' off the crust, in consequence of tender teeth, and not too many of 'em; which Gamp himself, Mrs. Chuzzlewit, at one blow, being in liquor, struck out four, two single and two double, as was took by Mrs. Harris for a keepsake, and is carried in her pocket at this present hour' (xlvi). Mrs. Gamp deserves to have her crusts carefully trimmed; in return, she is willing to give us all the gossip of her personal life, exposing both her weakness and her strength. Like her gat-toothed sister, she has managed the strength and courage to triumph over a harsh life without, somehow, even becoming hardened. They are both, primarily, social creatures, radiating 'extreme good humour and affability' (xlvi).

That she needs a prop for this courage is not surprising, nor is it surprising that such an artistic woman would require more than liquor for support. Mrs. Gamp's defence against loneliness, her 'talisman against all earthly sorrows' (xlix) is, of course, Mrs. Harris, who completes and supports her creator. Therefore, when Betsey Prig utters those vicious words, 'I don't believe there's no sich a person!' (xlix), the entire comic world shudders; for she is threatening Mrs. Gamp with a kind of annihilation. Even John Westlock senses the terrible danger and gives Sairey support more sensitive and kind than anything we would have thought he could manage: 'Never mind. . . . You know it is not true' (XLIX). Mrs. Gamp is, we see, horribly vulnerable. Because she goes so deep into human reality, a great deal more is at stake with her than with Pecksniff, and her triumph is therefore a great deal more expressive. She manages her victory, as we might expect, through words, finally even luxuriating in the possibilities of the role of martyr: ' "But the words she spoke of Mrs. Harris, lambs could not forgive. No, Betsey!" said Mrs. Gamp, in a violent burst of feeling, "nor worms forget!" ' (XLIX). We all sense by now that she can be shaken, perhaps, but never toppled.

Mrs. Gamp, then, gives the most basic support to the reality of the joyful human spirit and its ability to survive. When old Martin denounces her at the end and tells her to take less liquor, our one consolation is the assurance that she will surely ignore this stupidity. She does, in fact, transform his moral rigidity into something so plastic and artful as to repudiate immediately old Martin's code:

> Mrs. Gamp clasped her hands, turned up her eyes until they were quite invisible, threw back her bonnet for the admission of fresh air to her heated brow; and in the act of saying faintly— 'Less liquor!—Sairey Gamp—Bottle on the chimney-piece, and let me put my lips to it, when I am so dispoged!'—fell into one of the walking swoons; in which pitiable state she was conducted forth by Mr. Sweedlepipe, who, between his two patients, the swooning Mrs. Gamp and the revolving Bailey, had enough to do, poor fellow. (LII)

These three go off, we are sure, supporting one another in a real comic world.

And it is appropriate to end with these two fine supporters and companions, Young Bailey and Poll Sweedlepipe, who complete the comic pattern and add to it the necessary frills, the pure exuberance and soaring joy it must have. Young Bailey, first of all, has a gift of parody which is reminiscent of Sam Weller's but is without Sam's cynicism. He is, perhaps, a slightly freer, lighter version of the Artful Dodger, borrowing his predecessor's use of endlessly happy irony: 'I say, . . .

young ladies, there's soup to-morrow. She's a-making it now.
Ain't she a-putting in the water! Oh! not at all neither!' (IX).

Bailey is a 'remarkable boy, whom nothing disconcerted or
put out of his way' (IX), because he has absolute self-confidence
and with this sureness adds solidity to the final society. He is
extremely anti-American (in the best sense), acting 'in defiance
of all natural laws' (XXVI) and is so assured in his actions that
he is even able to convince Poll Sweedlepipe that he does
indeed need a shave, putting entirely to rout the limiting
'evidence of sight and touch' (XXVI). But the most important
testimonial to his greatness comes straight from the comic
seer; Mrs. Gamp immediately connects him with the principle
of worldly accommodation and affectionately recognizes him
as a partner in the artist's war: 'There's nothin' he don't
know; that's my opinion. . . . All the wickedness of the world
is Print to him' (XXVI). Together, he and Poll form a comic
union of youth and age, combating the real mischief of moral
rigidity, despair, and circumstance.

When Bailey is presumed dead, Poll senses that the most
beautiful life-principle has been lost from the comic society,
and his lament is the most poignant and perhaps most central
comment in the novel: 'Their office is a smash; a swindle
altogether. But what's a Life Assurance Office to a Life!
And what a Life Young Bailey's was!' (XLIX). It turns out,
however, that Bailey is not dead; the tension is relieved as he
comes in at the end 'all alive and hearty', resurrected to join
with his 'lovely Sairey' and the 'tender-hearted Poll' (LII).
And what a life that will be!

7 David Copperfield

LAUGHTER AND POINT OF VIEW

'Again, I wonder with a sudden fear whether it
is likely that our good old clergyman can be
wrong, and Mr. and Miss Murdstone right, and
that all the angels in Heaven can be destroying
angels.' (IV)

'THE world would not take another Pickwick from me now',[1]
Dickens wrote as he began work on *David Copperfield*. The
truth was that the world as he saw it would no longer maintain
the beautiful vision of *Pickwick*, and *David Copperfield* was to
be an exploration of the external pressures which severely
limit the possibilities of creating the internal Eden Pickwick
had proposed. The comic society, though rather tenuous in
several other of Dickens's novels, is here pushed to the distant
outskirts of the world and is embodied only in a collection of
the most distinctly misfit: the imprisoned, the alienated, the
mad, and the dying. The comedy of accommodation hinted at
in *Martin Chuzzlewit* is emphatically denied here. Jonas
Chuzzlewit has taken over much of the world, and the presumably invincible Bailey is now shown, in David, to be
terribly vulnerable. There are no resurrections; only the very,
very sad recording of defeats, limitations, compromises. *David
Copperfield* is no comedy, but a farewell to comedy. It is, in
fact, the most reluctant farewell to comedy on record.

For David is extremely sensitive to the comic vision; he is
born in the midst of gentleness and joy, and he never forgets
that atmosphere. It is certainly his misfortune that the Murdstones enter his life, but it might also be said that it is equally

---

[1] To Dudley Costello, *Nonesuch Letters*, ii. 150, 25 Apr. 1849.

unfortunate that he had enjoyed such an idyllic childhood before the murderers arrived. He is thrown directly from a rich and imaginative Eden into a mean and restricted cash-box version of reality. He leaves for Yarmouth from a home which has nothing but joy and returns to a home which has none. No transition and no connection are ever established between these worlds, and as a result it is not possible for him to find in life either complete commercial rigidity or full imaginative joy.[2] Although he later enters pretty fully into the Murdstonean ethic, he never absolutely abandons the perspective of his fragile and pathetic mother: 'What a troublesome world this is, when one has the most right to expect it to be as agreeable as possible!' (IV). David is always haunted by the sense of something missing, 'the old unhappy loss or want of something', and, like his mother, has the comic sense that things ought to be better, that one has a right to Eden. But the comic and commercial, the lovely and the firm, are never brought together, and David becomes something of a representative nineteenth-century man, for whom the realm of the imaginative, the spiritual, and the ideal is divorced from the realm of the pragmatic, the commercial, and the real. And, in place of a resolution, he adopts a very representative operating principle: a self-congratulatory firmness, modified by a compensating sentimentality. One can say, of course, that he comes to terms with his world, but the price he is asked to pay is enormous.

He must, as he says so often, 'discipline' his heart.[3] It has struck many readers that this is a terribly reductive formula for a humane and responsive existence, that it is priggish, escapist, ugly, and narrow, that it denies the values that count—those of Dora, the Micawbers, and Mr. Dick—and that this 'disciplining' is partly a euphemism for desensitizing, falsifying, sentimentalizing. All these charges are true; they

[2] The thematic reading used here is developed further in two articles of mine: 'The Darkness of *David Copperfield*', *DiS*, i (1965), 65–75, and 'The Structure of *David Copperfield*', *DiS*, ii (1966), 74–95.

[3] For a reading of the novel which accepts this phrase as an adequate statement of the theme see Gwendolyn B. Needham, 'The Undisciplined Heart of David Copperfield', *NCF*, ix (1954), 81–107. Several interpretations of the novel which start from an autobiographical premise are also associated with the notion of developing discipline and control; the best is by Edgar Johnson, *Charles Dickens*, ii. 677–90.

are fully supported by the novel. But it is equally true that the novel is never ironic in the sense of attacking its hero; it is never critical of David's decisions. But it is very sad about them. *David Copperfield*'s famous tone of melancholy[4] is created by more than its bittersweet reminiscences; it is perhaps more to the point that these are reminiscences of defeat, of a world now lost. David's course, from joy to a pain so intense that it admits of no escape but only of more or less inadequate evasion, is one which is at the centre of the experience of the last two centuries. Indeed, it helps explain the novel's immense and continuing popularity. The primary means of the attempted escape are also common ones: the important comic values are denied, and trivial antithetical values are loudly proclaimed. David tries very hard to turn his novel into a celebration of prudence, distrust, discipline, rigid and unimaginative conduct, and the commonest sense. It is a cause both of his pain and of the novel's greatness that he has terrible difficulty ever accepting these values; their inadequacy and irrelevance are signalled over and over again.

There are really two major kinds of signals: the commercial values do not help David, and, in addition, they are disproved by the beauty and power of the improvident and the undisciplined in the novel. First of all, David's own proclamations of prudent sanity are outgrowths of a rather complete fantasy life, an unhealthy substitute forced on him first by the Murdstones, later by Steerforth, and even by his aunt, rescue by whom ironically pushes him into the delusory world of the Strongs and the Wickfields and finally into the aura (not the arms) of Agnes, who is a vaporous and shadowy attitude rather than a woman. The firm pragmatism David mouths, in other words, is never solidly realized in his existence and is, therefore, largely a compensation for the fact that he can accept fully neither the comic reality of the Micawbers nor the black reality of the Murdstones. He is thus forced, subtly but insistently, into the position of impotence and delusion where, with Agnes, he believes that 'real love and truth are stronger in the end than any evil or misfortune in

---

[4] The discussion most tactfully and fully responsive to the subtlety of this tone is in George H. Ford's Introduction to the Riverside edition of the novel (Boston, Mass., 1958).

the world' (xxxv). On the next page, David says that Agnes is indeed strong in 'simple love and truth', and it is these *simple* qualities which he thinks will somehow deal with the complexity of Uriah Heep or Murdstone or Steerforth. This blind trust in a vague Providence can, in the end, lead to the awful suspicion that 'all the angels in heaven' really are 'destroying angels' (IV). The same reliance also often renders David passive and impotent. When Rosa Dartle viciously attacks Mr. Peggotty, for example, David can only sputter, 'Oh, shame, Miss Dartle! shame!', and he later listens next door while Rosa verbally flays the newly found Em'ly. It is lucky that there are active comic agents, such as Micawber, Traddles, Mr. Dick, and Mr. Peggotty, around to participate actively and creatively in arranging their lives. These people and others like them also establish a strong value system directly opposed to David's (and Murdstone's) firmness. It is a subversive structure which is constantly in evidence. Micawber, for instance, the architect and most enthusiastic builder of this system, does not simply wander in and out of the plot; he appears strategically and on schedule as apologist and propagandist of his sense of comic community.

Thus, as in many of Dickens's earlier novels, there is a basic dualism, a split between the comic world of the imagination, and the threatening and hostile world of practical or commercial 'reality'. In *David Copperfield* this split receives its most subtle and mature treatment. The novel also makes the most complex use of the rhetorical humour Dickens had mastered. Laughter is used to establish values, themes, and, paradoxically, the atmosphere of melancholy. *David Copperfield* is one of the funniest of Dickens's novels but also one of the saddest; for all of the fun is enlisted on the side of forces which are finally extinguished.

The crucial issue, then, is related to the technical one of point of view: the relation of the novel's established values to those gradually accepted by David and the control of our attitude toward both sets of value. It seems to me essential that we recognize that David is, in many key ways, neither the voice of the author nor the voice of the novel. In any case, there are three clearly distinguished stages in the novel, in which the conditions of David's life, the values suggested, and the rhetoricial techniques all shift radically and significantly:

i. *Childhood joy.* Chapters I–III. This section, though quite short, is extremely important in that it establishes an image of Eden which is never absent from David's mind but which is realized later only in tantalizingly brief snatches. The laughter in this section not only supports the comic values associated with David's happy childhood but, interestingly, encourages us to reject as harmless many of the threats which will later become more precisely defined and much more dangerous.

ii. *Isolation and fear.* Chapters IV–XIII. This black period, the period of Murdstone, Creakle, and the warehouse, functions as a direct contrast to the first and makes impossible for David the openness, spontaneity, and trust necessary for comedy. The humour in this section is similar to that in *Oliver Twist*, acting as rhetoric of attack in order to demand our sympathy for and identification with David. It also begins to build, through Micawber, an alternate system.

These first thirteen chapters are the novel's most crucial ones in determining the character of the hero; they are also among the finest in English literature in forming a complete fusion with their subject and creating a total imaginative identification with the child: George Orwell said that when he first read the early chapters, 'the mental atmosphere . . . was so immediately intelligible to me that I vaguely imagined they had been written *by a child*'.[5] They suggest the absolute necessity of comic joy; they also suggest its impossibility. These chapters urge us to identify with David, to sympathize with a value structure, and then to recognize that the two will likely never come together. The rest of the novel can be seen as the development of these dichotomies and of this rhetoric of frustration and melancholy.

iii. *Fantasy and firmness.* Chapters XIV–LXIV. The remaining chapters explore David's attempts to deal with the hostile world about him, his dependence upon fantasy, and his pathetically ironic drift towards Murdstonean firmness and sentimentality. Laughter here is asked continually to reinforce the comic value system, identify the split between this system

---

[5] *Dickens, Dali and Others*, p. 17. Attacks on the last two-thirds of the book are as common as praise for the first third, expressing, I rather think, the effectiveness of Dickens's rhetoric, not his failure.

and the hero, and try to heal it. It trails off altogether as David moves to Agnes and Micawber moves to Australia. The impossibility of a comic society must finally, and sadly, be admitted.

1

In Chapter III, Em'ly relates her vision of a future filled with wealth, generosity, and gentility, to which David responds, 'This seemed to me to be a very satisfactory, and therefore not at all improbable, picture.' The equation of the satisfactory with the probable only holds in Paradise, but this is where David seems to be for the first years of his life: a 'garden at the back . . . a very preserve of butterflies, as I remember it, with a high fence, and a gate and padlock; where the fruit clusters on the trees, riper and richer than fruit has ever been since, in any other garden' (II). The padlocked gate and high fence are subtle and ominous hints, of course, but they are quiet ones, and we are encouraged to imagine, with the boy, that his Eden is complete. Even crocodiles are imaginatively transformed to vegetables, and all predation and terror are banished from this happy, non-competitive world, supported throughout this section by a basically protective humour. Like other issues in this first section, however, the crocodiles become harder and harder to dismiss as the novel goes on, and this first deceptive allusion begins a chain of more and more significant references to animals, reflecting more and more closely the darker themes of the novel, and causing the initial laughter at the crocodiles to backfire. The transposition of animals and human beings suggests a basic and threatening inhumanity.

As David's position at home changes from that of a petted and much-loved only child to that of a victimized and lonely outcast, he gradually appears, both to himself and to the Murdstones, as less than human. Finally, the Murdstones complete this dehumanization by forcing on him a placard, *Take care of him. He bites.* The irony packed into the word 'care' emphasizes the brutality of this treatment as does David's complete acceptance of his animality. After looking for the dog that is to wear the sign and finding it is for him, he rejects utterly his own humanity and suffers a 'dread' of himself (v).

The transfer from Murdstone to Creakle does not at all change his feelings. The other boys pretend that he is a dog, and he soon looks at Creakle's school as a veritable kennel, twice referring to the boys as 'miserable little dogs' (vii), who bait the poor 'bull or bear', Mr. Mell, and who are harassed by a keeper who whips them, asking at the same time, 'Did it bite, hey ?' (vii).

David begins to adopt this dehumanizing vocabulary himself, not, however, to attack but only to achieve comfort in a fantasy life. No doubt unconsciously but still consistently, he speaks of good people as harmless domestic animals and evil people as dangerous predatory beasts. For example, Mr. Chillip is 'an amiable bird' (i); Barkis is 'like a horse' (iii); David's brother is 'a poor lamb' (ix); Dr. Strong is like 'a blind old horse' (xvi); Traddles says he is a 'fretful porcupine' (xli); Dora's aunts are 'little birds' (xli); Dora is 'a Mouse' (xliv); and Mr. Dick and Aunt Betsey are like 'a shepherd's dog' and 'a sheep' (lii). On the other hand, Mr. Murdstone is like a vicious dog (iii); Miss Murdstone is a 'Dragon' (xxxviii); and together they are 'two snakes' (iv); the Goroo man lives in a 'den' and has the 'claws of a great bird' (xiii); Steerforth (after his seduction of Em'ly) is 'a spotted snake' (li); Mrs. Markleham is 'a crocodile' (xlv); Rosa Dartle is 'lynx-like' and shows the 'fury of a wild cat' (xxix); and Uriah Heep is called at various times a 'serpent' (xlix), a 'red headed animal' (xxv), an 'Ape' (xxxv), an 'eel' (xxxv), a 'red fox' (xxxv), and he and his mother are likened to 'two great bats' (xxxix).

David is tempted to make his life over into a kind of fairytale, but even then a dark fantasy emerges: what chance, for instance, do the lambs and mice have against the serpents, the apes, and the wild cats ? Our first laughter at the crocodiles thus supports a comic and non-predatory world, which is ultimately seen as impossible.

The deceptive humour of the crocodiles is only one example of a technique often repeated in the first section; in many ways the very first chapter functions as a kind of reverse paradigm of the entire novel, bringing up nearly all of what will be the major threats, only to dismiss them in humour. Thus the initial Eden is a complete one, established in delight and fully protected by our laughter. The dark life which comes later reverses the opening of the novel virtually point-by-point, insisting that we recognize explicitly the loss of the beauty and joy of the garden. Even the mild jokes on the heroic birth which open the novel are preludes to the anti-heroism of the inactive protagonist. The first extended joke, however, involves the sale, as a safeguard against drowning, of the caul with which David was born. It is bought by an old lady who never goes near the water and is nevertheless (or therefore) cited as proof of the efficacy of cauls. The joke not only brings up the key symbol of the sea,[6] later to be identified explicitly with death, but also introduces the central thematic issues of prudence, delusion, and egoism, only to ask us to dismiss them in laughter. In much the same way, Miss Betsey flounces on the scene to suggest the comic possibilities of what are later to be seen as very dark tendencies: rigidity and iron composure. Her composure, further, is clearly compensatory, and the jeweller's cotton she stuffs in her ears suggests the forcible exclusion of unpleasant threats. Her vision of young Betsey Trotwood Copperfield, who 'must be well brought up, and well guarded from reposing any foolish confidences where they are not deserved' (I), foreshadows David's later disciplining of his heart; and her blunt, mad attack on Dr. Chillip prefigures all the mad and hostile clashes with which the novel is filled. Of course, all these issues are prefigured in a negative way: they are banished from serious consideration. Their later appearance, therefore, comes with greater force and poignancy.

Even at this early stage there are hints of the fall to come, primarily those connected with 'The Gentleman in the Black Whiskers' who takes David off on a trip and exposes him to the first dehumanizing laughter of exclusion: the boy is 'Bewitching Mrs. Copperfield's incumbrance', and he is forced to propose a toast, 'Confusion to Brooks of Sheffield!' (II). The characters' laughter here does not reflect the expansive, protective humour found elsewhere in this section, but hostile and aggressive impulses. More ominous still is Mr. Murdstone's failure to join in the day's general merriment. David's future

---

[6] For a fuller discussion of this symbol and other image patterns in the novel see my article, 'Symbol and Subversion in *David Copperfield*', *Studies in the Novel*, i (1969), 196–206.

stepfather even goes so far as to reject hostility itself if it has a communal quality. He is a man who resists all notions of community and is therefore the most dangerous to a comic society.

Significantly, David is shipped off to Yarmouth while Murdstone steps in to take his place at home, thus creating the pattern of escape and retreat the boy will be tempted to follow throughout. Peggotty's boat-house is indeed the centre of a potentially comic world, where all darkness is drained off in laughter at Mrs. Gummidge, a wonderful parody of misery. David is an alien in this world, however, and instinctively sees it as a 'retreat', not as a creative and burgeoning garden but as an evasion of a threat he cannot possibly fight. The magnitude of those threats and the impossibility of David's combating them have already been hinted at, then, as early as the third chapter. More important, our laughter has identified the qualities which the novel never ceases to regard as paramount and which are never seen as any less real than the values of Murdstone, just more difficult to establish. Perhaps the key joke in the whole section is a very quiet one: Murdstone, David says, asked for and received a flower from Mrs. Copperfield: 'He said he would never, never, part with it any more; and I thought he must be quite a fool not to know that it would fall to pieces in a day or two' (ii). David's natural realism is thrown against Murdstone's hypocritical sentimentality, forecasting not only the later union of firmness and evasion but establishing the child's perspective as clearly superior. David is completely unsentimental; his early comic world has been to him totally real and has never needed falsification to produce happiness. Our laughter is enlisted in support of the child and his values, and in opposition to the hideous Murdstone. Even after we recognize that Murdstone is not dismissable and that David's comic perspective is lost, the humour continually forces us to remember that for a brief time there was this lovely world.

2

But not for long; the Murdstones move in and establish a reign not only of physical cruelty but also of the gloomiest kind of self-mastery based on self-distrust: 'Control yourself, always control yourself!' (III). The 'firmness' on which they take their doctrinal stand is rooted in a vicious Calvinism, which distrusts spontaneity, natural affection, the basic goodness of undisciplined and unrestrained man, in short, the very bases of comedy; and the real conflict in the novel is between their 'control' and Micawber's wild self-indulgence, between cash-boxes and steaming punch. At this point, however, Murdstone's values are in complete control, and our laughter is often used much as it was in *Oliver Twist*, to identify the cruelty in these values, to expose the shadow of cruelty in ourselves, and to push us closer to the alienated child. The rhetoric in this section, then, is a rhetoric of attack, tempting us to be momentarily amused at what turn out to be dangerous threats, at Miss Murdstone's being a 'metallic lady altogether' who snaps, 'Generally speaking . . . I don't like boys. How d'ye do, boy?' (IV), or at her brother's elaborate puzzles involving double-Gloucester cheeses. We soon notice, though, that Miss Murdstone's dehumanizing, somewhat mad, treatment of David is really an accurate sampling of later confrontations, and Mr. Murdstone's puzzle, at which 'Miss Murdstone [is] secretly overjoyed', is only a type of the malicious wit common to all the many sadists in the novel. The hostility latent in this wit—and in any laughter it may have aroused— is unmistakably exposed in the horrible beating David receives for failing with the puzzle. Even worse than the beating, however, is the alienation of the boy from love and comfort, the door Murdstone symbolically throws up between David and his mother and nurse. The humour connected with the Murdstones, then, is meant finally to draw us closer to David and to his pain, confusion, and isolation.

It also enables us to understand better why he turns to romantic tales and eighteenth-century novels for 'my only and my constant comfort'. But instead of building an expansive and healthy imaginative life as it might this single comfort tends to become a narcotic, sustaining but dangerous. David still sees himself 'sitting on my bed, reading as if for life' (IV). It is, literally, for *life*. He begins here the fantasy role which never leaves him, although it does change form: from Steerforth and the story-telling in the dark, to the vague second childhood at Dover, to the tragically disrupted comic life with Dora, and finally to the less-than-substantial Agnes. Murdstone really gives David two choices: firmness or escape. He finally chooses to try for a combination, but now he only wants to escape. The awful fact is that these terrifying and impossible choices are being forced on a boy far too young to make them by himself. But he is completely alone; the good people are all on the other side of the locked door.

It is an interesting secondary function of the humour in this section to trivialize many of these good people or eliminate them from consideration. Mr. Barkis the carrier, for instance, is introduced as one of the most freakishly inhuman of Dickens's comic grotesques: 'I offered him a cake as a mark of attention, which he ate at one gulp, exactly like an elephant, and which made no more impression on his big face than it would have done on an elephant's' (v). This impassive man is a kind of joke on the absence of response and the non-humanity of the supposedly human. His affections are somehow connected to his gastric juices, and he decides then and there to make a play for the maker of those cakes, even though he has some considerable trouble getting her name straight. His magnificent phrase, 'Barkis is willin''', seems a joke on the failure of commitment, a perfect image of a kind of absorbent stomach-creature that gulps everything into itself and renders human notions of intelligence and emotion ludicrous. He appears, in other words, as an apparent 'relief' figure to drain our apprehensions and to release some of the intensity created by David's plight. Barkis seems to be a comic Murdstone, no more human but not in the least threatening.

As it happens, though, Barkis truly is willin', and this curiously touching phrase begins really to separate him from Murdstone's values and to associate itself with openness and friendliness, with a limited but genuine comic expansiveness: 'I'm a friend of your'n. You made it all right, first. It's all right' (x). In the midst of hostility, meanness, and cruelty, this declaration is terribly important. It belies altogether the basis of any laughter at this 'great stuffed figure' (x). What happens here is that we are forced to recognize how unlikely and how rare are the manifestations of friendship in this black world, and how very precious are those who are willin'. We are also asked to take a much closer look at Barkis, and when we do, we see that this supposed comic grotesque is a very functional character indeed. After marrying Peggotty, he becomes obsessed not so much with money as with the prudent resolve to protect that money. His crazy box stands as a parody indictment not only of Murdstone's value system, but, ironically, of David's as well. He pokes at his box and announces:

'Old clothes.'
'Oh!' said I.
'I wish it was Money, sir,' said Mr. Barkis.
'I wish it was, indeed,' said I.
'But it AIN'T,' said Mr. Barkis, opening both his eyes as wide as he possibly could. (XXI)

Significantly, however, he continues, 'more gently': 'She's the usefullest and best of women, C. P. Barkis. All the praise that any one can give to C. P. Barkis she deserves, and more! My dear, you'll get a dinner to-day, for company; something good to eat and drink, will you?' (XXI). He is an insanely disjointed man, a daffy mixture of the generous and the 'near', and we see him, finally, as a heightened and dramatic symbol of the open and willing heart corrupted by the ossifying pressures of prudence, as a signal of the potential beauty of man but also of the great dangers of the world. His death encapsulates his functional humour. Flopped over on his box, literally protecting it with his life, he manages, just at the end, to show the inner strength of his comic and generous impulses:

'C. P. Barkis,' he cried faintly. 'No better woman anywhere!'
'Look! Here's Master Davy!' said Peggotty. For he now opened his eyes.
I was on the point of asking him if he knew me, when he tried to stretch out his arm, and said to me, distinctly, with a pleasant smile:
'Barkis is willin'!'
And, it being low water, he went out with the tide. (XXX)

This death is one of the most costly in the novel; it removes one of David's willing friends. The comic carrier, initially too weak and too far away really to help the boy, has become, by the time of his death, a comic indictment of the firmness David is moving towards. Our laughter at Barkis has helped to increase our sense of the importance of joy to David and to determine later how far he is moving away from the values of the carrier. Mr. Barkis has, in his way, presented a form of hope to David, but the form has been too distorted for the boy to recognize it, and the alternate pressures have been far too strong.

The more common function of our laughter in this section, in fact, is to insist on the strength of the camp of the firm and the hostile, and the more usual jokes are of the deceptive kind exemplified by the waiter whom David meets on his way to Creakle's school. The waiter seems at first to be very much like Sam Weller, hearty, open, and witty. He 'very affably' calls to David, using Sam's own terms, 'Now, six-foot! come on!' Even the stories he devises to cheat David of his food are so resourceful and wild with such apparently undirected hostility that we are very likely to laugh: A gentleman 'in breeches and gaiters, broad-brimmed hat, grey coat, speckled choker', he says, 'came in here . . . ordered a glass of this ale— *would* order it—I told him not—drank it, and fell dead. It was too old for him. It oughtn't to be drawn; that's the fact' (v). He does, indeed, seem not only witty but, as David says, 'so very friendly and companionable' that it comes as a shock that he is *only* a cheat, malicious and cruel. When David tells him he is going to school 'near London', the waiter invents a story of a boy at the same school, just David's age, whose ribs were broken 'with whopping'. He then insists on taking one of David's shillings as a tip and joins with the crowd in laughing at the boy's huge appetite. The apparent friendliness has been a guise, and the wit has been hostile and self-serving, isolating and hurting the helpless child. Dickens then rubs our noses in the consequences of this reversal, insisting over and over in the next few pages on David's loneliness ('more solitary than Robinson Crusoe'), his feeling of abandonment (no one calls for him at the booking-office, and he thinks for a time that 'Murdstone had devised this plan to get rid of me'), and his dehumanization (the clerk 'presently slanted me off the scale, and pushed me over to him, as if I were weighed, bought, delivered, and paid for').

He then moves to Creakle's school, where the deceptive

humour is continued. We are invited to share in a kind of Hobbesian laughter at the man with no voice at all, but it is soon apparent that Creakle is no weakling to be dismissed. He is, rather, a continuation of Mr. Murdstone: 'I am a determined character. . . . That's what I am. I do my duty. That's what I do' (VI). 'Duty', we begin to understand, is a convenient euphemism which many characters—Murdstone, Creakle, Aunt Betsey, Mrs. Steerforth, Mr. Wickfield, Agnes, and later even David—use to cover sadism, sexual perversion, weakness, or incapacity. The world at Creakle's, then, is just as dark as the one at home, and David again turns to the only escape at hand, this time made more sinister in the figure of Steerforth, who begins by simply continuing the role of the waiter, cheating the boy of his money. He then forces David to retell his old stories in the dark, which even the young boy admits 'may not have been very profitable to me' since it encouraged all 'that was romantic and dreamy' (VII) in him. Steerforth does nothing to protect David from Creakle's mistreatment and, as a fantasy figure for the younger boy, is dangerous both to him and to others. The older boy symbolically joins hands with Creakle in expelling the one kindly figure, Mr. Mell, suggesting, in relation to David, the deadly union of determination with fantasy. More important, Steerforth does not really deflect the training in firmness away from David; he only encourages the dangerous tendencies to fantasy escape.

So David really has no choice. The forces of blackness close in around him and eventually make all happiness alien to him, isolating him from other men and implying that, in the face of his situation and the ugly world it suggests, all laughter is really self-centred and reprehensible. This attack on laughter is most pointedly illustrated by the undertaker, Mr. Omer, and his family. Mr. Omer is a character out of *Martin Chuzzlewit*, a relative of Mr. Mould's, who tries to build joy out of darkness, operating his business rather as if it were a confectioner's shop. In the environment of *David Copperfield*, however, such efforts seem callous, perhaps hideous. The ability to whistle to the happy rat-tat-tat of the hammer on the coffin is no longer applauded. David is met by Omer on his way home from school at the time of his mother's death. The

undertaker takes David to his shop to measure him for mourning clothes and to check up on the progress of Mrs. Copperfield's coffin and the love-making of his daughter and his
partner Joram. For a considerable space, the narrative focus
is removed from David, and we are allowed to bask in the
comic glow:

> 'Father!' said Minnie, playfully. 'What a porpoise you do
> grow!'
> 'Well, I don't know how it is, my dear,' he replied, considering
> about it. 'I *am* rather so.'
> 'You are such a comfortable man, you see,' said Minnie. 'You
> take things so easy.'
> 'No use taking 'em otherwise, my dear,' said Mr. Omer.
> 'No, indeed,' returned his daughter. 'We are all pretty gay here,
> thank Heaven! Ain't we, father?' (IX)

It sounds for a moment very much like a voice from Mrs.
Todgers's. Soon, however, ugly hints intrude. 'I knew your
father before you', Mr. Omer says in his continually amiable
way, but then he continues, 'He lays in five and twen–ty foot
of ground, if he lays in a fraction. . . . It was either his request
or her direction, I forget which.' The fact that this is said
'pleasantly' makes it all the more ghastly. The joy begins to be
as excluding and alienating to David as Murdstone's cruelty,
and Dickens begins to insist more openly on the cruelty of any
laughter. The three bustle David into a chaise and boisterously
roll off, with Mr. Omer chuckling while Joram steals kisses
from Minnie. Joram 'didn't appear to mind me at all', David
says, and the humour has tempted us to be equally neglectful
of the outcast and orphaned boy. He admits finally that he is
'afraid of them'. 'I do not think I have ever experienced so
strange a feeling in my life', he says, adding that he felt 'as if
I were cast among creatures with whom I had no community
of nature'. Anyone who can laugh, then, is a 'creature', unfeeling and awful. The image is one of an inverted Mrs.
Jarley's or Mrs. Todgers's: the joy creates discomfort and
excludes those who need it most. Ultimately it reinforces the
pessimistic vision at the heart of the novel that sees a world
in which the comic life is open only to a very few—and not at
all to the hero.

It has been closed for him by the Murdstones, who have so

mangled his youth that a part of his psychic life is now frozen.
He sees all joy as past, as contained in the brief time before
firmness entered his life: 'From the moment of my knowing of
the death of my mother, the idea of her as she had been of late
had vanished from me. I remembered her, from that instant,
only as the young mother of my earliest impressions, who had
been used to wind her bright curls round and round her finger,
and to dance with me at twilight in the parlour. . . . The
mother who lay in the grave, was the mother of my infancy;
the little creature in her arms [David's dead brother], was
myself, as I had once been, hushed for ever on her bosom' (ix).
By the time the Murdstones send him out for his 'fight with
the world' in the warehouse, he has already lost the chance for
what he most wants and needs: the sort of life presented so
brilliantly and so completely by the enemies of Murdstone and
Grinby, cash-boxes, and firmness—Mr. and Mrs. Micawber.
This great pair function to express periodically throughout the
novel the beauty and importance of comic existence; because
they do this so very well, they are the major cause of the
book's final sadness. They remind us of nothing so much as of
the life that has been stolen from David.

   A. O. J. Cockshut has made the perceptive comment that
it is never possible to give proportionate space to the Micawbers, that one, very literally, cannot say nearly enough.[7] The
tendency (as is evident here) is to talk about analysing them
rather than doing it. This is partly because Mr. Micawber is
perhaps the most organically complete of comic characters;
even his clothes (particularly the ornamental eye-glass and
the 'imposing shirt-collar') are a part of his perfectly harmoniz-
ing style, suggesting the wonderful comic notion that man has
the power to create himself. The difficulty, however, comes
also from the enormously rich and various functional role

   [7] *The Imagination*, p. 114. Others, like G. K. Chesterton, assert that it is
impossible really to say anything at all about him: 'All the critics of Dickens,
when all is said and done, have only walked round and round Micawber wondering what they should say. I am myself at this moment walking round and round
Micawber wondering what I shall say. And I have not found out yet' (*Appreciations and Criticisms*, p. 139). Among the best discussions are those by
Bernard Schilling, *The Comic Spirit* (Detroit, Mich., 1965), pp. 98–144, by J. B.
Priestley in *The English Comic Characters* (London, 1925), and by William
Oddie, 'Mr. Micawber and the Redefinition of Experience', *Dickensian*, lxiii
(1967), 100–10.

Mr. and Mrs. Micawber play. They climax a great line of
Dickens's comic characters and carry on the role of Sam
Weller as tutor and seer, Dick Swiveller as parodist, Sairey
Gamp as imaginative creator. They not only combine these
parts but are truly greater than their sum. And in the novel
they fail. All their kindness, their creative genius, their courage,
and their infinite resiliency cannot keep David from the trap
of the sentimental and the firm. But they do create a system
of values which, with the help of characters like Mr. Dick,
Peggotty, Barkis, and Miss Mowcher, and with the great
support of our laughter, maintains one-half of the conflict
in the novel: the approved but impossible life of the imagination.

It is often and truly said that Micawber builds worlds of
delight out of words, but he finds joy not only in words but in
arranging his unnecessary quizzing-glasses, not only in writing
letters but in creating a 'library' out of a few books and a dres-
sing table. Even more significant, his presence even distinguishes his house, making it 'unlike all the other houses in the
street—though they were all built on one monotonous pattern'
(xxvii). He is, above all, ornamental, which is to say, a walking attack on prudence and practicality. He and his wife live
deeply in the commercial world only to make fun of it and
turn potential sources of anxiety into rituals of cheer, motives
for exquisite melodrama, and, most important, into exaggerated depths from which to rebound into joyous celebrations:
'I saw her lying (of course with a twin) under the grate in
a swoon, with her hair all torn about her face; but I never
knew her more cheerful than she was, that very same night,
over a veal-cutlet before the kitchen fire, telling me stories
about her papa and mama, and the company they used to
keep' (xi). The principle seems totally to be one of resilience:
the more the Micawbers are pushed downward the higher they
spring back. In fact, much of the deepest-rooted humour of
the Micawbers is based on this paradoxically mechanical elasticity, the sense that they do rebound automatically, rather like
a rubber ball.

But beyond this there is the deep power of their conscious
and courageous fight against an almost overwhelmingly dark
and threatening social system. They act out a burlesque of

their troubles, distancing their pain, of course, but also humanizing the almost inhuman. All disasters are welcomed as proof of their own exceptional humanity, giving rise to scenes of potential grand suicide, tragic sacrifice, and magnificent decisions of alliance: ' "Mr. Micawber has his faults. I do not deny that he is improvident. I do not deny that he has kept me in the dark as to his resources and his liabilities, both," she went on, looking at the wall; "but I will never desert Mr. Micawber!" ' (xii). A tradesman's bill is a small price to pay for the chance to play Cleopatra every day or two. And behind the ring of the phrases and the echo of a million melodramas is the continual thrill of the assertive, unrestrained, and glamorized ego of comedy: 'All I have to say on that score is, that the cloud has passed from the dreary scene, and the God of Day is once more high upon the mountain tops. On Monday next, on the arrival of the four o'clock afternoon coach at Canterbury, my foot will be on my native heath—my name, Micawber!' (xxxvi). By welcoming these small disasters from the commercial society and creatively transforming them, the Micawbers avoid the really greatest threats of that society: dehumanization and despair. They have found the great and complex secret of joy in a commercial world.

This secret is very difficult to decipher fully, but at least a few parts of it are clear. First, the Micawbers have absolutely renounced the system and (except for the brief lapse with Uriah Heep) make no concessions in their war against it. Dickens here separates completely the notion of the good heart from the notion of commercial success and thereby creates a greater Pickwick, incidentally solving the problem of what Mr. Pickwick did 'in the city' all those years. Micawber is a coalescence of the notions embodied in Mr. Pickwick and Sam and a clear renunciation of the Brownlow–Cheeryble concept. Second, they carry on the great subversive tradition of attacking the system by parody. Mr. Micawber is active here, particularly in his recurrent burlesque of the alert and ruthless businessman waiting to spring on the first opportunity, but the major burden is carried by his wife, whose 'business habits' and 'prudent suggestions' (xxxvi) he has learned to depend on. 'My disposition', she says, 'is eminently

practical' (LVII), and she proves it over and over again with
rigorous analyses which ought to make all corporate flunkies,
government commissions, and faculty advisory groups blush:
'"We came," repeated Mrs. Micawber, "and saw the Medway.
My opinion of the coal trade on that river is, that it may
require talent, but that it certainly requires capital. Talent,
Mr. Micawber has; capital, Mr. Micawber has not. We saw,
I think, the greater part of the Medway, and that is my
individual conclusion"' (XVII).

But the Micawbers really spend comparatively little time
on such negative parody functions. They are probably the
most open and expansive of Dickens's comic characters,
accepting with resounding confidence in themselves and their
powers the whole range of the shabbiest existence and refusing
any sort of escape or falsification. They suggest not only that
life is bearable but that it can be wonderful: 'Experientia does
it—as papa used to say' (XI). *Experientia* certainly does it for
the Micawbers at any rate; it provides them with a chance to
dedicate their lives to joy. There is no image so firmly associated with them as that of Mr. Micawber working happily in
the midst of lemon-peel and sugar, rum, and steaming water,
making a punch instead of a fortune and, as David says,
enjoying himself more than any man he ever saw. '"But
punch, my dear Copperfield," said Mr. Micawber, tasting it,
"like time and tide, waits for no man"' (XXVIII). The subversive substitution is clear; Micawber transforms the clichés of
the Murdstone economy into justifications for parties. The
Micawbers are grandly anti-Malthusian, blissfully arguing that
'in our children we [live] again, and that, under the pressure
of pecuniary difficulties, any accession to their number [is]
doubly welcome' (XXVIII). Whatever doubts Mrs. Micawber's
prudent family have on this point simply provide Mr. Micawber
with an opportunity for splendid Byronic denunciations of
that socially prominent group. The mean, niggardly, frightened
spirit of order and balance was never more blatantly flouted
than by Mrs. Micawber's always-busy 'Founts' or, for that
matter, by Mr. Micawber's epistolary style, which takes arms
specifically against the previous century's leading proponent
of the organized and the clear-headed: 'I am about to establish myself in one of the provincial towns of our favoured

island (where the society may be described as a happy ad-
mixture of the agricultural and the clerical). . . . Our ashes, at
a future period, will probably be found commingled in the
cemetery attached to a venerable pile, for which the spot to
which I refer has acquired a reputation, shall I say from China
to Peru ?' (xxxvi).

Finally, the Micawbers are powerful because they love.[8] They
are not only unembarrassed in their show of warmth to one
another, but also to others, particularly David. This warmth
is manifested most openly in the touching scene where, in
leaving London, Mrs. Micawber looked down from the coach,
saw how small David really was (she had been in the friendly
habit of thinking of him as an equal), called him up on the
coach, 'and put her arm round my neck, and gave me just
such a kiss as she might have given to her own boy' (xii).
Every speech of Mr. Micawber's asserts, though more indirectly, the same warm response. He comes into the blacking
warehouse and begins his magnificent oratory to David, inter-
rupting it with an inevitable 'in short'. As inevitable as the
self-parodying 'in short', however, is its accompanying manner:
'with a smile and in a burst of confidence', with an offer, in
other words, of intimacy and connection. In the midst of the
mad hostility of cheating waiters, vicious tinkers, and raving
Goroo men, Micawber's undefensive warmth is strangely high-
lighted. Even his endless stream of letters suggests his fight
against the silence and systematic alienation of Murdstone's
system. The Micawbers are great, finally, because they offer,
even in the face of this threat, not mutual protection but
mutual fun. Their comic society is undefensive and open.
'Friend of my youth, the companion of my earlier days'
Micawber loves later to call David, associating himself not
only with the friendly Mr. Barkis but also, and more specifically, with Falstaff's great and equally anti-prudent battle-cry,
'They hate us youth'. Indeed they do, and there are few like
Micawber who can not only live with hatred but transform
it for his family and for others, even briefly for David, into
happiness.

But it is too late for David fully to accept the secret of

[8] This point is persuasively made by Douglas Bush, 'A Note on Dickens'
Humor', *From Jane Austen to Joseph Conrad*, p. 88.

existence offered him by the Micawbers. All trust, openness, and hope for joy have been either extinguished or perverted in him. In addition, the Micawbers are forced to leave London, taking with them the answer both necessary and unavailable to David. Left alone and without consolation of any sort, David runs away to Dover and to his Aunt Betsey. His flight through the countryside, significantly, is like a tour through the Chamber of Horrors: the donkey-driver, the tinker, the Goroo man, all fly out and terrify him with their mad, uncaused hostility. Even in Dover, no one will tell him where his aunt lives, simply because he is asking. The shopkeepers there, with their immovable coldness, are paradigmatic of the nightmare world, alternately chasing and rejecting the boy: 'not liking my appearance, [they] generally replied, without hearing what I had to say, that they had got nothing for me' (XIII). They surely do not, but David has nowhere else to go.

Aunt Betsey is a gentle and kindly person, but she does not have Mr. Micawber's secret. Instead of highly developed elasticity, she has a compensatory firmness; she lacks optimism, creative power, and imaginative hope. She and Mr. Dick are themselves partly on the run, she from her husband, Mr. Dick from the relatives who threaten to lock him up. In the artificial firmness which resolutely attacks not real enemies but donkeys, and in the mad, gentle man who holds his head like 'one of Mr. Creakle's boys after a beating' (XIII), might be seen a combined image of what David finally becomes. This retreat at Dover allows David to view his life 'like one in a dream' (xv), and the repeated references to new beginnings carry an ironic sense. He moves into an artificial and very fragile haven, where Aunt Betsey counsels him to be firm, where Agnes takes Steerforth's place as reading partner, and where, in 'the soft light of the coloured windows in the church' (xvi), Uriah Heep and Jack Maldon can be dismissed in fantasy.

Aunt Betsey and Mr. Dick do try very hard, but in the end this collection of outcasts is too defensive to help the boy much, and the humour connected with them is deceptive. Nowhere is this deception more crucial than in Aunt Betsey's encounter with the Murdstones. The refinement and reserve of much of this scene seem to induce the kind of 'laughter of the mind' advocated by George Meredith.[9] Meredith sees the true Comic Spirit as 'a most subtle delicacy' (p. 3) employed in a truly cultivated way. Its function is calmly to expose Folly, to pour the light of common sense on the overblown, the disproportionate, and the self-important (p. 48). Miss Betsey's comments to the pompous Jane Murdstone provide just this kind of deflation:

> 'I so far agree with what Miss Trotwood has remarked,' observed Miss Murdstone, bridling, 'that I consider our lamented Clara to have been, in all essential respects, a mere child.'
> 'It is a comfort to you and me, ma'am,' said my aunt, 'who are getting on in life, and are not likely to be made unhappy by our personal attractions, that nobody can say the same of us.' (XIV)

Jane Murdstone is, at the end of the interview, left sputtering and angry, and her exposure seems complete. But what of the silent Mr. Murdstone? Meredith says the Comic Spirit pursues Folly to the end, 'never fretting, never tiring, sure of having her' (p. 33). But here there are strong indications that the enemy is not really overcome.

Far from being defeated, in fact, Jane Murdstone does reappear as Dora Spenlow's companion to harass David, and Mr. Murdstone is left to pursue his wicked ways, unencumbered by a child. Aunt Betsey's 'victory' has thus produced a disturbingly ironic result: Murdstone is relieved of a boy whom he had already thwarted to his satisfaction and who could now be nothing but a hindrance. He is left free to extend his malevolence to other weak mothers and helpless boys (see LIX). The originally benign scene thus becomes, by the end of the novel, a very dark one. The Comic Spirit which had seemed so effective is rendered powerless, and the civilized laughter is shown to be incomplete and inadequate. The final suggestion is that this kind of Murdstonean power is not available to the good, and in this light Agnes Wickfield's simple trust is misplaced and her position very dangerous. There are, it seems, two honourable positions open: the imaginative and happy subversive warfare of the Micawbers or a retreat from the battle. One either renounces the terms of the fight or is beaten.

---

[9] 'An Essay on Comedy', *Comedy*, pp. 3–57.

3

The basic pattern of the novel, then, has been established. Only the outcasts are loyal and open to David; those in power are rigid and hostile. The boy then moves, in the rest of the novel, to look for an opening that is never there for long. Except for the comic joy of the outcasts, not available to him anyhow, he finds only the happy but dangerously flabby second childhood of the Wickfields or the hard, successful commercialism of Murdstone. The rest of his life can be seen as an attempt to combine the last two. Much of our laughter functions in this last section to remind us of the Eden David has lost, to show that the black world makes it impossible for him, and to suggest how limited his responses are.

He moves through a tragic marriage to the acceptance of simple notions of a disciplined heart, to a final union which seems to resolve none of the basic problems. He joins the firmly successful and the blurring escapists, the Agnes who is not only unable to stop Uriah Heep's subtle attacks on the Wickfield firm but who actually urges her father to enter into a partnership with Heep because she felt 'it was necessary for Papa's peace' (xxv). Peace indeed! It is significant that those who are opposed to Murdstone are equally opposed to this sort of peace, and, when they are shipped off to Australia at the end, it is suggested, perhaps, that they are irrelevant to the mature David but more likely that they are incompatible with nineteenth-century England. The letters from Micawber keep coming, though, to remind us of what is missing, and the humour is used more and more to define a lost world and to point towards the ironic position David moves close to: a gentler version of Murdstone, who likewise doesn't know that the flowers will wither in a day or so. Two instances of this sad and deceptive humour are especially prominent: the marriage to Dora and Micawber's exposure of Heep.

The Micawbers have all along been conducting a kind of triumphal Progress, parodying commerce and business in all the provinces of England and promoting their own brand of comic society. They function rhetorically to redefine all the important values and to measure David's increasing distance from them, as he stuffily warns Traddles against his friends (xxviii) and finally calls Micawber 'slippery' (xxxvi). These

judgements, echoed, incidentally, in George Orwell's perverse
conclusion that Micawber is nothing but a 'cadging scoundrel',[10]
simply indicate two increasingly incompatible systems. Micawber's borrowing, as W. H. Auden points out in reference to
another great borrower, Falstaff, is an important sign of
community,[11] establishing a necessary interdependence. In
return for money, Micawber gives language, punch, and happiness; these seem insufficient returns only to a perspective
which takes money seriously, as David certainly does and as
Micawber certainly does not. But Micawber does take joy
seriously, and his positive function becomes more emphatic,
moving to a climax in the wonderful denunciation and exposure of Uriah Heep (LII).

That Micawber ever gets into the clutches of Uriah suggests,
I suppose, the extreme power of commercial forces which can
enmesh, even briefly, such a clear-sighted enemy. There is
even the darker suggestion that Micawber must engage himself
for a time in their camp in order to acquire weapons, that only
those who are in some way corrupted can fight at all. But there
is, concurrently, the sense that Mr. Micawber is arranging for
himself a new part to play, with new lines, new poses, new out-
fits, and new opportunities for exercising his wild imagination
in mock forecasts of doom: 'For anything that I can perceive
to the contrary, it is still probable that my children may be
reduced to seek a livelihood by personal contortion, while Mrs.
Micawber abets their unnatural feats by playing the barrel-
organ' (XLIX). Notice no factories or warehouses appear here;
even his misery is fun. Finally, the general situation simply
allows an extremely apt and aesthetically satisfying movement
from the mysterious, secretive, and reserved back to the open,
confident, and trusting. Mr. Micawber's organic unity is disrupted—'his very eye-glass seemed to hang less easily, and his
shirt-collar . . . rather drooped' (XLIX)—and must be put right.

Equally significant is the nature of the villain. Uriah
Heep is really a kind of Alfred Jingle, resilient, courageous,
witty, and very bitter. He is the product of a hypocritical

[10] *Dickens, Dali and Others*, p. 67. Douglas Bush rightly remarks that 'one
might as well call Jack the Giant-Killer a homicidal maniac' ('A Note on
Dickens' Humor', *From Jane Austen to Joseph Conrad*, p. 90).
[11] 'Notes on the Comic', *Thought*, xxvii (1952), 70.

benevolence which produced charity schools that taught both humility and firm assertiveness, and his response to David's simple reflections is both cutting and valid:

'It may be [David said] profitable to you to reflect, in future, that there never were greed and cunning in the world yet, that did not do too much, and over-reach themselves. It is as certain as death.'

'Or as certain as they used to teach at school (the same school where I picked up so much umbleness), from nine o'clock to eleven, that labour was a curse; and from eleven o'clock to one, that it was a blessing and a cheerfulness, and a dignity, and I don't know what all, eh?' said he with a sneer. 'You preach, about as consistent as they did.'

He is right in attacking the soft-headed, the sentimental, and the insensitive realism that measures things against death and smugly assumes that anyone will choose the most *profitable* course. To this rightness he adds a surprising wit, suggesting both intelligence and, since he is so clearly cornered, real courage:

'You know what *I* want?' said my aunt.
'A strait-waistcoat,' said he.

But Uriah is vindictive. He is the apotheosis of the hurt and vengeful figure, part victim and part villain, who had appeared earlier as Jingle, Fagin, Sim, and Quilp. Micawber's victory is not over evil—only David views the fight in such narrow terms—but over the sensitivity that is pushed into violence and bitterness. Micawber affirms not goodness but comic optimism.

And he does so with the richness and rounded, complete perfection that characterizes all his actions. The exposure is, first of all, wonderfully arranged by Micawber, who uses his considerable talents as a stage-director to get every effect right. He uses, of course, a letter as the means of the exposure, not because it is in any sense necessary (Micawber is always an enemy of the necessary) but because it is a fitting medium of the dramatic and the openly and articulately communicative. He provides himself with a simple but brilliantly appropriate prop, a ruler. He transforms this instrument of precision and order first to a kind of wand used to point the grandest phrases and provide the most emphatic flourishes

and then to a mock duelling weapon to keep Uriah at bay. It
is all very much like an extremely imaginative child playing
in an office, and it carries, on a much higher level, the same
implicit criticism of the office. Micawber also masquerades as
a firm and aggressively insistent champion of the right—he is
called 'immovable'—and functions thereby as an indirect
lesson to all the truly firm that it is comic flexibility that
really is *profitable*.

The unique greatness of his triumph lies in its absolute lack
of real personal vengeance. All his energy is directed toward
gaiety, toward the relish that he has and that he gives to
others in the endless fun available in words: 'In an accumula-
tion of Ignominy, Want, Despair, and Madness, I entered the
office—or, as our lively neighbour the Gaul would term it, the
Bureau—of the Firm, nominally conducted under the appella-
tion of Wickfield and—HEEP, but, in reality, wielded by—
HEEP alone.' He is obviously spurred on not so much by the
desire to set things right as by the exquisite possibilities in
the name Heep. His letter is really a collection of 'triumphant
flourishes', and the real victory is one of language. As he
reaches the end of his charges, he is unable to hold on to the
logical and orderly listing he had been straining to follow and
he breaks out, just at the end, in a final phrase that destroys
the logic but gives a mad and wonderful hint of the joy beyond
logic: 'All this I undertake to show. Probably much more!'
He completes the act decorously by folding up his letter and
handing it 'with a bow to my aunt, as something she might
like to keep'. The letter, we see, is what counts—not Heep.
The scene ends with Micawber back in the arms of his wife,
re-forming the comic unit and, like the Phoenix he is always
invoking, starting off again on a life of improvidence, re-
freshed and confident: ' "Now, welcome poverty!" cried Mr.
Micawber, shedding tears. "Welcome misery, welcome house-
lessness, welcome hunger, rags, tempest, and beggary! Mutual
confidence will sustain us to the end!" '

Ultimately, though, the full context of the novel does not
absorb the comic triumph. Even in the midst of the exposure
scene, it is suggested that the narrator misunderstands the
important nature of the conflict. He can even make fun of
Micawber: 'And as individuals get into trouble by making too

great a show of liveries, or as slaves when they are too numerous rise against their masters, so I think I could mention a nation that has got into many great difficulties, and will get into many greater, from maintaining too large a retinue of words.' This comes at the end of a paragraph wherein David parades his fagged-out worldly knowledge, tiredly minimizing the power of Micawber and missing the real point completely. Micawber has really just separated the two worlds in the novel, his world of comedy from the world of commercial reality. He cannot, it seems, establish his as victorious for the representative David. Even his own restoration is really a restoration to a position from which he can make no more exposures, and the atypicality and limitations of his triumph become more emphatically insisted on as its inability to influence David is added to its apparent inability really to affect Uriah. We see Uriah, in the end, joined with Littimer in an institution run by Creakle, surrounded by an approving and admiring society. He is obviously poised for a leap back into the commercial fray, no doubt made more cagey by his last experience. The sad conclusion is that neither victory nor happiness is available to David, maybe not to his world, and the triumphant joy is finally cancelled.

Even more deceptive is the humour attending the idyllic courtship and the later marriage of David and Dora. The tone throughout these chapters is tender, protective, and very sad, in consonance with the saddest and most significant of the hero's actions. He says he 'was wandering in a garden of Eden all the while, with Dora' (xxvi), but the truth is that he cannot stay there, nor can he allow her to. The garden and the lovely child are destroyed, and with them the possibility of comic life.

Dora's position is at the heart of a kind of fragile and tender comedy: 'I heard the empress of my heart sing enchanted ballads in the French language, generally to the effect that, whatever was the matter, we ought always to dance, Ta ra la, Ta ra la! accompanying herself on a glorified instrument, resembling a guitar' (xxvi). But even before the marriage there are shadows on her dedication to dancing; the ominous Miss Murdstone turns up as a 'protector' ('Who wants a protector?' Dora significantly asks, in her comic openness) and Julia Mills is around to play vampire to their joys and miseries: 'though she mingled her tears with mine . . . she had a dreadful luxury in our afflictions. She petted them, as I may say, and made the most of them.' David admits, 'she made me much more wretched than I was before' (xxxviii). She is a deceptively funny symbol of the secret desire of the world to destroy the happiness of the young and the beautiful: 'Ye May-flies, enjoy your brief existence in the bright morning of life!' (xxxiii). Though she often sounds very much like Micawber and, like him, loves nothing so much as a well-mixed metaphor—'the oasis in the desert of Sahara must not be plucked up idly'—she is actually mean and twisted, and any laughter at her is turned back on us. But surviving and nearly obliterating these shadows is this valid image of Dora as innocence, purity, and love: 'sitting on a garden seat under a lilac tree, what a spectacle she was, upon that beautiful morning, among the butterflies, in a white chip bonnet and a dress of celestial blue' (xxxiii). The butterflies recall the 'preserve of butterflies' in David's own childhood garden, and Dora certainly recalls the boy's equally lovely and fragile mother. David is reaching for an Eden that was once there but can be no longer, not so much because he senses any pattern of incest but because he is not allowed to accept the Micawber values which Dora holds. She does, however, impress them on him for a time; the engagement flies, as it should, directly in the face of prudence. But David, with awful irony, thinks his judgement superior to hers, and even the adult narrator seems to have no real notion of what he has lost: 'What an unsubstantial, happy, foolish time it was!' (xxxiii). Such language simply indicates the extreme distance between the comic reality of the engagement and the narrator's businesslike version of reality. The clash of these two worlds is made clear throughout, as Dora confronts him with the irrefutable logic of comedy:

'My love,' said I, 'I have work to do.'
'But don't do it!' returned Dora. 'Why should you?'
It was impossible to say to that sweet little surprised face, otherwise than lightly and playfully, that we must work to live.
'Oh! How ridiculous!' cried Dora.
'How shall we live without, Dora?' said I.
'How? Any how!' said Dora. (xxxvii)

But David is unhappily caught by alternate values, which, ironically, he calls 'the source of my success': 'habits of punctuality, order, and diligence', 'thorough-going, ardent, and sincere earnestness' (XLII), and other such labels of the commercial ant-hill. And he moves to a marriage in which, again and again, he finds that he 'had wounded Dora's soft little heart, and she was not to be comforted' (XLIV). The gentle humour is, thus, deceptive; the clash of the two worlds causes real misery.

It is true that the marriage begins in laughter—the dinner-party at which Traddles is served the unopened oysters, for instance—but as it goes on Dickens insists more and more on the pain. Dora is pushed to acknowledge her limitations in David's world and to plead with him pathetically to relegate her to a low position in it: 'When I am very disappointing, say, "I knew, a long time ago, that she would make but a child-wife!" When you miss what I should like to be, and I think can never be, say, "still my foolish child-wife loves me!" For indeed I do' (XLIV). Still David shoves account books at her until 'she would look so scared and disconsolate, as she became more and more bewildered, that the remembrance of her natural gaiety when I first strayed into her path, and of her being my child-wife, would come reproachfully upon me' (XLIV). But the proper reproaches never really help; David is sensitive, but he is unable to escape his sense of unhappiness and his own limited scale of values. He actually tries to accept Annie Strong's stiff and unimaginative formula as adequate for his own situation: 'There can be no disparity in marriage like unsuitability of mind and purpose', and he adopts her phrase, 'the first mistaken impulses of my undisciplined heart' (XLV), as an important explanation of his existence. As a result, he tries to discipline his wife's wonderful spontaneity and to 'form her mind', accepting the false assumption that life needs moulding to laws, rules, and patterns.

In doing so, David turns his back on comedy and on his wife. She finally admits, 'I was not fit to be a wife' and argues that 'I know I was too young and foolish. It is much better as it is' (LIII). The Edenic Dora is made to wish for death, certainly the final rebuke to those firm 'habits of punctuality'. David has stepped briefly into the role of Murdstone. Beginning in full accord with comic values, he has become their enemy. The novel suggests no criticism of David, no moral judgement against him, only that the society of rich comedy is now far away on the other side of the world, ringing in the last echoes of Micawber's speech but about to disappear completely as a true social possibility from Dickens's novels.

8 *Little Dorrit*

THE ATTACK ON COMEDY

There was old people, after working all their
lives, going and being shut up in the workhouse,
much worse fed and lodged and treated altogether, than—Mr. Plornish said manufacturers,
but appeared to mean malefactors. Why, a man
didn't know where to turn himself, for a crumb
of comfort. As to who was to blame for it,
Mr. Plornish didn't know who was to blame for it.
He could tell you who suffered, but he couldn't
tell you whose fault it was. (I. xii)

In an early review in *Blackwood's* E. B. Hamley lamented that
in what he called the 'wilderness' of *Little Dorrit* 'we sit down
and weep when we remember thee, O *Pickwick*!'[1] Given a
comic perspective, the reaction is proper; for *Little Dorrit* is
the direct antithesis of *Pickwick*. Dickens's great novel of
imprisonment is not just dark and gloomy; it is specifically
anti-comic. Just as *David Copperfield* was a reluctant farewell
to comic values and society, so is *Little Dorrit* an attack on
them. It turns the world of *Pickwick* inside out.

Anti-comedy is a term used widely and indiscriminately
now, but it has a precise application to the central vision of
Little Dorrit, where the cardinal principles of comedy are all
brought up, only to be attacked, dismissed, or treated with a
bitter and complex irony, as in the great justification of prison
life given by the sodden Dr. Haggage:

'Nobody comes here to ask if a man's at home, and to say he'll
stand on the door mat till he is. Nobody writes threatening letters
about money to this place. It's freedom, sir, it's freedom! . . .
Elsewhere, people are restless, worried, hurried about, anxious

---

[1] 'Remonstrance with Dickens', *Blackwood's*, lxxxi (1857), 497.

respecting one thing, anxious respecting another. Nothing of the
kind here, sir. We have done all that—we know the worst of it;
we have got to the bottom, we can't fall, and what have we found ?
Peace. That's the word for it. Peace.' (I. vi)

Dr. Haggage sounds deceptively like Dick Swiveller, who
could transform his single room into 'chambers' with the power
of his imagination. But Swiveller, Micawber, Sairey Gamp,
and others of this line are all triumphant; Haggage is defeated.
His true consolation is the certainty that he has 'got to the
bottom'. Micawber falls back for a spring, but the debtors here
fall back for good. The *freedom* is a freedom from real contact,
and the *peace* is equivalent to death. With bitter irony,
Dickens then insists, through the rest of the novel, that the
prison is simply a microcosm of the social world, with its
snobbery, unreal distinctions, and vicious self-delusions, and
that all men really share the same isolation. Haggage's defence,
then, is the callous defence of the Barnacles: a justification
of the impossible *status quo*. Even further, his argument rests
not really on the comic term, freedom, but on the religious
term, peace, making extremely apt Dickens's description of
the doctor's speech: a 'profession of faith'. Haggage's peace is
a perversion of the true peace later represented in Amy Dorrit,
and his doctrine is no less than blasphemy. He is, ultimately,
one of the damned.

These are harsh but fitting terms for a novel rooted so deeply
in Christian pessimism, and they help explain why Haggage's
justification is, at the same time, funny and terrifying. *Little
Dorrit* does not finally make any terms at all with this world.
At its climax, the heroine says, 'Take all I have, and make it a
Blessing to me!' (II. xxix). Blessings can come only with
renunciation, and union can come only when it turns out that
all she has is nothing at all. 'We cannot but be right if we put
all the rest away, and do everything in remembrance of Him'
(II. xxi), Little Dorrit tells Mrs. Clennam, suggesting the
really deep pessimism of the novel: the 'all the rest' that is to
be renounced is truly all the rest of the world.

At any rate, these radical Christian terms are not amenable
to a comic society and can be used only for the darkest humour:
'Into this mixture, Mrs. Clennam dipped certain of the rusks
and ate them; while the old woman buttered certain other

of the rusks, which were to be eaten alone. . . . She then put on the spectacles and read certain passages aloud from a book —sternly, fiercely, wrathfully—praying that her enemies (she made them by her tone and manner expressly hers) might be put to the edge of the sword, consumed by fire, smitten by plagues and leprosy, that their bones might be ground to dust, and that they might be utterly exterminated' (I. III). The technique of this joke appears primitive but is really quite subtle. The selection of Old Testament texts is compared to the selection of rusks, both are made to appear arbitrary, and are humorously called 'certain'. Behind this, though, is the deceptive fact that however random the selection of rusks, the selection of texts is certain indeed. Even further, Mrs. Clennam's ego, originally seen as the butt of the joke, is presented finally as frightening. Egoism here is not funny but literally damnable, and Mrs. Clennam's egoistic and masochistic religion has absolutely no comic resonance.

It supports but makes miserable her own life and nearly paralyses the life of her son. Arthur is, in fact, as much a victim of Murdstonean repression as was David; he describes his childhood as 'austere faces, inexorable discipline, penance in this world and terror in the next' (I. II). There are numerous other parallels between this novel and *David Copperfield*. Both deal with various attempts to escape from the dark commercial world; both deal also with the dangers and attractions of masochism as a response to injustice—Miss Wade, for instance, is an almost exact parallel to Rosa Dartle, and her earlier relation to Henry Gowan is very much like Rosa's to Steerforth; both novels focus most centrally on the course of a sensitive and injured hero. But, in most ways, these courses are opposites. Arthur, unlike David, is fully conscious of being deeply infected himself, realizes the impossibility of a comic life with Pet (Dora), and moves not to commercial success but to its inverse: a failure which hurts others, public humiliation, imprisonment, and finally an anti-commercial marriage. *Little Dorrit* makes explicit the darkness hinted at in *David Copperfield* and in place of the earlier novel's sadness offers savagery, grotesquery, and black humour.

The difference in tone is immediately apparent, but the extent to which specific tendencies of the earlier novel are reversed perhaps is not. Mrs. Plornish, for example, is first introduced as a copy of Mrs. Micawber, 'hastily re-arranging the upper part of her dress' after nursing a child. The image is immediately branded on her: 'This was Mrs. Plornish, and this maternal action was the action of Mrs. Plornish during a large part of her waking existence' (I. xii). Children are not only nursing but are crawling on the floor, suggesting profusion and joy, but when Arthur compliments her on her crawler, Mrs. Plornish responds, while soothing the baby in her arms, 'he *is* a fine little fellow, ain't he, sir? But this one is rather sickly' (I. xii). The poverty of Bleeding Heart Yard, unlike that of the Micawbers, is the kind that causes suffering and kills. Dickens demands that we acknowledge both the humour and the pain, and the pure Micawber comedy is disallowed. Even more revealing, perhaps, is the treatment of Maggy, the poor idiot whose mind was permanently imprisoned when she was ten years old. She is protected by Little Dorrit, just as Mr. Dick is protected by Aunt Betsey, and when Maggy first comes boisterously on the scene, rolling on the ground with her potatoes, she seems to be a direct descendant of Richard Babley. The developing differences become enormous, though, and indicate the radically different methods of the two novels. Maggy's physical grotesquery, first of all, is stressed in exactly the ways Mr. Dick's was played down:[2] she has 'large bones, large features, large feet and hands, large eyes and no hair. Her large eyes were limpid and almost colourless. . . . She was not blind, having one tolerably serviceable eye' (I. ix). Mr. Dick's recurrent fear of his threatening relatives is menacing but always distant; Maggy's past pain, however, is epitomized in her pathetic references to the hospital: 'Such beds there is there!' Little Dorrit explains, 'She had never been at peace before' (I. ix), and Maggy stands finally as a symbol of the terrors of institutionalized cruelty and institutionalized 'peace'. She is also more realistically presented and is thus much harder to accept sentimentally: 'Maggy was very susceptible to personal slights, and very ingenious in inventing them' (I. xxiv).

---

[2] In the original version, Mr. Dick was to have greeted David by running his tongue back and forth across the window and squinting at him 'in a most terrible manner'. Both the tongue and the squint were removed in proof; see Butt and Tillotson, *Dickens at Work*, p. 130.

Dickens insists that we have all the reactions: affection, pity, distaste, amusement, and irritation, but none of them alone. Maggy can participate in no such comic triumphs as Mr. Dick's fine reconciliation of Dr. and Annie Strong, because *Little Dorrit* finally does not believe in comic triumphs.

I will examine later in more detail the nature and causes of this anti-comic tendency of the novel, but it is first necessary to insist that the terms are relevant. There is a general suspicion among critics that the darkness of the novel precludes comedy. For example, '*Little Dorrit* is without doubt Dickens' darkest novel. No other of his novels has such a somber unity of tone.'[3] The first sentence is probably true; the second one certainly is not. Is Flora sombre? is the Circumlocution Office? is Fanny Dorrit? is, for that matter, Rigaud? Surely the tone of the novel is richly various. Though the final view is certainly pessimistic, it is supported with all the resources of Dickens's rhetoric not with something as sterile as 'a somber unity of tone'. It is also a commonplace of criticism to assert that Dickens is in some way tired, that the treatment is forced and mechanical.[4] But it seems to me that his humorous imagination is fully engaged, manifesting itself in characteristically bizarre and yet functional ways in relation even to the most minor details: to the nameless tout who follows Arthur at Calais 'in a suit of grease and a cap of the same material', shouting, 'Hi! Ice-say! You! Seer! Ice-say! Nice Oatel!' (II. xx), to the Barnacle home just off Grosvenor Square which smells like 'extract of Sink' (I. x), and even to Frederick Dorrit's bedroom, where 'the blankets were boiling over, as it were, and keeping the lid open' (I. ix). I do agree that the nature of the humour is highly deceptive, in the sense that it is almost never pure, almost never presented without either accompanying blackness or staccato reversals. The reader very often is presented with the difficult mixture of feelings Arthur has when he first sees the adult Flora, 'wherein his sense of the sorrowful and his sense of the comical were curiously blended' (I. xiii). It is the major function of Dickens's humorous rhetoric to effect this curious

---

[3] Miller, *Charles Dickens*, p. 227.
[4] See Forster's *Life*, ii. 182. G. K. Chesterton put this view most concisely: 'Clennam is certainly very much older than Mr. Pickwick' (*Charles Dickens*, p. 230), but it is usually stated more flatly.

blending. The technique is presently so common that clichés—black humour, grotesque humour, and the like—have developed round it, but it has never been used more effectively in consonance with major aspects of the novel. Here the black humour supports the structural and tonal irony and shows us that it is, as the originally planned title of the novel insisted, 'Nobody's Fault' only because we live in a world of nobodies.

The relationship of this kind of humour to the particular genre of the novel, then, seems to me the most interesting issue in regard to *Little Dorrit*. Similarly, the major questions involve, first, the causes and nature of the novel's radically anti-comic tendencies and, second, the rhetorical use of this mixed, grotesque humour.

1

Little Dorrit dramatically inverts many of the techniques and assumptions of comedy. In the first place, as Lionel Trilling says, 'The imagination of *Little Dorrit* is marked not so much by its powers of particularization as by its powers of generalization and abstraction.'[5] Though there is, in fact, much particularization, it is true that the details do coalesce around a general pattern more firm and clear than in any other novel. There is a consistent tendency to relate all details to the pattern; for example, '[Arthur] perhaps had a misgiving also that Britannia herself might come to look for lodgings in Bleeding Heart Yard, some ugly day or other, if she over-did the Circumlocution Office' (I. x). This generalizing habit creates an immediate problem for comedy, which relies always on the personal and direct, and distrusts abstractions as falsifying. The tendency to abstract also reduces the comic and ego-satisfying sense of the uniqueness of experience and personality. Abstraction tends to group and to pluralize: '[He wondered] how many thousand Plornishes there might be within a day or two's journey of the Circumlocution Office' (I. XII). *David Copperfield* would never have asked how *many* Micawbers, the whole point being the special quality of the *one* Micawber.

[5] Introduction to the Oxford Illustrated edition, p. xv. The main arguments of Trilling's fine essay pervade subsequent criticism, and they are used extensively here. Further references will be cited in the text.

The generalizations do not always work against humour, it must be insisted, but only against comedy. In some cases, in fact, they allow for rich satire. Bar, for instance, whom Trilling cites as evidence of the abstract qualities of the novel (p. xv), is really not so much an abstraction of all lawyers as he is essence of lawyer: 'Bar was a man of great variety; but one leading thread ran through the woof of all his patterns. Every man with whom he had to do was in his eyes, a juryman; and he must get that juryman over, if he could' (II. xii). The sneer behind 'great variety' is almost audible. Bar is, very simply, his profession, suggesting his reduced, funny, terrifying, and representative state. For the most part, though, the novel's generalizations move away from the comic form altogether and approach the stern moral tone of the sermon. The rhetoric of application is the rhetoric of the parable, insisting always on the pertinence of the details, particularly the dark details, to the reader's life. Mr. Meagles's fawning and stupid adulation of the Barnacles, for example, is termed 'a weakness which none of us need go into the next street to find' (I. xvii). And it is certainly no 'amiable weakness'.

Little Dorrit is more darkly moral than any novel before it. It takes so stern a view of moral responsibility that any laxity is seen not as comic but as evil. The bitterly ironic notion of 'Nobody's Fault' pervades the novel, as each guilty character justifies his existence and elaborately explains his present evil. In the end, all of the explanations—Miss Wade's, Rigaud's, Mrs. Clennam's, Ferdinand Barnacle's, Arthur's—are equally valid and equally inapplicable. The novel distrusts justifications and holds up the non-explaining Amy Dorrit as a reproof to all its other characters. Everyone else is a self-deceiver, more or less dangerous (Mrs. Clennam) or sad (John Chivery). In comedy, self-deception is equally central, but it is brought up to be purged by laughter; here, however, the dark side of the trait is explored: 'The family fiction' by which William Dorrit lives in prison and exploits his friends and children is seen as emblematic of the condition of England, so deeply embedded that dynamite, not laughter, is needed to purge it. In this black world, the work of the creative imagination is likely to be seen simply as lying, and Dick Swiveller is inseparable from the Circumlocution Office.

In no other way is *Little Dorrit* so basically anti-comic as in its distrust of the creative imagination. Earlier novels had envisaged a general social condition almost equally black, but had ordinarily allowed for at least a private solution: that of Sam Weller, or Dick and the Marchioness, or even Sairey Gamp. Here the man least guilty and most admired, however, is an engineer, Daniel Doyce. Trilling says that Doyce 'stands for the creative mind in general' and that, in him, Dickens made his fullest 'claim for the virtue of the artist' (p. xv), but surely this is a misreading. In this novel the cynical and entirely condemned Gowan is closer to the creative artist than is Doyce. The engineer 'spoke in that quiet deliberate manner, and in that undertone, which is often observable in mechanics who consider and adjust with great nicety' (I. x). He is precise, careful, restricted, and, finally, pragmatic: he is interested, above all, in 'useful' inventions. His records are admired for their clarity; he alone is able to know, to get into things and see them, even if they are only things. And he alone, in this novel where the language comes close to getting away from people, can explain an idea 'with the direct force and distinctness with which it struck his own mind' (II. viii). Doyce is not only too limited to represent the creative mind; he is, in many ways, its antithesis. He is merely clear; he is not joyous, resilient, imaginative, or, in any real sense, creative. It is a key to the desperation and bitterness informing this novel that something so very limited as pragmatic clarity, attacked over and over again in earlier novels, is admired. It also suggests that *Little Dorrit* is, at least in one major strain, deeply reactionary in its celebration of the practical and in its implicit disenchantment with the powers of the liberating and extroverted imagination.

Over and over again, in the most acerbated passages in all of his writings, Dickens suggests that the true liberation is to 'exterminate the brutes', that the true philanthropy is murder: 'Assuredly [Blandois] did look then, though he looked his politest, as if any real philanthropist could have desired no better employment than to lash a great stone to his neck, and drop him into the water' (II. vii). There is no leniency here and no trust; Mr. Pickwick's kind are now called 'amiable whitewashers' (I. xi) and are armed not with bags of money

but with guns. The bluntest statement of this ethic of retaliation is given by a jolly hostess, a 'smiling landlady', who
is something of a reversed Mrs. Lupin: 'I know nothing of
philosophical philanthropy. But I know what I have seen. . . .
And I tell you this, my friend. . . . That there are people whom
it is necessary to detest without compromise. That there are
people who must be dealt with as enemies of the human race.
That there are people who have no human heart, and who must
be crushed like savage beasts and cleared out of the way' (I.
xi). There is every sign that this hopeless indignation has the
approval of the novel.[6] Its pessimism and hatred disallow
comedy.

But the attack on comedy goes even further. Although the
novel is, as Trilling says, '*more* about society than any other
of the novels' (p. v), it really repudiates the notion of society.
Little Dorrit not only deals with human isolation but sees that
isolation as largely inescapable; perhaps, in a dark sense, it is
even better than community. The last words of the novel
suggest the horrible condition of such society as there is: 'as
they passed along in sunshine and shade, the noisy and the
eager, and the arrogant and the froward and the vain, fretted,
and chafed, and made their usual uproar'. The blessedness
Amy Dorrit gives to Arthur has absolutely no effect on the surrounding society, and the clear sense is that the expansive
social redemption envisaged by comedy is impossible. Society
is seen simply as a collection of the harassed, and the real
problem is not the comic one of rejuvenating society or finding
one's place in it; one searches, rather, for a way to purify one-
self of the social taint. The sickness of the commercial society
is infectious, a point made over and over again in some of the
most deceptive of Dickens's jokes. The good-hearted turnkey,
for instance, devotes enormous energies to the generous notion
of giving money to his god-daughter, Little Dorrit. He simply
wants to will it to her and to ensure at the same time her safety
from her grasping relatives. Unable to isolate her from her own
small and ugly society, though, 'the turnkey thought about it

[6] It is true, of course, that Mrs. Clennam's version of bitter retaliation is not
approved of, primarily because it is unbalanced and not properly directed.
It is also true that the answer suggested by Amy Dorrit is not that of the
landlady, but this only indicates, I think, that the landlady's response is not
fully adequate. There is no real sense in which it is wrong.

all his life, and died intestate after all' (I. vii). His philan-
thropic notions are corrupted by being cast in the form of
money, anyhow, but the most serious point of the joke is the
insidious evil of social assumptions and the impossibility of
dealing with society on its own terms. The novel attacks
philanthropy almost as vigorously as it does the Circumlocution Office; both operate within and thus share the onus
of the corrupt system. The truly meek alone have a chance here
and then only in so far as they renounce social membership.
In *Pickwick* victory was seen as a release from prison; here
it is seen largely as an acceptance of imprisonment. The human
ego, which is supported by comedy, is attacked, and Arthur
is reborn not into comic and social triumph but into blessed
meekness, not only an anti-social but an anti-comic virtue.

Given this dark view of society, Dickens also repudiates
specifically the comic strategies for dealing with it he had
earlier supported. Subversive warfare (as in Sam) is seen as
self-destructive revenge; making the best of it (as in Sairey)
is seen as complicity; reversing its terms (as in Micawber) is
seen as masochism. The novel offers full explorations of the
subtle variations of self-defeating and dangerous plans for
dealing with society that fall short of the extreme and only
proper one finally adopted by Arthur. The most prominent
position in *Little Dorrit* combines self-pity with ingenious and
often sly kinds of vengeance. Mrs. Clennam assumes that virtue
comes in arranging a balanced and equal torture: 'He withers
away in his prison; I wither away in mine; inexorable justice
is done; what do I owe on this score!' (I. viii). Her sense of
'inexorable justice' is linked to Miss Wade's embittered vision
and her sado-masochistic response to that vision, and while
both are, in their way, *just* answers, justice is a comic term
which depends on a sane and balanced universe. In the universe of *Little Dorrit* it simply is not applicable.

The fullest treatment of vengeance, in the complex figure of
Rigaud, makes this point clearly. Rigaud, though ominous
and satanic, has his roots in Alfred Jingle. Like Jingle he
adopts the parody pose of a gentleman. 'It's my game', he
announces at once, and he continually pretends to justify himself by comparison to all others who live 'by their wits'. He
sees through the social façade and nearly triumphs over it,

but his 'playfulness' is now viewed as evil and his satire on the commercial world as collusion. He suggests, finally, that any touch with society is destructive; that one can never 'take things as they are'. All the relaxation, the sense of community, and the pleasure of witty revenge necessary to comedy are repudiated.

So, to a very large extent, is the notion that human beings can and will effect a comfortable change. This optimistic belief in the efficacy of education is at the heart of comedy, but here only a radical transformation can possibly help. Both the narrator and, ironically, Ferdinand Barnacle agree that things never really change for the better. The narrator knows that Mr. Meagles and Henry Gowan never will and never can be reconciled: 'When were such changes ever made in men's natural relations to one another: when was such reconcilement of ingrain [*sic*] differences ever effected! It has been tried many times by other daughters, Minnie; it has never succeeded; nothing has ever come of it but failure' (I. xxviii). Solid and *natural* relations are now seen in terms of distrust and dislike. Even darker is Ferdinand's laughing assurance that people will learn nothing at all from the Merdle swindle: 'The next man who has as large a capacity and as genuine a taste for swindling, will succeed as well. Pardon me, but I think you really have no idea how the human bees will swarm to the beating of any old tin kettle' (II. xxviii).

And thus there is an undercurrent of black fatalism in the novel, even in its circular form, where characters swing back to meet each other and move from one prison to another. There is some sense in which Miss Wade's acrid way of explaining life is exactly right: 'In our course through life we shall meet the people who are coming to meet *us* . . . and what it is set to us to do to them, and what it is set to them to do to us, will all be done.' The narrator adds that her tone 'implied that what was to be done was necessarily evil' (I. ii). Her ironic perspective tends to undercut even such faint hope as the novel allows and to imply that kindness defines exclusion and that misery is partly caused by joy. Her suspicion that a subtle condescension lies behind apparent consideration is more than partially justified in relation to her own life and, more importantly, in relation to the Meagles's treatment of Tattycoram. Though her logic is perverse, it is not mad, and one of the reasons the novel is so distinctly anti-comic is that it makes us feel sympathy not only for Miss Wade but for her vision of a world that is ruled by smug self-interest and cruelty.

The last and most obvious reason for the term, anti-comedy, is indeed this blackness. Though the novel deals with the comic theme of illusion and reality, it suggests that happiness is illusory and that the only reality is misery: 'Reality on being proved—was obdurate to the sight and touch, and relaxed nothing of its old indomitable grimness—the one tender recollection of his experience would not bear the same test, and melted away' (I. XIII). In one extraordinary passage the impulse of *Pickwick Papers* is specifically reversed: 'And he [Arthur] thought—who has not thought for a moment, sometimes?—that it might be better to flow away monotonously, like the river, and to compound for its insensibility to happiness with its insensibility to pain' (I. XVI). So, in almost the same language, had argued *Pickwick*'s Dismal Jemmy: 'Did it ever strike you, on such a morning as this, that drowning would be happiness and peace?' (v). The vision which was once hurriedly dismissed as perverse, even ridiculous, has now become established. In the world of *Little Dorrit*, even the wonderful and hospitable inns of *Pickwick* have become 'cruel houses', out to cheat any traveller (II. XVIII). The mock cruelty of Quilp has become the real physical cruelty of Flintwinch, and everywhere is bleak hopelessness and terror.

2

But this black, anti-comic novel is filled with laughter. By mixing the humorous with the vicious, the sad, the terrifying, and the disgusting, Dickens establishes a tone which disrupts our comfortable relation to the novel and which engages us in a rhetoric that defines the loneliness and emptiness common to all the novel's characters. It is a grotesque and hopeless world, but these qualities are made to move us most deeply when they are touched, briefly and poignantly, by the sanity and hopefulness of laughter. The dark world is in fact made all the darker by Dickens's explicit insistence on the absence of the important comic qualities. The humour continually urges us to acknowledge the importance of what is missing and, correspondingly, the force of the darkness that is present.

The humour in *Little Dorrit* is almost always joined with the most serious and grim issues, as, for example, in the description of Arthur's childhood Sundays:

> There was the dreary Sunday of his childhood, when he sat with his hands before him, scared out of his senses by a horrible tract which commenced business with the poor child by asking him in its title, why he was going to Perdition?—a piece of curiosity that he really in a frock and drawers was not in a condition to satisfy—and which, for the further attraction of his infant mind, had a parenthesis in every other line with some such hiccupping reference as 2 Ep. Thess. c. iii. v. 6 & 7. . . . There was the interminable Sunday of his nonage; when his mother, stern of face and un-relenting of heart, would sit all day behind a bible—bound, like her own construction of it, in the hardest, barest, and straitest boards. (I. iii)

The appeals for sympathy, the statements of cruelty, the record of repression and frustration are interwoven with jokes on the same subject. There is no question of comic relief or of reversal; the funny and the frightening are simply coincident. As a result the pain is doubly emphasized, precisely because the perspective for laughter is absolutely denied Arthur. There never was the freedom or joy in his childhood from which he could see, for a moment, the fun in 2 Ep. Thess. c. iii. v. 6 & 7.[7] The fact that this liberated perspective is for a brief moment given to us establishes, by contrast, the repression of the im-prisoned child, marched to chapel 'morally handcuffed to another boy' (I. iii).

Occasionally, instead of the staccato reversals, the humour is maintained a little longer in order to emphasize more dramatically the black and real alternative. Mrs. Bangham,

[7] The reference to 2 Thessalonians is, by the way, extremely apt. The chapters cited are a part of a general discussion of iniquity and suggest that the duty of the Christian is to isolate himself from a dark world. The allusion thus not only is consonant with Mrs. Clennam's Calvinism but also supports the novel's vision of Christian pessimism and alienation:

> 6. Now we command you, brethren, in the name of our Lord Jesus Christ, that ye withdraw yourselves from every brother that walketh disorderly, and not after the tradition which he received of us.

> 7. For yourselves know how ye ought to follow us: for we behaved not ourselves disorderly among you.

for instance, who is called in as 'fly-catcher and general attendant' at the birth of Amy Dorrit, is a wonderful comic presence,
garrulous, open, and cheerful, with the ability of Sairey Gamp
to twist every occasion into pleasantness and comfort. She
even does it with the huge flies that blacken the walls of the
debtor's room:

> 'P'raps they're sent as a consolation, if we only know'd it. . . .
> And to think of a sweet little cherub being born inside the lock!
> Now ain't it pretty, ain't *that* something to carry you through it
> pleasant? . . . And you a crying too?' said Mrs. Bangham, to rally
> the patient more and more. 'You! Making yourself so famous!
> With the flies a falling into the gallipots by fifties! And everything
> a going on so well!' (I. vi)

The jokes on providence, imprisonment, and death are barbed,
but they come off so quickly that Mrs. Bangham begins to look
like a genuinely comic figure, economizing all our pity and
disgust and turning them into amusement. Her partnership
with Dr. Haggage turns the delivery into a wild, brandy-filled
party and further supports the comedy. Finally, however, the
tone switches abruptly: 'Three or four hours passed; the flies
fell into the traps by hundreds; and at length one little life,
hardly stronger than theirs, appeared among the multitude of
lesser deaths' (I. vi). Untouched by this irony, Mrs. Bangham
and Dr. Haggage are back at fetching and drinking brandy
immediately after the birth. Comic joy is seen as callous escape,
and the humour has supported only an illusion of happiness.
The joke's disguises come suddenly off, reveal a black truth,
and then are put on again. The laughter mixes with the shock
and the pity and supports the pathos of the little girl, the
central hope of the novel and 'hardly stronger' nor, we feel,
more socially significant than the flies who die by the hundreds.

As the novel proceeds, the technique of shifting perspective
becomes refined until it sometimes appears in adjacent sentences, where the distant and polite is juxtaposed against the
committed and the savage: 'Mews Street, Grosvenor Square,
was not absolutely Grosvenor Square itself, but it was very
near it. It was a hideous little street of dead wall, stables, and
dung-hills' (I. x). Similarly, the mixture of the awful and the
funny becomes so subtle that it often appears in a single word,

as in the recurrent joke on Arthur's suppressed love for Pet Meagles, in which he is termed 'Nobody'. These techniques are then applied to two basic kinds of humour, governing two large areas of the novel: first, a functional and negative humour growing out of the Circumlocution Office to the Barnacles and the Merdles, Mr. Casby, Mrs. General, Mr. Dorrit, his daughter Fanny, even to Mr. Meagles and the tenants of Bleeding Heart Yard, and, second, a thin and sad positive humour radiating from Flora Finching and touching lightly a few others, among them Affery and John Chivery.

By far the most prominent is the humour which is centered in the heart of *Little Dorrit*'s society, the Circumlocution Office. It is a humour which reveals the full horror of that institution and the aptness of its symbolic duty as representative of England itself. The Circumlocution Office is, above all things, both a symbol and a prime cause of the national paralysis. Their motto, 'How Not to Do It', suggests not doing things the wrong way but not doing them at all. They stand to preserve the ossified *status quo*. Their officialized inactivity manifests itself, most significantly, in the specifically modern substitutes for true activity: sheer bulk and meaningless flurry: '. . . within the short compass of the last financial half-year, this much-maligned Department (Cheers) had written and received fifteen thousand letters (Loud cheers), had made twenty-four thousand minutes (Louder cheers), and thirty-two thousand five hundred and seventeen memoranda (Vehement cheering)' (II. viii). The Circumlocution Office obligingly carries out the principles of Parkinson's Law.

But it is more than inactive; it is fiercely inactive, and much of the humour subtly disguises the fierceness only to reveal it later with extra force:

If another Gunpowder Plot had been discovered half an hour before the lighting of the match, nobody would have been justified in saving the parliament until there had been half a score of boards, half a bushel of minutes, several sacks of official memoranda, and a family–vault full of ungrammatical correspondence, on the part of the Circumlocution Office. (I. x)

The *ungrammatical* correspondence seems at first to be just delightful Dickensian exuberance, the 'squiggle on the edge of

the page' Orwell noted.[8] That squiggle is delightful in this case
because it directs attention away from the danger of the Office
and suggests its ludicrous incompetence. Dickens then proceeds, however, in paragraphs too long to quote here, to build
a chorus of parallel clauses, beginning and ending with 'it',
until we begin to sense that the way in which the Circumlocution Office is ungrammatical is that it reduces all grammar
to the sputtering, spitting, impersonal particle. The Office,
finally, is anything but impotent: 'Because the Circumlocution
Office was down upon any ill-advised public servant who was
going to do it, or who appeared by any surprising accident in
remote danger of doing it, with a minute, and a memorandum,
and a letter of instructions, that extinguished him' (I. x). It
extinguishes all who try to get in the way of its grand object:
the denial of the human ability to know, the establishment of a
madhouse world of institutionalized blankness which simply
throws back all inquiry and reduces all humanity to the same
inhuman level. 'Upon my soul you mustn't come into the place
saying you want to know, you know' (I. x) is, in this sense,
the key joke in the novel.

The Circumlocution Office is manned and guided by the
Barnacles, parasites not so much on England as on life itself.
The Barnacles, in fact, are not enemies of England so much as
they *are* England, a cross-section which includes the snobbish
and the open, the austere and the friendly, the mean and the
kind. The real problem with the Barnacles and therefore with
the country is that they have no moral sense at all. They are
all, like three of their younger members, 'doing the marriage
as they would have "done" the Nile, Old Rome, the new singer,
or Jerusalem' (I. xxxiv). It's all one to them; they are equally
at home as spectators at a wedding or at the national decline.
The point is that they are only spectators. They share the
national disease, too, of being unable quite to catch hold of the
language: Lord Decimus proposed 'happiness to the bride and
bridegroom in a series of platitudes, that would have made
the hair of any sincere disciple and believer stand on end; and
trotting, with the complacency of an idiotic elephant, among
howling labyrinths of sentences which he seemed to take for
high roads, and never so much as wanted to get out of'

[8] *Dickens, Dali and Others*, p. 61.

(I. xxxiv). The humour is dark indeed; for in this madhouse world, it is suggested, any words will do, since everybody is nobody and nothing is to be done.

The most consistent humour, however, is connected to the 'best and brightest of the Barnacles' (II. xxviii), the amiable Ferdinand, in some ways the friendliest person in the novel. Very much like Sam Weller, Ferdinand is a wit and a cynic: 'I can give you plenty of forms to fill up. Lots of 'em here. You can have a dozen if you like. But you'll never go on with it' (I. x). But unlike Sam he is very much a part of the system; he implies by his presence that the Circumlocution Office can easily contain hostile elements, that it is impervious to this or any human attack, and that laughter certainly can't help. Ferdinand really recognizes the power of the institution and, in his light way, is as vitriolic as Miss Wade and as blasphemous as Mrs. Clennam, proposing that the Circumlocution Office is established by Providence: 'You'll say we are a Humbug. I won't say we are not; but all that sort of thing is intended to be, and must be.' Echoing Mr. Perker, he suggests that 'it is the point of view that is the essential thing'. Both he and Perker present the difficult spectacle of the good man inside the vicious system, and both require a simultaneous response of affection and condemnation. Ferdinand's vision is deeper, though, and consequently more bitter. He argues that the real purpose of the Circumlocution Office is to support the most natural of all human inclinations—isolation: 'You have no idea how many people want to be left alone. You have no idea how the Genius of the country . . . tends to being left alone.' The black humour of this insight is completed with the final truth that the Circumlocution Office is only England itself: 'Our place is not a wicked Giant to be charged at full tilt; but, only a windmill showing you, as it grinds immense quantities of chaff, which way the country wind blows' (II. xxviii).

Both the chief cog and the chief victim of this national grinding windmill is Mr. Merdle, 'the man of his time' and 'the name of the age' (II. v). He is married to a perfect bosom, used not to nurture little Micawbers but to hang jewels on. Mrs. Merdle is, as she so often says, the perfect image of Society and, at the same time, a parody of a human being. She is a kind of continual check to comedy, forever parading by inversion her inhumanity: 'My feelings are touched in a moment'; 'I am the creature of impulse.' But her bosom is huge only because it 'seemed essential to her having room enough to be unfeeling in' (I. xx).

She is dangerous, certainly, but she is no Mrs. Corney, presumably because Merdle hasn't even enough substance to be henpecked. When he enters—purely by accident, since he is only running from the butler—a room where his wife is present, he mumbles, 'I beg your pardon . . . I didn't know there was anybody here but the parrot' (I. xxxiii). This complex joke works first by identifying the artificial Mrs. Merdle and her bird, but it hints, beyond this, that Mr. Merdle is fit company only for a parrot. Because there are many such jokes, we are soon likely to build up really a large supply of laughter at this epitome of loneliness and detachment, a man who 'stopped, and looked at the table-cloth; as he usually did when he found himself observed or listened to' (II. xii). He is the archetypally alienated man—'Let Mrs. Merdle announce, with all her might, that she was at Home ever so many nights in a season, she could not announce more widely and unmistakably than Mr. Merdle did that he was never at home' (I. xxxiii)—and his condition, though irresistibly funny, is also pathetic.

It is, further, ominous; for in the end we are asked to laugh at the primal condition of the novel, which might be called nobodiness. Merdle's position suggests that the insidious social machine elevates those most capable of being nothing, that he becomes a funny and terrifying God of Nobodies, the grand cipher. The climax of this dark humour comes at the time of his death, in a series of some of the finest scenes in Dickens. Merdle visits Fanny and Edmund, needing to borrow, significantly, a penknife, having no kind of potency about him. As he leaves to exert himself to one perverse act of will, Dickens suddenly shifts the perspective to Fanny, and Merdle waltzes off to commit suicide: 'Waters of vexation filled her eyes; and they had the effect of making the famous Mr. Merdle, in going down the street, appear to leap, and waltz, and gyrate, as if he were possessed by several Devils' (II. xxiv). This combination of the ridiculous and the awful is characteristic of the treatment of Merdle. It is capped only by the final black joke, appropriately involving Merdle's enemy, the Chief Butler:

'Mr. Merdle is dead' [said Physician].
'I should wish,' said the Chief Butler, 'to give a month's notice.'
'Mr. Merdle has destroyed himself.'
'Sir,' said the Chief Butler, 'that is very unpleasant to the feelings of one in my position, as calculated to awaken prejudice; and I should wish to leave immediately.' (II. xxv)

Nobody has been killed, and a new Nobody will take his place. There is no reason for feeling in the world of the Chief Butler and other non-humans, and the humour brings home the full terror of the situation.

This group, the Merdles, the Barnacles, and the Circumlocution Office, are at the centre of the negative humour, and radiating out from this centre are the same falsity, snobbery, rigidity, and dangerous inhumanity, touching almost all the characters in the novel and completely infecting many of them. One of the most corrupt is 'The Last of the Patriarchs', a darkly ironic phrase attached repeatedly to Christopher Casby, who has established his reputation by having been 'formerly town-agent to Lord Decimus Tite Barnacle' (I. xiii). It is clear that in this connection he picked up much of that family's secret and became a kind of deputy Barnacle himself. The humour associated with him functions most obviously to support the general attack the novel makes on appearances, particularly, in the case of this 'boiling-over old Christian' (I. xxxv), on merciful and kindly appearances. The Patriarch seems, in one way, to be very much like Mr. Pecksniff: 'I heard from Flora . . . that she was coming to call, coming to call. And being out, I thought I'd come also, thought I'd come also.' Dickens says that the Patriarch's manner made his declaration seem 'worth putting down among the noblest sentiments enunciated by the best of men' (I. xxiii).[9] But Pecksniff could transform platitudes into comfort by the exercise of his great artistic style; with Mr. Casby the repetitions indicate not style but emptiness and reflect not on his imagination—for he has

---

[9] The treatment of Mr. Pecksniff is, on the surface, almost identical. He merely repeats Mrs. Lupin's words, but, the narrator says, 'Anybody would have been, as Mrs. Lupin was, comforted by the mere voice and presence of such a man' (III).

none—but on the pathetically deluded condition of the listeners
whom he impresses. He is a vacant head with benign white
whiskers, but the condition of nothingness—or nobodiness—
is not completely funny. He is simply a reduced version of the
central nothing, Mr. Merdle, and he is, as it turns out, dangerous
in the same way: he is behind the misery of Bleeding Heart
Yard.

He is also behind Mr. Pancks, one of Dickens's most complex
humorous eccentrics, representing, most prominently, the man
who transforms himself into a snorting and puffing machine
both to satirize the system and to fit into it. His reflections on
the position of man in a commercial economy are both funny
and accurate: 'Keep me always at it, and I'll keep you always
at it. There you are with the Whole Duty of Man in a commercial country' (I. xiii). The 'it' is undefined both because
there are no distinctions between functions in 'a commercial
country' and because it ties Pancks to the mad and powerful
indefiniteness of the Circumlocution Office. Arthur is never
sure that his friend isn't joking when he says such things, but
their quality of humorous exaggeration is conditioned by the
fact that they do seem to describe Pancks pretty well. He is,
in fact, a man caught in the commercial trap, the basically
good man who, ironically, helps corrupt Arthur. He does, at
the end, break out of that trap in one of the few scenes of
liberation in this novel of imprisonment, but even his revenge
on Casby is deceptive. It is purely personal and humorous, not,
as we are likely to hope, social and comic. He does not change
the condition of Bleeding Heart Yard; he only frees himself
from the Circumlocution Office bondage.

But that escape, even though limited, is made doubly important by its difficulty and obvious rarity; for the Circumlocution Office is everywhere, perhaps nowhere more clearly
than in Mrs. General, who seems to come naturally, as a representative of Society, to the Dorrits along with their new-found
wealth. Her dedication to the surfaces and to the proprieties
ties her, ironically, to Blandois and to the novel's deep distrust
of the basic assumption of the realistic comedy of manners:
that surfaces reflect depths. In *Little Dorrit* the surface either
falsifies the real or simply varnishes an emptiness. Mrs. General,
for instance, is dedicated entirely to a life defined by others:

'But, like other inconvenient places . . . it must be seen. As a place much spoken of, it is necessary to see it' (II. i). While this is, at least potentially, sad, it is actually dangerous, as is her whole notion of 'forming the mind', that is to say, the lips, by repeating 'Prunes and Prism', as if it were a religious incantation. This half-funny phrase not only indicates a reduction of life to the level of manikins; it is also an instance of one of the most interesting symbols that recurs in the novel: the malign or ignorant use of language to reflect a world where communication is dying and where one hangs on to sense only tenuously. Mrs. General is really another zero, one of the globular things that split off from the Circumlocution Office and assume a mock identity. While this recognition of Mrs. General's nothingness is, in itself, funny, the concurrent recognition that her social function is to hollow others out is not. 'A truly refined mind will seem to be ignorant of the existence of anything that is not perfectly proper, placid, and pleasant' (II. v), she says, and since, in this dark novel, nothing is really proper, placid, or pleasant, she is counselling a life in the void. Mrs. General is, finally, the humorous *and* dangerous agent of falsification.

But it is not really Mrs. General who infects the Dorrit family; she simply comes to them when they need her, in order to put the finishing touches on tendencies that have been fully developed—even in the Marshalsea. Swinburne said of the Patriarch of the prison, 'Mr. Dorrit is an everlasting figure of comedy in its most tragic aspect and tragedy in its most comic phase.'[10] This expresses very well the mixed response one must have to this exceptional figure. He turns the potentially comic fact that he is a 'very amiable and very helpless middle-aged gentleman' (I. v) into a terrible weapon against his children. He is an excellent 'Father of the Marshalsea' but of nothing else, a symbol of an institution but a black parody of parental love and responsibility. He gets 'relish'— Mr. Micawber's term, we remember—only from condescension and from such things as Mr. Nandy's 'infirmities and failings', which he loves to point out 'as if he were a gracious Keeper, making a running commentary on the decline of the harmless animal he exhibited' (I. xxxi). He is, as much as Merdle, a

[10] 'Charles Dickens', *Quarterly Review*, cxcvi (1902), 29.

symbol of petrified nothingness, who is paid liberally by all who know him for being and doing nothing so well.

It is difficult, however, to react simply to Mr. Dorrit, principally because he is both despicable and funny, both self-deluding and self-conscious: 'While he spoke, he was opening and shutting his hands like valves; so conscious all the time of that touch of shame, that he shrunk before his own knowledge of his meaning' (I. xix). After a comic speech to his institutional children, he retires to persuade Amy to flirt with young John Chivery. He is stirred by her response, however, into a brief glimpse of his own ugly meaning and to tears of self-pity which reveal 'his degenerate state to his affectionate child'. The narrator then makes explicit the necessity of a complex response to this weak man: 'Little recked the Collegians who were laughing in their rooms over his late address in the Lodge, what a serious picture they had in their obscure gallery of the Marshalsea that Sunday night' (I. xix).

After his release, Mr. Dorrit becomes a truer copy of Merdle, similarly afraid of servants, similarly powerful, and similarly alienated from his own home. Though still a partially humorous figure, he becomes more and more representative of a generalized condition of man, 'so full of contradictions, vacillations, inconsistencies, the little peevish perplexities of this ignorant life' (II. xix). When he finally breaks down, in the climactic scene where the world of Society is equated with the world of the Marshalsea, the humour is the blackest in the novel. Mr. Dorrit is a victim of the system and victimizer of his children, both prisoner and jailer.

We see his influence most clearly in his daughter, Fanny, who is a kind of Elizabeth Bennet gone wrong. Possessed of spirit and great retaliatory wit, she alone in the family appears capable of generating comedy, of seeing through Mrs. General and Mrs. Merdle and demolishing their false world in her grand and 'irrepressible' way. But she really hasn't a chance; she is forced not to attack but to compete with Mrs. Merdle, and, thus, her happy rebellion against Mrs. General is only superficial. She invariably and wittily rejects any suggestion Mrs. General makes, but 'she always stored it up in her mind, and adopted it another time' (II. v). Given her training, there is no course open to her but Mrs. General's, and she finally becomes 'almost as well composed in the graceful indifference of her attitude as Mrs. Merdle herself' (II. vi). She finally marries Mrs. Merdle's son, another vacuum, and mixes, for the rest of her life, triumph and misery. In the last view we have of her, she is continuing the system of vengeance and cruelty, making 'little victims' of her own children. She is true to her upbringing; if Amy is the Daughter of the Marshalsea, Fanny is surely the daughter of the Circumlocution Office.

As we move further out from the centre, the influence of that Office becomes more subtle and less easy to detect, but it is strong everywhere. It actually touches almost all of the good people, most notably Mr. Meagles, Dickens's final repudiation of the good man of the establishment. Meagles is a more complex and much darker Brownlow, who is not only good-natured, 'comely and healthy, with a pleasant English face', but actually goes 'trotting about the world' (I. ii). His insularity—he 'never by any accident acquired any knowledge whatever of the language of any country into which he travelled' (I. ii)—and condescension to foreigners, however, are seen as incipient Podsnappery. Meagles, like Mrs. General, simply shuts out what he doesn't want to hear, suggesting not only an inability to learn but also a smug capitulation to all things English. And in this novel nothing is more English than the Circumlocution Office. Meagles's 'curious sense of a general superiority to Daniel Doyce' (I. xvi) reflects a frame of mind which really assumes the primacy of the Barnacle values, and he is as much a Barnacle–Merdle worshipper as anyone. Even after losing his daughter to a man he knows very well is a scoundrel, Meagles reflects happily on the Barnacles in attendance at the wedding, 'It's very gratifying. . . . Such high company!' (I. xxxiv). Dickens is quite explicit finally about the egoism and snobbery that tie Merdle to the Circumlocution Office: 'Clennam could not help speculating . . . whether there might be in the breast of this honest, affectionate, and cordial Mr. Meagles, any microscopic portion of the mustard-seed that had sprung up into the great tree of the Circumlocution Office' (I. xvi). This good and amiable man's lack of full humanity is made more and more clear:

'Now would you believe, Clennam,' said Mr. Meagles, with a

hearty enjoyment of his friend's eccentricity, 'that I had a whole morning in What's-his-name Yard—'

'Bleeding Heart?' (I. xxiii)

And, at the end of the novel, Dickens's rhetoric establishes definitely the sad limitations of Meagles:

'You remind me of the days,' said Mr. Meagles, suddenly drooping—'but she's very fond of him, and hides his faults, and thinks that no one sees them—and he certainly is well connected, and of a very good family!'

It was the only comfort he had in the loss of his daughter, and if he made the most of it, who could blame him? (II. xxxiii)

He escapes blame only because he could not escape the Circumlocution Office. His fault is everybody's fault, and his humour is mixed always with this dark insight.

Darker still is Dickens's treatment of the poor. Even the tenants of Bleeding Heart Yard do not escape the same corrupt attitudes which lie behind slums and poverty. They are actually part of the system that exploits them:

'Ah! And there's manners! There's polish! There's a gentleman to have run to seed in the Marshalsea Jail! Why, perhaps you are not aware,' said Plornish, lowering his voice, and speaking with a perverse admiration of what he ought to have pitied or despised, 'not aware that Miss Dorrit and her sister dursn't let him know that they work for a living. No!' (I. xiii)

Everyone, it appears, finds his nothingness to worship, overlooking entirely the suffering their snobbish gods cause. The elaborate and extended jokes concerning Mrs. Plornish's mastering the Italian language—'Me ope you leg well soon'— are immediately connected to a general Bleeding Heart Yard prejudice against foreigners, partly the result of long and careful training 'by the Barnacles and the Stiltstalkings' but also going beyond even their leaders' bigotry: 'They believed that foreigners had no independent spirit, as never being escorted to the poll in droves by Lord Decimus Tite Barnacle, with colours flying and the tune of Rule Britannia playing' (I. xxv). Dickens does make it clear that the Plornishes are good people, generous, open, and warm, and Mrs.Plornish's linguistic pretences are undeniably funny. But we must also recognize that they are in part an offshoot of the Circumlocution Office.

All this Circumlocution Office humour is, in the end, much

like the country scene painted inside the Plornish house: 'No
Poetry and no Art ever charmed the imagination more than
the union of the two in this counterfeit cottage charmed Mrs.
Plornish' (II. xiii). The values of another world are there, but
they are 'counterfeit', unrealized, and to a large extent un-
realizable in this world. Even the best attempts to live by
these values are unsuccessful. There are, however, characters
who give it a good try and whose relative failure is expressed
in a kind of mixed humour quite different from the sort connected with the Circumlocution Office. Instead of infecting
the funny with the bitter or disgusting, it is qualified with
weakness, sadness, or a consciousness of limitations. The
character coming closest to a full comic existence is undoubtedly Flora Finching, but there are at least two others,
Affery and John Chivery, who, though much less complex, do
have distinct comic powers. Most often, however, we are asked
with these two to recognize not so much the fact of their comic
force but the degree to which it is severely qualified.

In another novel Affery would doubtless have been like
Mrs. Bedwin or Peggotty, a tender-hearted servant, secretly
wiser and more powerful than her master. Here, however, she
is so very limited, so much a real victim of physical cruelty,
that her comic powers have very little room in which to
expand. She expresses, above all things, the extremely limited
powers of the good, but she does so, significantly, in lines that
are, at least partly, funny. Discussing her marriage to Flintwinch, she explains, 'It was no doing o' mine. *I*'d never thought
of it.' 'What's the use of considering?' she proceeds, 'If them
two clever ones have made up their minds to it, what's left for
me to do? Nothing' (I. iii). The humour here works with the
central issues of power, will, and evil. Very quickly, though,
we see that Affery really *is* 'swallowed up' (I. v) in her husband
and Mrs. Clennam, and that those two clever and evil ones
render her good-hearted instincts nearly powerless: 'Why if it
had been—a Smothering instead of a Wedding . . . I couldn't
have said a word upon it, against them two clever ones' (I. iii).
It is almost a smothering, and even though she does rouse
herself in the end to do some good and, more important, suggest that the human will is not entirely without power, the
good she does is limited, and our dominant impression of her

is of a woman who is, indeed, lucky to get off without being killed. The amusement is there but it is never pure, being so mixed with sensations of cruelty and danger.

John Chivery, on the other hand, appears at first to be an excellent economizer of these sensations, a character who can turn the energies of pity into laughter. Any person so happily and ingeniously concerned with his own epitaph we are likely to feel can hardly be hurt by death, much less by any smaller enemy. He is so much a 'sentimental son of a turnkey' (I. xviii), anticipating so quickly any dolorous feelings, that he seems likely to be able to turn them off for us. He also plays the sort of role we are used to in earlier Dickens novels: the weak-headed but gentle lover, who is perfectly willing to accept at the end a secondary reward or none at all. The heroine invariably offers him not love but Christian kindness. Here, however, Little Dorrit meets him with a look 'of fright and something like dislike', and the potentially funny character almost instantly changes to a serious one: 'The mournfulness of his spirits, and the gorgeousness of his appearance, might have made him ridiculous, but that his delicacy made him respectable' (I. xviii). Finally, the humour is turned to a sadness which, if sentimental, is probably the most effective sentimentality in all of Dickens: 'As she held out her hand to him with these words, the heart that was under the waistcoat of sprigs—mere slop-work, if the truth must be known—swelled to the size of the heart of a gentleman; and the poor common little fellow, having no room to hold it, burst into tears' (I. xviii). His pain is the pain of all the 'common little fellows', and the brilliant aside on the 'slop-work' suggests that he feels the hurt of all the poor who try for something better. His epitaphs, then, while still funny, are, at the same time, the darkest expressions of the comic ego in Dickens. Behind the fun is the sense that if John is to have any rewards they will be in death:

Here lie the mortal remains of JOHN CHIVERY, Never anything worth mentioning, Who died about the end of the year one thousand eight hundred and twenty-six, Of a broken heart, Requesting with his last breath that the word AMY might be inscribed over his ashes, Which was accordingly directed to be done, By his afflicted Parents. (I. xviii)

His satisfactions are there, but they are certainly extreme.

As the novel proceeds, John's delicacy and loyalty are made more and more important, but his ridiculousness never disappears: 'The world may sneer at a turnkey, but he's a man—when he isn't a woman, which among female criminals he's expected to be.' For once, Dickens's rhetoric, conscious of its own brilliant effects, simply explains itself: 'Ridiculous as the innocence of his talk was, there was yet a truthfulness in Young John's simple, sentimental character, and a sense of being wounded in some very tender respect, expressed in the burning face and in the agitation of his voice and manner, which Arthur must have been cruel to disregard' (II. xxvii). One must not disregard his pain, and it is very difficult to disregard his humour.

With Flora,[11] there is even more to balance and to hold in mind. This great comedienne functions, finally, as the most important attack on comedy. She is to Arthur, as the narrator says the past is to 'most men', the repository of 'all the locked-up wealth of his affection and imagination' (I. xiii), and when she again appears, it is with a 'fatal shock'. She reminds Arthur that all happiness is illusory and that the only constant is misery. Her humorous attempts to revive the old days only make the pain sharper, and it is, ironically, her attempt to be what he wants—the Flora of the past—that makes the affair both funny and sad. Flora's implicit repudiation of our sense of the past is, more basically, a repudiation of the continuity necessary for comedy, of the sense of a stability that underlies growth and makes possible such formulae as 'they lived happily ever after'. Here it is implied that the natural order of things is one of decay, not growth, and that only disillusionment is stable. *Little Dorrit* is a very sharp attack on the very reminiscent tone that made *David Copperfield* so strong. Eden is not lost here; rather it is suggested

[11] The best comments on Flora are by Dickens himself. He wrote to Forster: 'There are some things in Flora in number seven that seem to me to be extraordinarily droll, with something serious at the bottom of them after all' (*Life*, ii. 183). In another letter he also touched very close to one of the basic reasons Flora makes us so sad: 'Indeed some people seem to think I have done them a personal injury, and that their individual Floras (God knows where they are, or who) are each and all Little Dorrits!' (*Nonesuch Letters*, ii. 785, to the Duke of Devonshire, 5 July 1856). Monroe Engel's statements on the 'terrible pathos' of Flora's 'divided awareness' seem to me perceptive and valid (*The Maturity of Dickens*, p. 131).

that, even if there ever had been an Eden, it was filled with weeds.

But Flora has more than these simple negative functions. Even if her final contribution to the novel is anti-comic, she is, by herself, a true comic character. Her motto, 'We do not break but bend' (I. xxiv), might be that of all the important comic characters. Like them, Flora has enormous internal resources for fighting the darkness. She combats loneliness, for instance, by providing both sides to a conversation: 'Oh good gracious me I hope you never kept yourself a bachelor so long on my account! . . . but of course you never did why should you, pray don't answer, I don't know where I'm running to' (I. xiii). There is the sense, of course, that she must keep talking or the other person will ruin things. But she *does* keep talking; not only that, she performs her favourite imitation of the past—'Papa! Hush, Arthur, for Mercy's sake!'—with 'infinite relish' (I. xxiii). Flora's verbal resources, in other words, are not purely negative and defensive; they are also happy and expansive.

More important, perhaps, is the fact that through it all she has preserved a powerful 'warmth of heart', a preservation that runs counter to the novel's main ironic direction, which implies that only the values of the Circumlocution Office are preserved. Flora, in this very basic way, offers a small but very significant comic hope. She is remarkably kind not only to Arthur and to Little Dorrit but to her symbolic legacy from the world, Mr. F's Aunt, a comic essence of hostility.[12] To some extent, I suppose, Mr. F's Aunt is a double figure, a symbolic completion of Flora, adding the maliciousness that has been drained out of her protector. More centrally, though, she serves as a satire on all the assurances of language and human knowledge, screaming out, with 'mortal hostility towards the human race', 'There's mile-stones on the Dover road!' (I. xxiii). To Mr. F's Aunt, all such facts are reasons for 'bitterness and scorn', and she madly but pointedly shouts out the fact of her disappointment and her humiliation. She also looks for a cause for this pain, gradually becoming more and more

---

[12] The relationship of Mr. F's Aunt to the principles of darkness and aggression in the novel is explored in a fine article by Alan Wilde, 'Mr. F's Aunt and the Analogical Structure of *Little Dorrit*', NCF, xix (1964), 33–44.

personal: 'You can't make a head and brains out of a brass knob with nothing in it. You couldn't do it when your Uncle George was living; much less when he's dead' (I. xxiii). She finally settles on Arthur as a representative cause: 'Drat him, give him a meal of chaff' (II. ix). The astonishing comic point is that her pain is uncaused and that her mad search for a source is, in the end, about as reasonable as anyone's. Mr. F's Aunt's vengeance is only an extension of Fanny's and Miss Wade's. Thematically, then, her position is not purely amusing, and the increasingly sharp focus of her hostility makes laughter more and more difficult. Still, her maliciousness highlights, by contrast, Flora's gentleness and kindness.

These last qualities are all the more impressive because they are so solidly founded in Flora. When Arthur tries lamely to assure her that he is happy to see her, she responds with a melancholy shrewdness:

'You don't seem so . . . you take it very coolly, but however I know you are disappointed in me, I suppose the Chinese ladies— Mandarinesses if you call them so—are the cause or perhaps I am the cause myself, it's just as likely.'

'No, no,' Clennam entreated, 'don't say that.'

'Oh I must you know,' said Flora, in a positive tone, 'what nonsense not to, I know I am not what you expected, I know that very well.' (I. xiii)

She understands Arthur's feelings and the cause of those feelings. Flora is amazing because, for all her imaginative games, she is not a self-deceiver. She sees disappointment and somehow manages to keep going. Unlike Arthur she does not really romanticize the past: 'Mr. F was so devoted to me that he never could bear me out of his sight . . . though of course I am unable to say how long that might have lasted if he hadn't been cut short while I was a new broom, worthy man but not poetical manly prose but not romance' (I. xxiv). She is a person who builds comic resiliency in the midst of pain, not, like Mrs. Gamp, transcending the pain, but holding it in balance with the joy. For us, as for Arthur, then, the 'sense of the sorrowful' and the 'sense of the comical' must be 'curiously blended' (I. xiii).

To make matters more complex, there are times when Flora presents a vulnerable side to us, even a slightly defensive one.

Her volubility is often really only a desire to talk, to get all her feelings out, and it expresses, at these times, a pathetic fear of silence: 'Good gracious, Arthur,—I should say Mr. Clennam, far more proper—the climb we have had to get up here and how ever to get down again without a fire-escape and Mr. F's Aunt slipping through the steps and bruised all over and you in the machinery and foundry way too only think, and never told us!' (I. xxiii). There is, further, a real sense in which Arthur is unkind to her: 'as Mr. F himself said if seeing is believing not seeing is believing too and when you don't see you may fully believe you're not remembered' (II. ix). Her desperate loneliness, thus, sometimes comes to the surface, and she appears terribly vulnerable:

'so true it is that oft in the stilly night ere slumber's chain has bound people, fond memory brings the light of other days around people—very polite but more polite than true I am afraid, for to go into the machinery business without so much as sending a line or a card to papa—I don't say me though there was a time but that is past and stern reality has now my gracious never mind—does not look like it you must confess'. (I. xxiii)

She really knows what 'stern reality' is, and it is horribly cruel to her. The mixture of the comic and the painful, the poetic flight and the sad moment of self-consciousness appears over and over again in her speech. She cannot, finally, rest on poetic platitude. Micawber would have wonderfully embellished the notion of 'oft in the stilly night'; he would certainly never have questioned it.

In the end, Flora is a picture of hopeless devotion rather sadly if imaginatively parodying herself: 'Papa sees so many and such odd people . . . that I shouldn't venture to go down for any one but you Arthur but for you I would willingly go down in a diving-bell much more a dining-room' (II. ix). This self-parody is, apparently, the only outlet for the comic spirit in the novel. Not only is the opening very limited, but it clearly takes great courage and spirit even to try for it. Flora has certain roots in earlier comic conceptions—the basic sexual humour of Rachael Wardle and Miggs, Sairey Gamp's happy parodies of the instability of existence, the transcendent use of language of Dick Swiveller and Micawber. She expands all these roles, adds a much deeper self-consciousness and presents, paradoxically, not only amusement but melancholy. At the close of the novel she is forced to admit 'that I don't know after all whether it wasn't all nonsense between us though pleasant at the time'. It is true that she bounces back with a Micawber spring—' "The withered chaplet my dear," said Flora, with great enjoyment, "is then perished the column is crumbled" ' (II. xxxiv)—but there is no possibility of triumph. She is left with Mr. F's Aunt and her loneliness. The best we can say is that she is not done for.

There is a certain aptness, then, in the final, wildly malicious response of Mr. F's Aunt: 'Bring him for'ard, and I'll chuck him out o' winder!' Whoever has killed comedy ought certainly to be chucked 'out o' winder!' But here, as elsewhere in the novel, the enemy can't be located. It is Nobody's Fault.

9 *Our Mutual Friend*

MR. PICKWICK IN PURGATORY

'My dear Boffin, everything wears to rags,' said
Mortimer, with a light laugh.

'I won't go so far as to say everything,' returned Mr. Boffin, on whom his manner seemed
to grate, 'because there's some things that I
never found among the dust.' (I. VIII)

Our Mutual Friend is very much like *Little Dorrit*, as everyone
knows; it is also very much like *The Pickwick Papers*, as very
few will admit. Gaffer Hexam's grisly Socratic examination
of his partner, Rogue Riderhood, raises issues as dark as any
suggested by Dr. Haggage: 'Is it possible for a dead man to
have money? What world does a dead man belong to?
T'other world. What world does money belong to? This world.
How can money be a corpse's? Can a corpse own it, want it,
claim it, miss it?' (I. I). This passage not only establishes the
main themes of the novel but also implies that there is one
gigantic illusion—money—which is exposed by the one firm
reality—death. But Gaffer's voice is not the voice of the novel,
and *Our Mutual Friend* finally transcends the bitterness of
Little Dorrit. The first clue to the difference lies in the former
novel's peculiarly ambivalent attitude towards the victims.
Dickens, the great novelist of the helpless, ends his career by
taking a darkly ironic view of the weak, and of the virtuous
weak at that, not the selfish William Dorrit but the selfless
and independent Betty Higden. Betty is very much admired,
but the position she is forced into is that most dangerous to a
comic society. Her understandable desire to avoid the workhouse amounts, ironically, to a repulsion to all those who
would help her. But even more central, her fierce self-suffici-
ency, developed as a necessity, keeps the orphan Johnny from

the hospital and the medical aid that the doctor implies might have saved his life: 'This should have been days ago. Too late!' (II. ix). The great, broad-shouldered English pride in self, nurtured both by a hard society and a courageous spirit, leads here to ignorance, isolation, and harm. Dickens suggests even that Betty's chief virtue has some ties to that of Mr. Boffin's slimy misers:

'Some of us will be dying in a workhouse next.'

'As the persons you cited,' quietly remarked the secretary, 'thought they would, if I remember, sir?'

'And very creditable in 'em too,' said Mr. Boffin. 'Very independent in 'em!' (III. v)

Our Mutual Friend attacks the anti-social retirement of *Little Dorrit*, its completely understandable but finally disastrous plan of defensiveness, and insists on the necessity of human ties, expansiveness, and social life. Rugged independence is sacrificed for the chance of comic communion.

The novel shows a full awareness of the dangers of openness and of the extreme difficulty of finding true selfhood and love, but, for all the filth, the ordure, the slime, the metaphoric transmogrification of people into birds of prey, and the vision of established society as a dismal swamp, *Our Mutual Friend* comes closer to the solution of *Pickwick* than any other Dickens novel. It has the same dark optimism. '*Our Mutual Friend* makes a happy return to the earlier manner of Dickens at the end of Dickens's life', said G. K. Chesterton, and George Orwell, agreeing, said that the return was 'not an unsuccessful return either. Dickens's thoughts seem to have come full circle.'[1] We have been taught by more recent critics that these statements must be qualified, but they do point to one outstanding similarity: both novels establish an expansive comic society, which is clearly removed from the awful depersonalized mass which goes by that name, but which is none the less authentically comic in its values and its promise. Both novels suggest that there is an opening for those willing to submit to a proper education. While the education in the later novel is much more harsh than was Mr. Pickwick's, the goal of that education, the discovery of the nature of true reality, is seen as promising, not delusive. In this sense the novel is much

---

[1] *Appreciations and Criticisms*, p. 207; *Dickens, Dali and Others*, p. 8.

brighter than was *David Copperfield*; here it is the good
people, not the villains, who are in close touch with the real.
One of the main humorous episodes, the tussle between Boffin
and Wegg, makes just this point. For much of the novel,
Silas appears to be much like Uriah Heep, less smoothly but
just as effectively manipulating reality so as to entangle the
good but naïve Mr. Boffin. In the end, of course, it is Wegg's
avarice and selfishness which are out of touch with reality,
and the pleasant comic surprise is that our laughter all along
has supported the true values. Finally, then, laughter is used
to attack illusion, and there is not the ironic sense here, as there
was in *David Copperfield* and *Little Dorrit*, that only happiness
is unreal. Certainly the commercial society, of which Wegg is
both an extension and a symbol, is largely based on the halluci-
nation of money, and our clarifying laughter works to expel
that society. But this expulsion does not upset the comic
solution; it only suggests that here, as in *Pickwick Papers*,
the true reality is personal and the true society very selective.

It is a true comic society, however, established with, among
other things, a basic sexual humour, freer and lighter than
anything since *Pickwick*. The Wilfer family, for instance,
contains great varieties of female aggression, not only in the
stony and shrewish Mrs. Wilfer but in her equally imperious
daughter:

'Dearest Lavinia,' urged Mr. Sampson, pathetically, 'I adore you.'
'Then if you can't do it in a more agreeable manner,' returned
the young lady, 'I wish you wouldn't.' (IV. XVI)

The humour here, as with *Pickwick*'s Mrs. Pott, attacks the
socially dangerous demands of women. Even more interesting,
however, is the almost equally strong attack on the victims
of female tyranny. Mr. Sampson shares in all the attacks, and
while the perpetual cherub, R. W., is pleasant enough, he
has so readily given up the fight that he is easily identified as
one source of his unhappily disrupted home, his daughter
Bella's corruption, and, incidentally, his own wife's demands
for power. The fact that he has 'no egotism in his pleasant
nature' would have made him something of a hero in *Little
Dorrit*, but it makes him a comic butt here. Laughter, then, is
asked to support not only the standard balance of the family

unit, which is the basis of the normal comic society, but also the importance of an assertive and confident ego.

There are other important parallels between this last novel and the first one. The very form of *Our Mutual Friend*, with its absence of a clear radial centre, even of clearly marked central characters,[2] provides the same comic sense of spontaneity and apparent discontinuity that misled early critics into calling both novels formless. More crucial, however, is the acceptance of the things of this world, even, if seen rightly, of money itself. Though the novel is certainly concerned with aberrant attitudes toward money, the central attack is not on money but on the exaggerated importance attached to it. As in all comedies, money is seen as the great generator of illusion,[3] but it contains within itself very positive forces. It is an index of personality and, even more, an instrument for the testing and development of personality. The neutral quality of money itself and its potential for good are themes so explicitly stated in the novel that it is difficult to see how they ever could have been missed: John Harmon argues, 'But all people are not the worse for riches' (IV. v), and Mrs. Boffin points out that old Harmon's money is at last 'beginning to sparkle in the sunlight' (IV. xiii). Perhaps the definitive attitude, however, is Rumty Wilfer's. When Bella admits that she hates poverty and loves very much what money will buy, her father very simply says, 'Really, I think most of us do' (II. viii). This majority response is precisely that of the novel, and it cheerfully rewards with baskets of money the characters who have been initiated into the comic society. Without money, after all, how could Mr. Pickwick have provided himself with milk punch?

But *Our Mutual Friend* is, one must admit, very largely an affair of muck and corpses, not of milk punch and cricket matches, and any comparison between the two novels must carry with it severe qualifications. The need for these qualifications is most apparent in the details of the novels. The 'Six Jolly Fellowship Porters', for instance, though 'a bar to soften the human breast' (I. vi), is no 'Leather Bottle', set in a

---

[2] This point is made by Miller, *Charles Dickens*, p. 292.

[3] Lionel Trilling, 'Manners, Morals, and the Novel', *The Liberal Imagination* (New York, 1957), pp. 203–4.

charming country village. The comfort is there, but it is of a very grim sort, and it is provided to the miscellaneous 'waterfront characters' who, we assume, are something like the two we know best, Gaffer and Riderhood, unprincipled and violent men. There is no effort to soften the dangerousness of these men, and in the late scene where Rogue robs the dying Betty Higden, their truly brutal unscrupulousness is made undeniable. Still, the humour associated with the inn and with its 'pepperer' of a mistress, Miss Abbey Potterson, tends to repudiate the force *Little Dorrit* was willing to put on killing off the incorrigibles. Miss Abbey rules her burly customers with exactly 'the air of a schoolmistress' (I. vi), and their complete and abject submission suggests that these thugs are really little boys at heart and that human nature, however perverted, has usually (though not always, as Riderhood himself makes clear) a sound core. Our laughter at Abbey directs our attention to the larger evil and confirms the novel's key argument that the dismal swamp is not created by these creatures but by the fastidious superficiality of Podsnap and Veneering. The point, thus, is far more complex than the similar situation in *Pickwick* but contains within it the impulse that had Mr. Pickwick recognize Jingle in prison and forgive him.

Similarly, the treatment of the unnamed 'foreign gentleman' in *Our Mutual Friend* uses very different means but arrives at much the same ends as the laughter evoked by the ignorant Count Smorltork in *Pickwick*. While the early novel simply assumed the superiority of England and her language in order to provide rather primal Hobbesian laughter, in *Our Mutual Friend* the perspective is completely shifted and the reader is denied the immediate comfort of bigotry. When Mr. Podsnap explains, with grandly patronizing lessons in pronunciation thrown in, that England is specially favoured by Providence, the foreign gentleman responds, 'It was a little particular of Providence; . . . for the frontier is not large' (I. xi). The foreigner has complete common sense, indeed sanity, behind him, and the humour is made to attack England's 'representative man'. But Dickens has never, even for a moment, asked us to identify with Podsnap, and so, though the laughter rejects one society, it builds, at the same time, a sense of the superiority of another kind of society, not yet fulfilled but

later to be populated by the Boffins, the Harmons, the Wray-
burns, and, one suspects, the Sloppys. The humour in both
novels, then, expels in order to confirm.

The means in *Our Mutual Friend* are, of course, different
and do fit the novel's most important tenet: that the first
condition of comedy is the full acknowledgement of social and
individual corruption. Though something of the same claim
might be made for *Pickwick*, it is certain that the corruption
envisaged here is much deeper and much more pervasive.
Just as *Pickwick* was a novel most closely associated with the
myth of Eden, so is *Our Mutual Friend* preoccupied with the
combined torture and hope of purgatory. The final goals are
no longer to be recaptured; they are to be arduously fought
for. Even Boffin's elaborate masquerade suggests that Dickens
now sees the attaining of comedy as something very difficult
and rare. The full sense of Eden being the natural condition
of man is certainly lost. The novel distrusts, in fact, many of
the assumed virtues of *Pickwick*'s Eden: innocence, benevolence, and passivity. *Our Mutual Friend* can be seen as an
attempt to find the early comic solution in a world whose
society is so vicious and so hardened that only a form of
rebirth is promising. Seen in comparison with any other
Dickens novel, however, *Our Mutual Friend* offers a real hope,
one which is a matured and more complex version of the
original vision from the wheelbarrow.

The sad fact is, however, that *Our Mutual Friend* does not
fully sustain this tougher comic vision,[4] and I think it likely
that the reader is forced to pay for the increasingly moving
Wrayburn–Hexam plot with the increasingly silly and trite
Wilfer–Harmon plot. Taylor Stoehr has suggested that the
novel is really one-half of a great novel,[5] and, while I think it
is only at the end that the second plot goes sour, he is generally
right. On the one hand we have the uncompromising artistic
tact that insists that Eugene 'might not be much disfigured
by-and-bye' (IV. xvi); on the other hand we have baby

---

[4] There is enormous controversy on this point, and many critics, of course,
do not agree that there is a failure. Of those who do, one of the most interesting
is Robert Barnard, who argues that the novel fails 'because Dickens was losing
his faculty for writing serious comedy' ('The Choral Symphony: *Our Mutual
Friend*', *REL*, ii [July, 1961], 93).

[5] *Dickens: The Dreamer's Stance* (Ithaca, 1965), pp. 206–7.

Harmon and his aviary. What goes wrong, perhaps, is that the spirit of the novel suddenly becomes too Pickwickian[6] in this section of the plot. Complex and troubling matters are treated as simple and remote. The suggested union between Jenny Wren and Sloppy, for instance, weakly flashes back to Mr. Winkle and Arabella Allen. But Jenny, in particular, is no Arabella Allen, and she can never be brought into conjunction with Sloppy's world—no matter how well he 'ornaments' her crutch handle. Though Dickens insists on Sloppy's delicacy in suggesting this ornamentation, such an operation is almost bound to seem callous or flippant, and the reduction of her pain and torment to a prospective family joke is indicative of the attempted oversimplification.

But the relaxation comes only late in the novel, and, despite this flaw, *Our Mutual Friend* is one of Dickens's most impressive novels. If not as consistent or unified either in method or in attitude as *Little Dorrit*, it is perhaps more courageous in what it attempts: the final destruction of the old, corrupt society and the fashioning of a new and open one. As always with Dickens, the process is supported fully by his humour, which here is used, perhaps more than in any other novel, as a structural element, binding together characters, attitudes, and different parts of the novel. Even the fine set pieces, where the narrator calls upon his most sarcastic rhetoric, are no longer allowed, as they sometimes were in *Bleak House* or *Hard Times*, to stand alone. Here they often signal the beginning of a recurrent humorous pattern, which clarifies and enforces the theme. One of the most important instances involves the brilliant satire of shares. Chapter x (Book I) opens with an extended and excited attack, in which the tempo builds with the anger:

Have no antecedents, no established character, no cultivation, no ideas, no manners; have Shares. Have Shares enough to be on Boards of Direction in capital letters, oscillate on mysterious business between London and Paris, and be great. Where does he come from? Shares. Where is he going to? Shares. What are his tastes? Shares. Has he any principles? Shares.

[6] I do not mean to suggest that the vision of *Pickwick* is in any way inferior. But, since the two novels work on very different assumptions and ask very different questions, the mixture is incongruous and startling.

The same motif appears then in discussing the Boffins' search for an orphan:

The suddenness of an orphan's rise in the market was not to be paralleled by the maddest records of the Stock Exchange. . . . The market was 'rigged' in various artful ways. Counterfeit stock got into circulation. Parents boldly represented themselves as dead, and brought their orphans with them. Genuine orphan-stock was surreptitiously withdrawn from the market. (I. xvi)

Later in the chapter, the same diction describes poor Sloppy: 'A considerable capital of knee and elbow and wrist and ankle had Sloppy, and he didn't know how to dispose of it to the best advantage, but was always investing it in wrong securities, and so getting himself into embarrassed circumstances.' The perverse and cruel substitution of commercial for human values is forcibly demonstrated by this organic humour.

Even more striking than this repetitive technique is the violent negative tendency of much of the humour. Though the ultimate purpose of the humour here is the same as in *Pickwick*, it is much more deeply aggressive, seeking primarily not so much to protect our natural goodness as to extirpate our corruption. It is a violent humour of rejection, very often Swiftian in its mode. The laughter evoked by *Our Mutual Friend* is not, as in other novels, pushed towards compassion or terror so much as towards disgust. Nowhere else in Dickens is the macabre so nearly nauseating as, for example, in the description of Mr. Dolls's death. He wanders, like other drunks, to Covent Garden Market, largely for 'the companionship of the trodden vegetable refuse, which is so like their own dress that perhaps they take the Market for a great wardrobe' (IV. ix), is seized with a fit, dies, and is carried to Jenny's home where 'in the midst of the dolls with no speculation in their eyes, lay Mr. Dolls with no speculation in his'.

But the humour is purgative so that, in the end, the reader may be able to reach the insight of Eugene. The novel is really an attack not on money but on egoism, and the most crucial theme is announced in the title: mutuality and its values of friendship and love. The old society has erected a system of camouflages and substitutes which makes love impossible and which turns the joy of life into a hysterical delusion, symbolized by the mad search for money. *Our Mutual Friend* destroys, as

comedy always has, the illusory and false in order to provide
for the comfort and happiness possible in reality. Despite the
fact that the illusion is monstrous and the destruction immense,
then, *Our Mutual Friend* shares the confidence of *Pickwick*
that the true reality is a comic one, and our laughter here
points us towards Dulwich once more.

But before one can find the way to Dulwich, it is necessary
to clear away all the impediments, which, in this case, amount
to all existing social beliefs and pressures and almost all
private inclinations. An extreme form of this humour of
expulsion is displayed very clearly in the first chapter, where
that creature of the slime, Gaffer, and his daughter Lizzie are
conducting their gruesome *fishing*, an important and disgusting
reversal of comic play. But Dickens does not treat this episode
solely as disgusting; the characters exhibit tendencies which
in other environments would certainly be funny. After Gaffer
runs through his ridiculous argument with Riderhood, where
he distinguishes his own honest corpse-robbing from Gaffer's
'sneaking' thievery of living men, he shoves off, 'composing
himself into the easy attitude of one who has asserted the high
moralities and taken an unassailable position'. The combination of amusement and horror acts to expel not only his
occupation, but his method: the creation of self-serving and
meaningless distinctions, the hollow smugness, the selfishness
which alienates him from his 'partner' and his daughter, and
from any sane conception of reality.

And his method is precisely that of society. Gaffer Hexam
is truly the double of Mr. Podsnap, and Mr. Podsnap is very
clearly a pillar of the English world. He and Veneering are
both, significantly, called 'representative' men, and though
Podsnap appears at first more substantial and though he
strains mightily to maintain his superiority to Veneering,
there is no difference. They are Boots, Brewer, Buffer, the
Payer-off of the National Debt, the Poem on Shakespeare, the
Grievance—all indistinguishable. At the same time, as representative men, they are the powerful men of the nation as
it is now conceived. The humour that seeks to reduce and

destroy them, therefore, might be called anarchic, or perhaps revolutionary.

Veneering is ripped apart with a technique amazing in its economy. 'What was observable in the furniture, was observable in the Veneerings—the surface smelt a little too much of the workshop and was a trifle sticky' (I. ii). One *observes* both the furniture and the Veneerings; and since no distinction is asked for, the implied simile vanishes. The Veneerings simply are furniture. They are manufactured people, so 'filmy' that they really do not exist. Dickens, interestingly, introduces the Veneerings and instantly reduces them. There is no trickery in the humour and no effort is made to identify Veneering with us. Though the final aim of the humour is to make us recognize Veneering and Podsnap as apt representatives of a good part of our own experience, Dickens makes it easy for us to use that knowledge without discomfort. However malicious his humorous attack, his rhetoric is amazingly gentle. The reader is very quietly pushed toward Eugene—by way of the Social Chorus.

The key irony of this last term lies in the fact that there is no community, no real society. The Veneerings have no friends, receive no attention, command no respect—nor does anyone else. Twemlow's continual worry about whether he is Veneering's 'oldest and dearest friend' makes this point very sharply. In this society there are no friends, primarily because the society does not allow membership to human beings: 'Oh! Mr. Boots! Delighted. Mr. Brewer! This *is* a gathering of the clans. Thus Tippins, and surveys Fledgeby and outsiders through golden glass, murmuring as she turns about and about, in her innocent giddy way. Anybody else I know? No, I think not. Nobody there. Nobody *there*. Nobody anywhere!' (II. xvi). This suggestion of bleak nothingness and Veneering's continual straining for social acceptance might, indeed, have been very sad. Veneering, however, is never at all touched by melancholy or any other feeling. He is the same whether deserted or accepted, very literally a man of surfaces, without depth or self-consciousness. As is very seldom the case in Dickens, the humour, though completely negative, is also completely pure. Since we can hardly feel a compulsion to pity Veneering, the hostility in our laughter is unchecked.

Sometimes, the humour becomes so very basic that it approaches the level of the dirty joke. When Podsnap first enters Veneering's house and mistakes Twemlow for his host, his wife follows suit, 'looking towards Mr. Twemlow with a plaintive countenance and remarking to Mrs. Veneering in a feeling manner, firstly, that she fears he has been rather bilious of late, and, secondly, that the baby is already very like him' (I. II). Though the appeal of the joke is a little unfocused; whether we respond to the ludicrous notion of adultery, the play on the theme of this 'oldest and dearest' friendship, or the idea of two such pieces of furniture as the Veneerings having sexual impulses, our amusement is urged to belittle the Veneerings and suggest their essential nothingness.

This nothingness is, further, made explicitly representative in Mr. Veneering's campaign for Parliament. His non-existent friends rally round him to do precisely nothing, and Podsnap's perfectly sound advice—'You ought to have a couple of active energetic fellows, of gentlemanly manners, to go about' (II. III)—unintentionally satirizes the entire competitive economy Veneering represents so ably. The work these people do, the energy they expend, amounts to a gigantic charade, rigged from the start to no one's advantage. It is not only a system of government that is being attacked here but a system of life as well, an organization and theory Dickens had fought against in every novel and which he here brings into compact shape as the dangerous and hilarious Podsnappery.

' "Let me . . . have the pleasure of presenting Mrs. Podsnap to her host. She will be," ' in his fatal freshness he seems to find perpetual verdure and eternal youth in the phrase, "she will be so glad of the opportunity, I am sure!" ' (I. II). Podsnap finds eternal (and fatal) freshness in clichés; he is a dark parody of the important rejuvenations celebrated in Eugene and Harmon. He lives off the formulated and falsifying language on which this society is built, particularly on the handy fiction of the 'young person'. The humorous attack latent in this phrase is only incidentally directed at prudery.[7]

---

[7] Dickens makes it clear, in fact, that Podsnap's prudery is based on notions which are actually prurient: 'And the inconvenience of the young person was that, according to Mr. Podsnap, she seemed always liable to burst into blushes

More important is the way in which the notion reduces all questions to the simplest and most evasive terms: 'It was an inconvenient and exacting institution, as requiring everything in the universe to be filed down and fitted to it' (I. xi). This sense of reduction is attacked over and over again in Podsnappery; for it does away with all comic variety and threatens to turn us all into Lady Tippinses, old, monotonous, and mean. The fact that there is 'no youth (the young person always excepted) in the articles of Podsnappery' (I. xi) suggests that the 'young person' is a selfish and somewhat filthy invention of the aged, without relation to the truly young.

In fact, Podsnap's whole inverted world amounts to an attempt to provide a comic existence for himself, and our laughter at Podsnappery is ultimately a rejection of inadequate or false solutions. Podsnap 'was quite satisfied. He never could make out why everybody was not quite satisfied, and he felt conscious that he set a brilliant social example in being particularly well satisfied with most things, and, above all other things, with himself' (I. xi). His satisfaction is, as we see in his poor daughter, completely self-contained and non-generating. It is based on rigorously maintained ignorance: 'I don't want to know about it; I don't choose to discuss it; I don't admit it!' (I. xi). His methodical world is only an imposition of his restricted ego ('getting up at eight, shaving close at a quarter-past,' etc.) on externals, reducing all the world to his own being: 'what Providence meant, was invariably what Mr. Podsnap meant' (I. xi). Podsnap is no less a blasphemer than Mrs. Clennam and, as a truly representative man, is much more dangerous. Laughter is made to work against his defensiveness, his stasis ('We know what France wants; we see what America is up to; but we know what England is' [IV. xvii]), his cruelty ('Then it [starvation] was their own fault' [I. xi]), and his cold and finally anti-social code, perfectly expressed as a series of exercises 'on the social ice' (II. viii). In the last chapter of the novel, the narrator assures us that, in the great comic tradition, Veneering's true

_____

when there was no need at all. There appeared to be no line of demarcation between the young person's excessive innocence, and another person's guiltiest knowledge' (I. xi).

emptiness is about to be exposed and that the social chorus is, for us, an irrelevant whine. The Podsnappian (or English) society is rhetorically destroyed.

Indeed it has had more than its share of death from the beginning, in Podsnap's parties where the guests move around like a 'revolving funeral' (I. xi) and in Veneering's ironic display of 'the bran-new pilgrims on the wall, going to Canterbury in more gold frame than procession, and more carving than country' (I. iii). Veneering's attempt to gild this great symbol of freshness and life makes the picture an appropriate, though unintentional, symbol of death. But the most prominent death's head is Lady Tippins. With her 'immense obtuse drab oblong face, like a face in a tablespoon, and a dyed Long Walk up the top of her head, as a convenient public approach to the bunch of false hair behind' (I. ii), Lady Tippins is subject to the most brilliant physical wit in Dickens. Her humour 'is enhanced by a certain yellow play in [her] throat, like the legs of scratching poultry' (I. ii). We are asked to laugh over and over again at the fact that she is old and ugly. The corpse of the drowned and mangled George Radfoot is 'not *much* worse than Lady Tippins' (I. iii), and in the end we see that this old 'dyed and varnished' lady is not just artificial; she is unreal: 'you might scalp her, and peel her, and scrape her, and make two Lady Tippinses out of her, and yet not penetrate to the genuine article' (I. x). She isn't there at all, and our laughter helps to get at her true nothingness and to define the way this 'yellow wax candle—guttering down, and with some hints of a winding sheet in it' (II. xvi) is emblematic of moribund Podsnappery. She is like one of Poe's innumerable grinning skulls who haunt gay parties and forecast their doom. Instead of terror, Dickens uses humour to help kill not only Lady Tippins but the whole rotten society of her 'lovers'.

As we move away from the centre of Podsnappery to its junior officers and its less direct manifestations, the intensity of the humorous attack is still not relaxed. The most negative and hostile humour, in fact, is directed at Fascination Fledgeby, who is a Veneering on the rise and, more important, an illustration of Podsnappery in action. Fledgeby represents the application of the 'getting up at eight' egoism to the young and the stupid. He is a pure economic creation[8] and a true nineteenth-century man, with a real genius in money matters and complete idiocy otherwise. His nickname refers sarcastically to his anti-social qualities: other people must actually talk for him, and Dickens flays this offshoot of the commercial society with deeply aggressive and emasculating wit, continually making the frightening and funny point that this impotent non-being is sure to succeed in this mad Podsnappian world. Fledgeby is always 'feeling for the whisker that he anxiously expected' (II. IV) and that is certain never to come, the point being the non-procreative qualities of Podsnappery. Our laughter is urged to support the argument that only the hollowed-out, the self-contained, the moronic, and the sterile rise to the top of this economic anti-society. But Fledgeby's economic success and his exactly corresponding guilt are attacked still further in a cruel but extremely effective scene of pure vengeance. Fledgeby, appropriately attired in 'a pair of Turkish trousers and a Turkish cap' (IV. VIII), is caned by Alfred Lammle, while Mrs. Lammle waits downstairs, politely holding her husband's cap. These fine details provide not so much distractions as excuses for enjoying the fierce aggression at the heart of this scene: 'Oh I smart so! Do put something to my back and arms, and legs and shoulders. Ugh! It's down my throat again and can't come up. Ow! Ow! Ow! Ah—h—h—h! Oh I smart so!' Jenny and the narrator then join with the Lammles to complete this primitive but probably highly satisfying physical vengeance, Jenny by putting pepper on the wounds and the narrator by so obviously relishing the spectacle of Fledgeby's pain: he is last seen 'in the act of plunging and gambolling all over his bed, like a porpoise or dolphin in its native element'. The brutal nature of this comedy suggests not only its very basic nature but a negative impulse so strong that it reaches back to the physical, to the desperate satisfaction of a truly frightened man. Edmund Wilson remarked that Dickens was 'now *afraid* of Podsnap';[9] the humour indicates that he is, at any rate, afraid of the more elemental Podsnappery manifested in Fledgeby.

[8] This is almost literally as well as symbolically true. His mother had agreed to marry his father only because she was unable to pay the bill he held (II. v).

[9] *The Wound and the Bow*, p. 78.

Like the Circumlocution Office, but even more thoroughly and dangerously, the spirit of Podsnappery radiates outward, swallowing the callous Charley Hexam and finally killing his schoolmaster-friend, Bradley Headstone. Dickens deceptively makes the whole basis of Headstone's tragedy originally the subject of a joke: 'Bradley Headstone, in his decent black coat and waistcoat, and decent white shirt, and decent formal black tie, and decent pantaloons of pepper and salt, with his decent silver watch in his pocket and its decent hair-guard round his neck, looked a thoroughly decent young man of six-and-twenty' (II. 1). His mind is a 'wholesale warehouse' of facts, and we are encouraged to laugh at one more unself-conscious automaton. He is even supported by an equally mechanical schoolmistress, Miss Peecher, who could 'write a little essay on any subject, exactly a slate long' (II. 1). But even Miss Peecher, we find, is not actually this superficial: 'If Mr. Bradley Headstone had addressed a written proposal of marriage to her, she would probably have replied in a complete little essay on the theme exactly a slate long, but would certainly have replied yes. For she loved him.' The point is that when the varnish of Podsnappery is applied to anyone who is not, like the Veneerings, all surface, or like Fledgeby, nearly a pure void, the result is a dangerous, potentially tragic repression. For the only time in this novel, Dickens's humour is purposefully misleading. He urges us to assume that Headstone and Miss Peecher are shallow, only to insist on the real terror of Podsnappery by dramatically showing us the results of such a mistake in the extended and moving picture of Bradley Headstone's frustration, the murder he commits, and his suicide. In a novel whose central theme is the attainment of true love, the major enemy is this agency which so distorts men and values as to make love of any kind impossible.

Not satisfied with this rhetorical indictment, Dickens includes two other indications of the power of Podsnappery which, again, clarify the nature of the enemy through humour. The Lammles and Mr. Twemlow represent, respectively, the possibilities within the Podsnap society of imaginative rebellion, or of virtuous and modified acquiescence. The Lammles' marriage, first of all, is another example of the commercial distortion of love. United by Podsnappery, however,

they acknowledge, in a moment of bitter clarity, their condition, and agree on a life of witty vengeance, which at
first seems to be a form of Sam Weller's sustaining war of the
imagination. They arrange a brilliant plan to make money,
get at Podsnap through his daughter, and, at the same time,
maintain a continual parody of Fledgeby. Their ability to
provide conversation for both of the ludicrously shy lovers
amounts to an imaginative creation of their protégés:

'But what,' said Mrs. Lammle, stealing her affectionate hand
toward her dear girl's, 'what does Georgy say?'
'She says,' replied Mr. Lammle, interpreting for her, 'that in her
eyes you look well in any colour.' (II. IV)

Despite this power, though, the Lammles haven't a chance
against Podsnap. They err, first of all, in imagining that
Podsnap really cares about his daughter, but the real failure
comes through Mrs. Lammle's perception of Georgiana's
affection for her. She responds to it and is henceforth beaten;
Podsnap has an easy time with anyone who can love. His
defeat of them is not, of course, personal but just another cool
item of business which follows 'shaving at eight'. The Lammles
are ruined, ultimately, because they try to bring personalities,
even fraudulent ones, into battle against the anti-person,
Podsnap. Finally, then, even Mrs. Lammle's existential tough-
ness—'though this celebration of to-day is all a mockery, he is
my husband, and we must live' (II. XVI)—is overthrown.
Despite the last courageous thrust against Fledgeby, they
cannot maintain the Micawber pose of gay deception. They
go off to a joyless life, only able to 'bear one another, and bear
the burden of scheming together for to-day's dinner and to-
morrow's breakfast—till death divorces us'. Podsnap has
attacked the rebellious imagination and left it worn and
suicidal: 'haggardly weary of one another, of themselves, and
of all this world' (IV. II).

It is equally hard on the man of virtue, poor frazzled Mr.
Twemlow, who tries to exist on its edges. Twemlow is clearly
a part of the Podsnap circle; he is one of the flies which flock
to the newly rich Boffins and is introduced as just another
'innocent piece of dinner-furniture' (I. II). The fact that he is
innocent only makes him easy prey. Though a well-meaning

man, Twemlow suggests a rejection of the passive and sentimental innocence Dickens had once looked so favourably upon.
As a 'Knight of the Simple Heart' (III. xiii), he echoes a part
of Mr. Pickwick quite distinctly, but here Pickwick's qualities
are completely ineffectual, almost undesirable. Twemlow often
becomes clearly not so much a character as a tendency—a
tendency, that is, to be cast out:

> For, the poor little harmless gentleman once had his fancy, like
> the rest of us, and she didn't answer (as she often does not), and he
> thinks the adorable bridesmaid is like the fancy as she was then
> (which she is not at all), and that if the fancy had not married
> some one else for money, but had married him for love, he and she
> would have been happy (which they wouldn't have been), and that
> she has a tenderness for him still (whereas her toughness is a
> proverb). (I. x)

He is too weak to know love at all except through the falsi-
fications of memory. As a hanger-on, Twemlow is exactly like
the impoverished—miserable and nearly undefined as a
separate person: 'Say likewise, my Twemlow, whether it be
the happier lot to be a poor relation of the great, or to stand
in the wintry slush giving the hack horse to drink out of the
shallow tub at the coachstand, into which thou hast so nearly
set thy uncertain foot' (II. xvi).

Twemlow, no doubt, is just what Oliver Twist would have
grown up to be, and, in another novel, he might have received
complete approval. But here, though victimized, his state very
likely arouses little compassion and a good bit of something
close to contempt: Twemlow 'is shorter than the lady as well
as weaker, and as she stands above him with her hardened
manner, and her well-used eyes, he finds himself at such a
disadvantage that he would like to be of the opposite sex'
(III. xvii). In his closing defence of Lizzie, we witness not so
much a revolution or even a change of heart as an ironic
display of the limitations of passive goodness. His position is
not only snobbish—'I think he is the greater gentleman for
the action, and makes her the greater lady'[10]—but uses the

---

[10] In *The Dickens World*, Humphry House argues that Twemlow's speech
demonstrates both sincerity and sophistry and that his 'ingenious phrasing
very imperfectly conceals a sort of satisfaction in the fact that Eugene is really
doing a very generous thing in marrying Lizzie, and that she is doing very well
for herself by marrying him' (p. 163).

very diction he has learned from Podsnappery: 'If the gentleman's feelings of gratitude, of respect, of admiration, and
affection, induced him (as I presume they did) to marry this
lady—.' Mew says the cat. . . .

On another level this humour of expulsion collects in a
massive examination of and a grand attack on mothers. Such
an attack marks an interesting and significant shift in Dickens's
practice; for in all past novels the indictment was laid on the
fathers. The absence of fathers or the perversion of the paternal
function had always symbolized the absence of authority,
potency, and moral direction, but here what is missing is not
moral direction but love. Our laughter is turned time and again
against the inversion, distortion, or neglect of maternal affections, in order finally to provide for a proper and valid love.
From Mrs. Fledgeby's pawnbroker view of motherhood, to
Mrs. Podsnap, Mrs. Veneering, Mrs. Wilfer, and Jenny Wren
and her poor child, we move through a gallery of perversion.
Even the potentially tender women are thwarted: Betty
Higden's ignorant tenderness does not help Johnny, and Mrs.
Boffin's search for an orphan child is never really rewarded.

So fundamental is this attack on false mothers that Mrs.
Podsnap is, in many ways, more frightening than her husband.
She is not merely likened to but identified with a 'rocking-
horse', suggesting her ridiculous stateliness as well as her
absence of direction or meaning and, perhaps more basically
and ironically, her enmity to childhood and joy. Her daughter
is a 'young rocking-horse', who 'was being trained in her
mother's art of prancing in a stately manner without ever
getting on' (I. xi), but again we see the dangers of applying a
superficial system to a person of any complexity. Her mother
may be so inhuman as to be delighted when 'friends of their
souls' were unable to come to Georgiana's birthday party:
'Asked, at any rate, and got rid of' (I. xi). But her daughter is
deeply human and is incapable of this rigid social accounting.
Her bleak admission to Mrs. Lammle, 'Oh! Indeed, it's very
kind of you, but I am afraid I *don't* talk' (I. xi), devastatingly
indicts her mother. Largely because of her natural warmth,
Georgiana is repulsed by Mrs. Podsnap's notion of society and
is, paradoxically, therefore forced to spend all her energies
trying to avoid human contact: 'Oh, there's Ma going up to

somebody! Oh, I know she's going to bring him to me! Oh, please don't, please don't, please don't! Oh, keep away, keep away, keep away!' (I. xi). She has learned that no society at all is more amiable than Podsnappian society. When she is briefly able to 'shrink out of the range of her mother's rocking, and (so to speak) rescue her poor little frosty toes from being rocked over', she creeps to Mrs. Lammle with perhaps the novel's most startling and revealing statement: 'You are not ma. I wish you were' (II. iv). We see her at the end as 'soft-headed and soft-hearted', loyal and generous to her 'first and only friend' (IV. ii) but obviously without much chance in the dismal swamp and still captivated by her dead, rocking-horse mother.

A more extensive rejection of the maternal and a somewhat milder picture of what is generally wrong is given in the Wilfer family. Rumty, the head of the family or 'master', as his wife so sardonically reminds him, is so shy and self-effacing that he shrinks from using an assertive first name and timidly offers only an initial, *R*. He has long ago resigned control to his wife. But it is not so much for an improper assertion of power that Mrs. Wilfer is attacked—in many ways she has simply moved into a power vacuum—but for her constant gloom, her selfishness, and her pomposity. She always speaks in lugubrious hyperbole and manages to make even her compliments grim: 'Pardon me . . . the merits of Mr. Boffin may be highly distinguished—may be more distinguished than the countenance of Mrs. Boffin would imply—but it were the insanity of humility to deem him worthy of a better assistant' (I. xvi). She is the 'corrective' to merriment, aptly compared to the Dead March in *Saul*. Her gloomy presence can, in fact, lead her children to wish 'either that Ma had married somebody else instead of much-teased Pa, or that Pa had married somebody else instead of Ma' (III. iv). Even darker, she can, when convenient, renounce her motherhood altogether: 'Your daughter Bella has bestowed herself upon a Mendicant' (IV. v).

For all this, however, she is really not much more than a comic butt, contributing to but not at the centre of the attack on mothers. She is not a killer, only a mild depressant. With the exception of R. W. (who, we gather, deserves his fate), she does very little harm, simply because she is so consistently ignored. She is forced to be so monumentally imposing because she desperately wants not so much power as attention. As we see that her own children sneer at her, our laughter likely joins their scorn in eliminating from serious consideration this potential tyrant. Her extinction is managed most effectively by her daughter Lavinia, a kind of Meredithian comic imp constantly in attendance on her:

'Papa and Mama were unquestionably tall. I have rarely seen a finer woman than my mother; never than my father.'
The irrepressible Lavvy remarked aloud, 'Whatever grandpapa was, he wasn't a female.' (III. iv)

Lavinia's sharp wit provides us with an opportunity to take revenge on all the aged and the revered, but most particularly to reject all the demands of the false mothers:

'Silence!' proclaimed Mrs. Wilfer. 'I command silence!'
'I have not the slightest intention of being silent, Ma,' returned Lavinia, coolly, 'but quite the contrary.' (III. xvi)

The triumphant and liberating humour is even likely to conceal the truly dark suggestion that no mother at all is better than most of the ones we see in the novel. We are asked to extinguish Mrs. Wilfer in order that we may escape from all mothers.

The obsession with inadequate mothers is grotesquely manifested in the inverted relationship Jenny Wren maintains with her father.[11] The little cripple sublimates some of her pain and bitterness into sharp harangues directed at her father, whom she imaginatively transforms into her child in order to provide herself with the moral authority for scolding. Though unquestionably victimized by the slimy Mr. Dolls, Jenny is no Little Nell, patient and loving, but a neurotic child, searching, even irrationally, for some outlet for her pain. Exactly reversing Nell's attraction to the small and helpless, Jenny hates children and contents herself with malicious plans for vengeance on them—'There's doors under the church in the Square—black doors, leading into black vaults.

[11] There is a good discussion of this interesting character by Richard J. Dunn, 'Dickens and the Tragic-Comic Grotesque', *Studies in the Novel*, i (1969), 153–5, but it is difficult to see how he can find her 'consistently admirable'.

Well! I'd open one of those doors, and I'd cram 'em all in, and then I'd lock the door and through the keyhole I'd blow in pepper' (II. i)—and on her future husband: 'When he was asleep, I'd make a spoon red hot, and I'd have some boiling liquor bubbling in a saucepan, and I'd take it out hissing, and I'd open his mouth with the other hand . . . and I'd pour it down his throat, and blister it and choak him' (II. ii).

Her 'beautiful' side is an imaginative life which, time and again, is identified with a wish for non-being. Even Riah's roof-top, where she sometimes feels light and happy, she instinctively associates with death: 'Don't be gone long. Come back, and be dead!' (II. v). Her game with Riah, in which he is her 'godmother', suggests exactly what is missing: kindness and unselfish love. Jenny's pathetic perversion of sexes and ages, of life and death, indicates how terribly difficult it is to find affection in this world. There is nothing in *Pickwick* to match the stern realism with which Jenny's search for love is handled.

But there is a movement here which is parallel to Pickwick's education, a purging of a different sort, which leads to a preparation for true comedy and true love. In Eugene and Lizzie, Bella and John, and the Boffins we are provided with a positive humour which directs us toward the comic goals. With Eugene, for example, though we are likely to approve of his brilliant attacks on mindless work and hysterical Protestant values of action—'If there is a word in the dictionary under any letter from A to Z that I abominate, it is energy. It is such a conventional superstition, such parrot gabble!' (I. iii)—it becomes clear that he fails utterly to direct his wit and moral imagination to any goals. His cynicism is dangerous but curable. He is, first of all, never captured by Podsnappery, and he has an implicit sense of the important human values: 'When your friends the bees worry themselves to that highly fluttered extent about their sovereign, and become perfectly distracted touching the slightest monarchial movement, are we men to learn the greatness of Tuft-hunting, or the littleness of the Court Circular? I am not clear, Mr. Boffin, but that the hive may be satirical' (I. viii). His lively sense of the ridiculous, though somewhat reminiscent of Henry Gowan's, keeps him sane and self-critical enough to enable him at least to find purgatory. His very imperturbability, however, indicates his moral stasis, and the partial unselfconsciousness he jokes about is pernicious. He can't tell Mortimer his motives because as yet he hasn't really troubled himself to look for them. Appropriately, it is largely his own limitations, his egoism and lack of moral direction, which goad Headstone to homicide:

'But I am more than a lad,' said Bradley, with his clutching hand, 'and I WILL be heard, sir.'
'As a schoolmaster,' said Eugene, 'you are always being heard. That ought to content you.' (II. VI)

His wit is sharp but uncommitted: 'The man seems to believe that everybody was acquainted with his mother!' (II. VI). And in treating Headstone in this way he is unintentionally moving towards Podsnappery, assuming that the absurd schoolmaster is superficial and powerless. Very simply, his comic detachment must be eliminated, and he must be made one with the river's redemptive slime before he can marry the corpse-catcher's daughter. Their marriage ceremony, conducted on the edge of death, is the perfect symbol of his comic rebirth, a rebirth which assaults the old society by the creation of a new and competing one.

Bella's case is not nearly so satisfactory. Although presumably tested by her trial with the Boffins and by her husband's gratuitous mystification, her early promise is largely thrown away. She announces at the beginning, 'I hate to be poor, and we are degradingly poor, offensively poor, miserably poor, beastly poor' (I. IV), but this potentially important theme is never really developed, and Bella's understandable hatred of poverty becomes a tiresome and frivolous attraction to baubles. Dickens makes motions toward educating Bella but then tries to recapture Dora in her. The chapter describing her wedding seems to me the most mechanical writing in Dickens, ending in hilarity so forced it becomes dismal: 'And oh, there are days in this life, worth life and worth death. And oh, what a bright old song it is, that oh, 'tis love, 'tis love, 'tis love, that makes the world go round!' (IV. IV). Bella's trial, finally, simply proves her constant. Her testing is far too easy, never approaching the 'fire and water' that Lizzie had forecast and that the pattern had demanded for her. The comic society is, thus, at least slightly disturbed by having to include such inadequately certified members.

Bella's teachers, the Boffins, also play important but largely unsatisfactory comic roles. Mrs. Boffin, like Mrs. Lupin and Mrs. Todgers, does a very workmanlike job of defining the chief concerns of the open comic society. Beginning as a rather elementary parody of 'Fashion', she expands to become an image of strong affection and an advocate of comfort and expansiveness: ' "That's it!" said the open-hearted Mrs. Boffin. "Lor! Let's be comfortable" ' (I. ix). Most important, she asserts the key comic doctrine, the primacy of feelings: 'It is ... a matter of feeling, but Lor how many matters *are* matters of feeling!' (II. x). Though really only at the periphery of the final comic society, Mrs. Boffin articulates most clearly its values: the old platitude that the world is best served with kindness and decency, which, as George Orwell points out, is not in Dickens such a platitude after all.

Mr. Boffin finally lends his support to this position, but only after a lengthy masquerade, the conclusion of which has pleased almost no one.[12] Nearly all critics have felt either that Boffin ought not to have changed or that, once changed, he should have stayed changed. Boffin is not only subject to some apparent deception on Dickens's part[13] but seems often far too much like the Cheerybles, trotting around without a real moral concern in the world and therefore peculiarly out of place in the complex and urgent environment of the novel. There is, however, a good deal of support for Boffin that is not often noted and which certainly ought to be cited. Most generally, we ought to grant the validity of Dickens's aim: the creation of a basic comedy displaying the permanence underlying apparent change. The Boffins, we are to assume (and there is no reason we should not), have already been educated. It is also true that Dickens allows a critical attitude to play around Boffin, particularly at the beginning—he is described

---

[12] Grahame Smith (*Dickens, Money, and Society*) calls the revelation that Boffin's miserliness has been a disguise 'one of the biggest disappointments in literature' (p. 182) and goes on to discuss the causes and consequences of 'the weakness of the Boffin strand' (pp. 182–3).

[13] The particular passage often referred to comes at the end of Book III, ch. xiv, where Dickens says Boffin, alone in the streets, looked 'very cunning and suspicious'.

as 'warming (as fat usually does), with a tendency to melt' (I. VIII)—suggesting that he is not nearly so complex as Eugene or John and that moral dilemmas will therefore be easy for him. One ought also to allow for the thematic relevance of his disguise and the fine opportunities it allows for attacks on commercialism: 'A sheep is worth so much in the market, and I ought to give it and no more. A secretary is worth so much in the market, and I ought to give it and no more' (III. v). Finally, Dickens does offer a very large number of clues throughout Boffin's miser period that might have (but apparently have not) signalled his intention very clearly. He makes it fairly plain that Boffin is deliberately leading Wegg and Venus on, encouraging their avarice and their fraudulent claims: he rolls his eyes greedily over a miser story and pointedly gasps to his readers, 'see what men put away and forget, or mean to destroy and don't!' (III. VI). There also are several indications of Mrs. Boffin's uneasiness in her role as conspirator: Bella is 'lost in speculations why Mrs. Boffin should look at her as if she had any part in' the upcoming dismissal of Rokesmith, and Dickens says the good lady later 'glanced at her husband as if for orders' (III. xv). This very dismissal, furthermore, provides Boffin with a chance to make his pedagogic point with elaborate unsubtlety: 'Luckily, [Bella,] he had to deal with you, and with me, and with Daniel and Miss Dancer, and with Elwes, and with Vulture Hopkins, and with Blewbury Jones and all the rest of us.' But the strongest clue provided is the final breakfast with the Lammles, where Mr. Boffin acts with delicacy and generosity, not only toward Georgiana but toward the married cheats themselves. Still, Mr. Boffin is called upon to lend enormous positive support to the comic centre, and the scene that reveals his constancy should bring the comic society into focus with a snap. But the slight mystification here and the unaccountable lapse of force in the treatment of Bella considerably weakens the comic satisfaction.

Bella and Boffin aside, however, the comedy is anything but flabby. This is, in fact, Dickens's toughest novel, and he is at some pains to eliminate the sentimental, the weakly romantic, even the too-easy benevolence. There is a great distrust of charity here, as indicated by the long burlesque of begging letters Mr. Boffin receives (I. xvii). Even quite genuine benevolence comes under attack, most pointedly in Charley Hexam's Ragged School. This 'temple of good intentions' is naïve and stupid in its romantic assumptions about children:

But all the place was pervaded by a grimly ludicrous pretence that every pupil was childish and innocent. This pretence, much favoured by the lady-visitors, led to the ghastliest absurdities. Young women old in the vices of the commonest and worst life, were expected to profess themselves enthralled by the good child's book, the Adventures of Little Margery, who resided in the village cottage by the mill. (II. i)

One can't help wondering where Little Nell would stand in this cynical light. In any case, good intentions are clearly not enough; solid and realistic knowledge is needed, not good works that simply flatter one's notion of how happy things really are. All benevolence becomes secret patronizing—'I wish someone would tell me whether other countries get Patronized to anything like the extent of this one!' (II. xiv)— and even the Reverend Frank Milvey and his wife are treated with more than a little suspicion: 'He accepted the needless inequalities and inconsistencies of his life, with a kind of conventional submission that was almost slavish; and any daring layman who would have adjusted such burdens as his, more decently and graciously, would have had small help from him' (I. ix). This masochist is married to a limited and bigoted wife, but as do-gooders go, they are fine people.

Sentimentality is just as vigorously pursued by this hostile humour as is benevolence, particularly when the sentimentality is Mrs. Veneering's: ' "Could it be, I asked myself," says Mrs. Veneering, looking about her for her pocket-handkerchief, "that the Fairies were telling Baby that her papa would shortly be an M.P. ?" ' (II. iii). No flaccid emotional substitutes are allowed here, and all weak longings are treated like Twemlow's dreams or poor Miss Peecher's fantasies, where 'a manly form, bent over the other, being a womanly form of short stature and some compactness, and breathed in a low voice the words, "Emma Peecher, wilt thou be my own?" after which the womanly form's head reposed upon the manly form's shoulder, and the nightingales tuned up' (II. xi). Contempt totally smothers any possible compassion. Even more startling is the treatment of Johnny, who is introduced as something of a brat, ' "holding his breath:" a most terrific proceeding, superinducing, in the orphan, lead-colour rigidity and a deadly silence, compared with which his cries were music yielding the height of enjoyment' (I. xvi). He bears his illness not with resignation but 'with a quiet air of pity for himself' (II. ix), and even the pathos of his death is qualified by the brutal reaction of Silas Wegg: 'Mr. Wegg argued, if an orphan were wanted, was he not an orphan himself, and could a better be desired? . . . [He] chuckled, consequently, when he heard the tidings' (II. x).

The love celebrated by this novel is made more firm because of the relentless, humorous elimination of all unauthentic and easy forms of it. The optimism of *Our Mutual Friend* is real, but it is based on very pessimistic premises. As the mock resurrection of Riderhood suggests, no light desires are satisfied in this world, and comic satisfaction can come only to the truly initiated. It is the function of humour both to narrow the grounds of the comedy and then to assert its importance.

Both of these functions, finally, are combined in the partnership of Venus and Wegg, who provide the most continuous humorous support for the comic pattern. Silas Wegg illustrates in harmless and dismissable ways most of the main themes of Podsnappery, and Venus is a happy reflection of the purgatorial testing and the positive new society. These roles are extremely important, but the characters are, I think, just barely adequate for them. Perhaps the main reason for this is that they hearken back to much simpler comic types; they are both completely unselfconscious and quite uncomplex. Dickens can even use them for some physical, Marx Brothers, humour, for example Wegg's slippery ascents and bouncing descents of the mounds. They are so nearly puppets that they can be played for the kind of visual humour not found in Dickens since Mr. Pickwick chased his wind-blown hat for several pages. Because they are so often simple, Venus and Wegg can lend very elemental support to the novel's most basic comic direction, but the responses they evoke cannot reach very far into the complexities of either Podsnappery or Eugene's purgatorial route. They do, however, accomplish a great deal, and it is only in comparison with earlier humorous supporters that their function seems insufficient. It is important to assert that there is nothing tired or strained about the treatment of these two. The conception is brilliant but too simple.

Silas Wegg illustrates the corruption of the social man and burlesques nearly all the traits we are asked to dismiss: meanness, avarice, vengefulness, selfishness. He is a miniature Podsnap, and our laughing attacks on him are meant to carry over to the rejection of his entire society, even Miss Elizabeth, Master George, Aunt Jane, and Uncle Parker. Wegg is introduced, we gather, in order to be immediately used as an economic parody. He has desperately established squatter's rights to a few square inches and tries to sell there a kind of imitation, Podsnappian comedy: dry nuts, wizened fruit, and corny halfpenny ballads. It is, indeed, a 'sterile' stall (I. v). The most apparent key to the humour evoked here, however, is in the treatment of Wegg's wooden leg, which is viewed as a natural extension of a man who 'was so wooden a man that he seemed to have taken his wooden leg naturally, and rather suggested to the fanciful observer, that he might be expected— if his development received no untimely check—to be completely set up with a pair of wooden legs in about six months' (I. v). Wegg is the epitome of this dead society, the stuff from which rocking-horses like Mrs. Podsnap are made. Further, since he is one of those 'quite as determined to keep up appearances to themselves, as to their neighbours' (I. v), the leg can be used over and over again, especially as it can be made to touch on pain, to establish a great tension[14] and therefore excellent Freudian humour: 'So gaunt and haggard had he grown at last, that his wooden leg showed disproportionate, and presented a thriving appearance in contrast with the rest of his plagued body, which might almost have been termed chubby' (IV. xiv). Venus's attempts to be delicate in reference to the antecedent of the wooden leg touch the grotesque so closely and sheer away so suddenly that they provide some of the funniest lines in the novel:

'Come! According to your own account, I'm [i.e. his bones] not worth much,' Wegg reasons persuasively.

[14] This term is borrowed from Dorothy Van Ghent's brief but excellent discussion of Wegg as 'death-in-life' ('The Dickens World', *SR*, 421).

'Not for miscellaneous working in, I grant you, Mr. Wegg; but you might turn out valuable yet, as a—' here Mr. Venus takes a gulp of tea, so hot that it makes him choke, and sets his weak eyes watering: 'as a Monstrosity, if you'll excuse me.' (I. VII)

The fact that Wegg refers to his bones as 'me' makes the joke more thematically relevant and more horrible. It is only because neither Venus nor Wegg is in the least touched by the macabre notion that the brilliant humour can be brought off. Their simplicity has its drawbacks, but also its great advantages.

Wegg has even more direct thematic functions. 'Balancing himself on his wooden leg' and fluttering 'over his prey with extended hand', he clearly repeats the 'birds of prey' motif, his professional declining and falling evokes images of decay and corruption, and he continually alludes to the main themes of money, virtue, and selfishness: 'It ain't for the sake of making money, though money is ever welcome. It ain't for myself, though I am not so haughty as to be above doing myself a good turn. It's for the cause of right' (II. VII). In all these cases our negative laughter is used to reject Wegg directly. In a few others, the humour reverses the terms, recognizing in Wegg perversions of important positive values, particularly the sense of trust (notice the image of the two partners each grasping a corner of the will) and the central issue of friendship.

The exposure of Wegg, then, is arranged as a climax because it is a final dismissal of all the dangerous values. While far less complex than the similar unmasking of Uriah Heep, the simplicity of this scene gives it a certain added strength. Unlike Uriah, Silas never really catches on and always bounces back with more outrageous cupidity. When Boffin offers to give him money enough to establish him again in his stall, Wegg begins listing what he has lost and adds a truly Podsnappian snobbery: 'There was, further, Miss Elizabeth, Master George, Aunt Jane, and Uncle Parker. Ah! When a man thinks of the loss of such patronage as that; when a man finds so fair a garden rooted up by pigs; he finds it hard indeed, without going high, to work it into money' (IV. XIV). Because of this offensiveness, his final placement is particularly apt; the true wisdom now doesn't reward the cheats but plops them into carts of night-soil with what is surely the most disgustingly evocative word in the novel, a loud 'splash'. So much for the values of Podsnappery.

With Mr. Venus, the situation is reversed and the comedy is, in the end, much more serious. He becomes, as his name indicates, a comic symbol of love, now created out of the grave. A central figure in this society, he is a man who, like most others, makes money from death. The physical dissociation that surrounds him in his trade mirrors the emotional alienation all over the society: his stock inventory concludes with 'human warious' (I. vii), a comic and terrifying comment on society's inhumanity. It is only his complete ignorance of the ghastly symbolism he lives with that can make his remarks funny.

Venus also adds further weight to Wegg's parody of Podsnappian commercialism. He is a kind of specializing Horatio Alger, who has cornered the bone and articulation market: 'I'm not only first in the trade, but I'm *the* trade' (I. vii). He is not, however, vicious like Wegg; he simply is not yet educated. And it is in his hilarious love affair with Pleasant Riderhood that his positive function becomes clearest. His tag line is first introduced as shockingly incongruous: 'She knows the profit of it, but she don't appreciate the art of it, and she objects to it. "I do not wish," she writes in her own handwriting, "to regard myself, nor yet to be regarded, in that bony light"' (I. vii). As it comes up again and again, however, the direction of the humour changes and the hostility is relaxed: '"The spectacle of those orbs [i.e. the stars]," says Mr. Venus, gazing upward with his hat tumbling off, "brings heavy on me her crushing words that she did not wish to regard herself nor yet to be regarded in that—"' (II. vii). The wonderful detail, 'with his hat tumbling off', does act as an economizer of seriousness, but it becomes increasingly clear that Venus's problem is the general problem of the novel stated in humorous terms: the conflict between love, on the one hand, and, on the other, money, social being, death, and corruption. Time and again Venus's parody makes this point. Lamenting Pleasant's refusal, he declares, 'my very bones is rendered flabby by brooding over it. If they could be brought to me loose, to sort, I should hardly have the face to claim 'em as mine' (III. vii).

But it isn't until the introduction of Pleasant Riderhood that the full seriousness of this comedy can be recognized. Pleasant is the victim of a hard life and has adopted a toughly realistic view of things: 'Show her a Funeral, and she saw an unremunerative ceremony in the nature of a black masquerade' (II. xII). Remarkably, though, she has managed to hold on to 'a touch of romance', at least 'of such romance as could creep into Limehouse Hole' (II. xII). It is the presence of this warmth in the middle of Limehouse Hole which adds a new perspective to the relationship and causes Venus's change in regard to Boffin to parallel the rebirth of Eugene. He affirms, likewise, in his happy renunciation of the articulating of lady's bones (not sacrificing those of men, children, and animals) the warm possibilities of comic society.

Though Dickens has not perhaps quite come full circle, his last completed novel does recapture the humorous directness of his first. Laughter is used to expel the villains and make the new world safe for love.

Bibliography

THE following bibliography is very highly selective and is intended only to point out the most important sources. In the case of Dickens criticism, where there are available excellent checklists and bibliographical studies (see Ada Nisbet, 'Charles Dickens', *Victorian Fiction: A Guide to Research* [Cambridge, Mass., 1964], pp. 44–153 and J. Don Vann, 'A Checklist of Dickens Criticism, 1963–1967', *Studies in the Novel*, i [1969], 255–78), I have listed only those studies which seem to me crucial to the themes and methods discussed here. As a result, many of the books found in the usual listings and in various ways basic to an understanding of Dickens are not included here. In the section on comedy, laughter, and humour the list is somewhat longer but still is restricted generally to those works most fundamentally related to the position taken in this book.

Dickens Criticism

AUDEN, W. H., 'Dingley Dell and the Fleet', *The Dyer's Hand and other Essays*, New York, 1962, pp. 407–28.

AXTON, WILLIAM F., *Circle of Fire: Dickens' Vision and Style and the Popular Victorian Theater*, Lexington, Ky., 1966.

BARNARD, ROBERT, 'The Choral Symphony: *Our Mutual Friend*', *REL*, ii (July, 1961), 89–99.

BUSH, DOUGLAS, 'A Note on Dickens' Humor', *From Jane Austen to Joseph Conrad*, eds. Robert C. Rathburn and Martin Steinmann, Jr., Minneapolis, Minn., 1958, pp. 82–91.

CHESTERTON, G. K., *Appreciations and Criticisms of the Works of Charles Dickens*, London, 1911.

—— *Charles Dickens*, New York, 1965.

CHURCHILL, R. C., 'Dickens, Drama and Tradition', *Scrutiny*, x (1942), 358–75.

CLAYBOROUGH, ARTHUR, 'Dickens: A Circle of Stage Fire', *The Grotesque in English Literature*, Oxford, 1965, pp. 201–51.

COCKSHUT, A. O. J., *The Imagination of Charles Dickens*, London, 1961.

COOLIDGE, ARCHIBALD C., Jr., 'Dickens's Humor', *VN*, no. 18 (1960), 8–15.

CROSS, BARBARA M., 'Comedy and Drama in Dickens', *WHR*, xvii (1963), 143–9.

DUNN, RICHARD J., 'Dickens and the Tragic-Comic Grotesque', *Studies in the Novel*, i (1969), 147–56.

DYSON, A. E., '*Barnaby Rudge*: The Genesis of Violence', *CritQ*, ix (1967), 142–60.

—— '*Martin Chuzzlewit*: Howls the Sublime', *CritQ*, ix (1967), 234–53.

—— '*The Old Curiosity Shop*: Innocence and the Grotesque', *CritQ*, viii (1966), 111–30.

FOLLAND, HAROLD F., 'The Doer and the Deed: Theme and Pattern in *Barnaby Rudge*', *PMLA*, lxxiv (1959), 406–17.

FRYE, NORTHROP, 'Dickens and the Comedy of Humors', *Experience in the Novel*, ed. Roy Harvey Pearce, New York, 1968, pp. 49–81.

JOHNSON, EDGAR, *Charles Dickens: His Tragedy and Triumph*, 2 vols., New York, 1952.

KETTLE, ARNOLD, 'Dickens: *Oliver Twist*', *An Introduction to the English Novel*, vol. i, London, 1951, pp. 123–38.

MCKENZIE, GORDON, 'Dickens and Daumier', *Studies in the Comic*. Univ. of Cal. Pubs. in Eng. viii, no. 2, Berkeley, Calif., 1941, pp. 273–98.

MCMASTER, R. D., 'Birds of Prey: A Study of *Our Mutual Friend*', *DR*, xl (1960), 372–81.

—— '*Little Dorrit*: Experience and Design', *QQ*, lxvii (1961), 530–8.

MARCUS, STEVEN, *Dickens: From Pickwick to Dombey*, New York, 1965.

MILLER, J. HILLIS, *Charles Dickens: The World of His Novels*, Cambridge, Mass., 1958.

ORWELL, GEORGE, 'Charles Dickens', *Dickens, Dali and Others: Studies in Popular Culture*, New York, 1946, pp. 1–75.

PRIESTLEY, J. B., 'The Great Inimitable', *Charles Dickens 1812–1870*, ed. E. W. F. Tomlin, New York, 1969, pp. 13–31.

PRITCHETT, V. S., 'The Humour of Charles Dickens', *Listener*, li (1954), 970–3.

SCHILLING, BERNARD N., *The Comic Spirit: Boccaccio to Thomas Mann*, Detroit, Mich., 1965, pp. 98–144.

SIMPSON, M. EVELYN, 'Jonson and Dickens: A Study in the Comic Genius of London', *E&S*, xxix (1943), 82–92.

SMITH, SHEILA M., 'Anti-Mechanism and the Comic in the Writings of Charles Dickens', *RMS*, iii (1959), 131–44.

SPILKA, MARK, *Dickens and Kafka*, Bloomington, Ind., 1963.

STEIG, MICHAEL, 'Dickens, Hablôt Browne, and the Tradition of English Caricature', *Criticism*, xi (1969), 219–33.

TRILLING, LIONEL, '*Little Dorrit*', *KR*, xv (1953), 577–90.

VAN GHENT, DOROTHY, 'The Dickens World: A View from Todgers's', *SR*, lviii (1950), 419–38.

WILSON, EDMUND, 'Dickens: The Two Scrooges', *The Wound and the Bow*, New York, 1947, pp. 1–104.

Comedy, Laughter, and Humour

AUDEN, W. H., 'Notes on the Comic', *Thought*, xxvii (1952), 57–71.

BAUDELAIRE, CHARLES, 'On the Essence of Laughter', *The Mirror of Art*, trans. and ed. Jonathan Mayne, London, 1955, pp. 133–53.

BERGLER, EDMUND, *Laughter and the Sense of Humor*, New York, 1956.

BERGSON, HENRI, 'Laughter', *Comedy*, ed. Wylie Sypher, Garden City, New York, 1956, pp. 59–190.

BRODY, MORRIS W., 'The Meaning of Laughter', *Psychoanalytic Quarterly*, xix (1950), 192–201.

CAMERON, WILLIAM BRUCE, 'The Sociology of Humor and Vice-Versa', *Informal Sociology*, New York, 1963, pp. 79–94.

CLUBB, MERREL D., 'A Plea for an Eclectic Theory of Humor', *Univ. of Cal. Chron.* xxxiv (1932), 340–56.

COOK, ALBERT, *The Dark Voyage and the Golden Mean, A Philosophy of Comedy*, Cambridge, Mass., 1949.

COOPER, LANE, *An Aristotelean Theory of Comedy*, New York, 1922.

CORNFORD, FRANCIS MACDONALD, *The Origin of Attic Comedy*, London, 1914.

DOOLEY, LUCILE, 'The Relation of Humor to Masochism', *Psychoanalytic Review*, xxviii (1941), 37–46.

DUBOIS, ARTHUR E., 'Comedy, An Experience', *ELH*, vii (1940), 199–214.

EASTMAN, MAX, *Enjoyment of Laughter*, New York, 1936.

—— *The Sense of Humor*, New York, 1921.

FREUD, SIGMUND, 'Humor', *International Journal of Psychoanalysis*, ix (1928), 1–6.

—— *Wit and Its Relation to the Unconscious*, trans. A. A. Brill, New York, 1916.

FRYE, NORTHROP, 'The Mythos of Spring: Comedy', *Anatomy of Criticism*, Princeton, N.J., 1957, pp. 163–86.

GRAY, DONALD J., 'The Uses of Victorian Laughter', *VS*, x (1966), 145–76.

GREGORY, J. C., *The Nature of Laughter*, New York, 1924.

GROTJAHN, MARTIN, *Beyond Laughter*, New York, 1957.

HUIZINGA, JOHAN, *Homo Ludens: A Study of the Play-Element in Culture*, London, 1949.

KAYSER, WOLFGANG, *The Grotesque in Art and Literature*, trans. Ulrich Weisstein, Bloomington, Ind., 1963.

KIMMINS, CHARLES W., *The Springs of Laughter*, London, 1928.

KOESTLER, ARTHUR, 'The Comic', *Insight and Outlook*, New York, 1949, pp. 3–110.

LANGER, SUZANNE, 'The Comic Rhythm', *Feeling and Form*, New York, 1953, pp. 326–50.

LUDOVICI, ANTHONY, *The Secret of Laughter*, London, 1932.

McARTHUR, HERBERT, 'Tragic and Comic Modes', *Criticism*, iii (1961), 36–45.

MATHEWSON, LOUISE, 'Bergson's Theory of the Comic in the Light of English Comedy', *Univ. of Nebr. Stud. in Lang., Lit., and Crit.*, no. 5, 1920.

MEREDITH, GEORGE, 'An Essay on Comedy', *Comedy*, ed. Wylie Sypher, Garden City, New York, 1956, pp. 3–57.

MUNRO, D. H., *Argument of Laughter*, Melbourne, 1951.

MYERS, HENRY A., 'The Analysis of Laughter', *SR*, xliii (1935), 452–63.

PIDDINGTON, RALPH, *The Psychology of Laughter*, London, 1933.

POTTS, L. J., *Comedy*, London, 1948.

RAPP, ALBERT, *The Origins of Wit and Humor*, New York, 1951.

SEWARD, SAMUEL S., Jr., *The Paradox of the Ludicrous*, Stanford, Calif., 1930.

SEWELL, ELIZABETH, *The Field of Nonsense*, London, 1952.

SOULE, DONALD, 'Comedy, Irony, and a Sense of Comprehension', *HAB*, xiii (1962–3), 37–54.

STYAN, J. L., *The Dark Comedy: The Development of Modern Comic Tragedy*, Cambridge, 1962.

SUTTON, MAX KEITH, ' "Inverse Sublimity" in Victorian Humor', *VS*, x (1966), 177–92.

SWABEY, MARIE C., 'The Comic as Nonsense, Sadism, or Incongruity', *JP*, lv (1958), 819–33.

—— *Comic Laughter: A Philosophical Essay*, New Haven, Conn., 1961.

SYPHER, WYLIE, 'The Meanings of Comedy', *Comedy*, ed. Wylie Sypher, Garden City, New York, 1956, pp. 193–258.

TAVE, STUART M., *The Amiable Humorist: A Study in the Comic Theory and Criticism of the Eighteenth and Early Nineteenth Centuries*, Chicago, Ill., 1960.

WATTS, HAROLD H., 'The Sense of Regain: A Theory of Comedy', *Univ. of Kansas City Rev.* xiii (1946), 19–23.

Index